L'Espagne Républicaine

French Policy and Spanish Republicanism in Liberated France

An Anti-Franco postcard distributed during the United Nations debate on Spain, 1946, by Spanish Republican exile groups.

L'Espagne Républicaine

French Policy and Spanish Republicanism in Liberated France

David A. Messenger

BRIGHTON • PORTLAND

Copyright © David Messenger, 2008, 2009.

The right of David Messenger to be identified as Author of this work has been asserted in accordance with the Copyright, Designs and Patents Act 1988.

2 4 6 8 10 9 7 5 3 1

First published 2008, reprinted 2009, in Great Britain by
SUSSEX ACADEMIC PRESS
PO Box 139
Eastbourne BN24 9BP

and in the United States of America by
SUSSEX ACADEMIC PRESS
920 NE 58th Ave   Suite 300
Portland, Oregon 97213-3786

All rights reserved. Except for the quotation of short passages for the purposes of criticism and review, no part of this publication may be reproduced, stored in a retrieval system, or transmitted, in any form or by any means, electronic, mechanical, photocopying, recording or otherwise, without the prior permission of the publisher.

British Library Cataloguing in Publication Data
A CIP catalogue record for this book is available from the British Library.

Library of Congress Cataloging-in-Publication Data
Messenger, David A.
  L'Espagne républicaine : French policy and Spanish republicanism in
    liberated France / David A. Messenger.
    p. cm.
  Includes bibliographical references and index.
  ISBN 978-1-84519-259-4 (h/c : alk. paper)
   1. France—Foreign relations—Spain. 2. Spain—Foreign relations—
  France. 3. France—Politics and government—1945–1958.
  4. Spain—Politics and government—1939–1975. 5. Spain—History—
  Civil War, 1936–1939—Governments in exile. 6. Political refugees—
  France—History—20th century. I. Title.
  DC59.8.S7M47 2008
  940.53′4408961—dc22
                                                                    2007022752

Typeset & Designed by SAP, Brighton & Eastbourne.
Printed by TJ International, Padstow, Cornwall.
This book is printed on acid-free paper.

CONTENTS

Series Editor's Preface	vi
Acknowledgements	ix
Introduction: France and Spain in the Aftermath of the Second World War	1
1 The French Refugee Crisis and Economic Warfare in Spain, 1942–1944	9
2 The Resistance and Spanish Republicanism in Liberated France, 1944–1945	30
3 French Politics and the Cause of Spanish Republicanism, 1944–1947	51
4 French Initiatives on Spain, 1945–1946	75
5 France, the West and the Spanish Question, 1946	97
6 French Acceptance of Franco's Spain, 1946–1948	122
Conclusion: France, Spain and Post-War Foreign Policy in Europe	139
Notes	143
Bibliography	175
Index	188

SERIES EDITOR'S PREFACE

David Messenger's book forms part of a fruitful and growing trend in European historical scholarship to bring the war back into post-war studies. In contrast to the standard periodization, which viewed 1945 as a kind of "ground zero", an increasing number of scholars are re-drawing those chronological and conceptual boundaries. Instead of the post-war *tabula rasa* that the original demarcation implied, scholars are now focusing on the lingering impact of the war in defining the possibilities and limits of the post-war era. What is emerging is a new periodization, in which the years immediately before and after the end of hostilities are being linked together, part of a historical "moment" that generates different questions than the traditional post-'.45 narrative.

One of the key characteristics of this historical "moment" is its fluidity and uncertainty, a moment when the future identity/ies of European society and politics were not yet fixed, not yet sucked into the Cold War dynamic that would soon impose its homogenizing framework on the continent. In contrast to traditional post-war histories, which jumped right from war to Cold War without taking a breath, the new historiography lingers on the liminal period in between, exploring the other future "reconstructions" being imagined. Such a perspective has sought, on the one hand, to recover the plurality of European experiences, and on the other, to provide a bridge between the post-war histories of East and Western Europe, which have been separated by Cold War categories. Messenger's analysis of French foreign policy debates between 1944 and 1948 over the "Spanish Question" fits precisely into this emerging framework. By lingering over the public and policy debates on this crucial European issue, Messenger argues, we can see the outlines of competing visions for reconstructing France and Europe in the post-war.

On the one hand, Messenger finds the more familiar Cold War discourse, which is already formulating the language of pragmatic *realpolitik* in the name of national security. On the other, there is the mostly-forgotten foreign policy discourse centered on notions of "justice" and the creation of a new social order. Some French historians have begun to explore what Messenger calls the "justice" discourse in terms of domestic politics. Rooted in the Resistance and the moral and political idealism of the struggle against fascism, the "justice" discourse was invested in the deepening and renewal of French democracy. What Messenger's book contributes, however, is the extension of this analysis into the realm of foreign policy. That is, as the French thought more broadly about the reconstruction of a democratic Europe, they were presented with two competing frameworks for the new Europe, one rooted in the power politics of *realpolitik* and the other in a "new politics" of human rights and democracy. The upshot is that France's experience of war and resistance did not leave a single legacy with a clear blueprint for the future, but competing interpretations that sparked vigorous debates.

What Messenger argues convincingly is that these debates are nowhere more clearly elaborated than in the question of defining France's relationship with authoritarian Spain. Messenger explores how the "*realpolitik*" attitude towards the Franco regime took shape during the last years of the war, over discussions about refugee policy and economic trade. But in the immediate post-war period, it is the "justice" model that dominates public discourse, the conviction that France should help Spanish Republicans unseat the authoritarian dictator and restore the democratic republic (which was, of course, what Spanish Republicans assumed the democratic victors would do).

While this view is widely held at first, Messenger demonstrates how both opinion and policy shift from the "justice" model to the "*realpolitik*" model by 1947–48. To make the case, he goes beyond traditional diplomatic sources to include the debates carried out in the public sphere, in newspapers and tracts written by associations and individuals connected with the Resistance. By incorporating this broader swathe of public opinion, the book aims to illuminate more than just a narrow conversation going on within the halls of the Quai d'Orsay, but a national debate in which many ordinary Frenchmen and women are passionately invested in what happens in France, Spain and Europe. It may be that the ordinary person's passion for settling the future of Europe was a legacy of the war itself, or both wars, in which the fate of individual nations was so clearly tied to the fate of Europe as a whole.

While the historical "moment" in which other visions of a European democratic order were being considered was fleeting in chronological terms, Messenger makes a convincing case that our understanding of war and reconstruction is greatly enriched by the effort to linger on that moment. On a basic level, he has demonstrated that it is impossible to understand the debates in French foreign policy in 1946 and 1947 without reference to the legacies of the war itself. Perhaps more importantly, by insisting that the transition from war to post-war was neither straightforward nor obvious, Messenger helps to restore a sense of historical contingency to European and French reconstruction. Thus, at the same time that he rescues the path not taken from the dustbin of history, he also sheds further light on the contested process by which the Cold War-dominated foreign policy framework emerged as dominant. The result is an

Series Editor's Preface

analysis whose implications go well beyond the few brief years under scrutiny, looking back to the war as well as into the future of Cold War diplomacy.

PAMELA RADCLIFF
University of California, San Diego

ACKNOWLEDGEMENTS

This book has been a work in progress for some time, and it is to the credit of many people that it has been completed in the form you have before you. Publication would not have been possible without the financial, intellectual and moral support of the institutions and individuals that I am delighted to thank and acknowledge below.

This project began as my doctoral dissertation and I am grateful to the University of Toronto School of Graduate Studies, Department of History and Centre for International Studies for funds that permitted my initial research. Subsequent funds from the Carroll College Faculty Development Fund, the Spanish Ministry of Culture's Program of Cultural Cooperation with American Universities and the University of Wyoming Department of History and International Studies Program allowed completion of the project.

Research for this book was carried out in numerous archives around Western Europe and the United States and I am grateful to the staffs of each and every one. I found wonderful workplaces in both the reading rooms of the *Archives du Ministère des Affaires Etrangères* in Paris and in the *Archivo General* in the *Ministerio des Asuntos Exteriores* in Madrid.

Thanks also are due to the helpful and encouraging archivists and staffs of the *Archives Nationales de France*, the *Institut Français d'Histoire Sociale*, and the *Bibliothèque Nationale Francois Mitterrand*, all in Paris; the *Bibliothèque Municipale de Toulouse*; the *Fundacìon Pablo Iglesias*, Madrid and the *Archivo General de Administracìon* in Alcala de Henares; the National Archives of the United Kingdom Public Record Office, Kew; the Churchill Archives Centre, Cambridge, the Cambridge University Library Manuscripts Room; and the National Archives and Records Administration of the United States in College Park, MD.

For assistance in finding housing around the globe I am thankful to Patty Fischer and Joe Piggott who steered me towards a wonderful apartment in Paris, to Michael Cox and Jennifer Purves who put me up in London, and to Lorne Breitenlohner who navigated for me both in London and Cambridge. Like many other researchers who entered Madrid tentatively for the first time, I am grateful to the late Tom Entwhistle for introducing me to his neighborhood and his engagement with the history of twentieth-century Spain.

Acknowledgements

Neither this book, nor my career for that matter, would have been possible without the support, encouragement and constructive criticism of many historians who have shaped this project in so many ways. The University of Toronto's Department of History provided an ideal atmosphere to complete a dissertation that sought to be multi-national in scope as well as grounded in the history of 20th century Europe. It also provided me with advice, wisdom and support necessary in embarking on an academic career. I wish to thank Sidney Aster, Ken Bartlett, Lorne Breitenlohner, Hilary Earl, Robert Hanks, Adrienne Hood, Timothy Jenks, Eric Jennings, Julia Kinnear, Michael Marrus, Francine McKenzie, Trish McMahon, Alison Meek, Ronald Pruessen, Mark Thompson, Gary Wilson and many others for making the department and graduate school at Toronto a great atmosphere to learn in. I also wish to thank the members of the Toronto French History and Social Sciences colloquium, especially David Higgs, Bill Irvine and Tim Le Goff, for augmenting my education and welcoming me as a colleague.

Many scholars have read portions of this work and provided insight and encouragement, most especially Michael Creswell, Desmond Dinan, Talbot Imlay, Samuel Kalman, Kenneth Moure, Pamela Radcliff, Lynne Taylor and Neville Wylie. In terms of making the argument into book form, I am grateful to the staff at Sussex Academic Press, especially the Editorial Director Anthony Grahame, and the historians who oversee the Studies in Spanish History series, José Alverez Junco, Nigel Townson and Pamela Radcliff. Thanks are also due to Amy Murphy for preparing the index. Finally, those individuals who made me welcome in my first full-time position at Carroll College in Helena, Montana and most recently at the University of Wyoming, deserve mention for their support of my work.

Parts of the text have previously appeared in two journals. Chapter 1 appeared as "Rival Faces of France: Refugees, Would-be Allies and Economic Warfare in Spain, 1942–1944", *International History Review* 27:1. Portions of Chapter 3 have appeared as "'Our Spanish Brothers' or 'As at Plombières': France and the Spanish Opposition to Franco, 1945–1948", *French History* 20:1, published by Oxford University Press. I thank these journals and their presses for their permission to include that material here.

The front cover is made up of the Spanish resistance newspaper *Solidaridad Espanola* (Toulouse), May 1945; source: Biblioteca Virtual de Prensa Histórica, Ministerio de Cultura, Madrid. The small colour illustration on the back cover is an anti-Franco poster, France, 1945. And the frontispiece is an anti-Franco postcard distributed during the United Nations debate on Spain, 1946, by Spanish Republican exile groups. I have been unable to determin whether the latter two illustrations are copyrighted in any way.

My work has been deeply influenced and shaped by two mentors who deserve special mention. Denis Smyth did more than supervise my disserta-

Acknowledgements

tion. He read the work, criticized it, encouraged it, and me, with wit, sincerity and grace in equal measure. I am truly grateful for his insight, support and modeling of the 'good life' as an academic and teacher. Bob Swartout was not only kind enough to offer me my first position at Carroll College, but also to read this work as a non-Europeanist and tell me where I needed to be clearer and more direct. He also demonstrated how to be a teacher, a scholar and a community leader each and every day he came to work. For this, I am greatly indebted.

Finally, I am grateful to my family for their support, financial and otherwise, and most especially for their encouragement over the years. My two grandfathers, Maurice Messenger and John W. Murray, passed on their love of history and contributed greatly to the direction my life has taken. My wife, Maureena Walker, has lived with this project as long as she has known me, followed me to the Rocky Mountain West, and made numerous other sacrifices. I am truly blessed to have her love in my life. I hope that one day my sons Will and Jack will see that more than European soccer kits resulted from my many absences in their early years. Finally, I dedicate this book to my parents, David and Anne Messenger. They taught me to dream, and then let me. This book is one result of that.

Of course, any omissions or errors in fact, judgment or interpretation are entirely my own.

For my parents

INTRODUCTION

France and Spain in the Aftermath of the Second World War

In his recent history of Europe since 1945, entitled *Postwar*, Tony Judt reflects that since the fall of Communism in 1989, many historians and commentators have come to realize that the shadow of the Second World War was much longer has that it was assumed in the midst of the Cold War.[1] Few historians today would accept the idea that the movement from war to Cold War was immediate and clearly demarcated.[2] Rather, the reconstruction of Europe that began as territories were liberated from Nazi rule in 1944 and 1945 was conceived of not in terms of a future conflict between capitalism and communism, but rather as a process that had to start with a "decisive reckoning with the past – with the pre-war elites who had sacrificed democracy to appease the dictators."[3]

In thinking of the early post-war era as one that integrated concerns of the war, and even the pre-war, to the immediate situation, a new historiography has emerged that challenges older ideas of periodization and division. In particular, the search for concepts that united pre-war thought, wartime experience and post-war debates about reconstruction has contributed to a reassessment of what mattered in Europe following the Liberation of territories and countries from Nazi occupation. Historians like Geoff Eley have emphasized internal politics in many states, and in particular the appearance of coalitions of socialists, communists and others, who favored "democracy and reform" much as the Popular Front movements of the 1930s had.[4] For these groups, reconstruction conceived in this manner was about "justice" above all, which included the prosecution of war criminals and collaborators, new economic planning, and the creation of a new and more just social order.[5] As democratic governments fought the war against fascism, and western intellectuals observed what was occurring in Europe, an analysis of the war that linked dictatorships and the violation of individual rights developed. In response, a reassertion of the value of rights to liberal democracy occurred, in language that spoke of 'human rights', 'justice' and 'universalism'.[6]

This was especially so in post-war France. Emerging from the collaborationist Vichy era, rebuilding from the devastation of war and occupation, France was also in the midst of its own political redefinition. Led by the wartime Resistance leader Charles de Gaulle, in coalition with a number of non-Gaullist resistance groups, the French political scene was at a moment Jean-Pierre Rioux has described as "unique" in the nation's history, for "the Right had collapsed with Vichy, and the Left, invested with all the moral authority of the Resistance, was now the natural spokesman for the national interest."[7] The renewal of democracy within France created a unique situation, for "ordinary people thought about the social contract and had an opportunity to renegotiate it."[8] Having lived through the experience of occupation, collaboration and resistance, the public as well as governmental and Resistance leaders all played a role in the process of legitimizing the new regime. For the renewed democracy, the question of justice was central.[9] Not only must the Republic be reestablished, but collaborators must be purged, traitors punished and reforms implemented. The Resistance vision for justice and renewal, described most clearly in the *Conseil National de la Résistance* Charter of March, 1944, had a powerful appeal to the public in the days and months following French Liberation.[10] The experience of defeat and occupation had led France and its citizens to conclude that a reform of their approach to politics and policy was required.

This book sets out to make the argument that that idealism of 1944 and 1945 around the concept of democracy, justice and rights was equally applicable in the realm of foreign policy and international order. This was especially so when activists in France turned their thoughts to the case of Spain. In a continent where most states were transforming themselves from one regime to another, either willingly or not, Spain did not change following the end of the war. It remained a semi-fascist dictatorship under the rule of General Francisco Franco. During the 1930s, Spain and its civil war captivated many, whether they saw it as "the last great cause", a dress rehearsal for the world war which followed or the first open battle of the twentieth-century conflict fought between capitalism and communism.[11] The influence of the conflict, and its various interpretations, lasted well beyond the victory of Franco's Nationalist forces in 1939. Moreover, new developments in 1944 and 1945 revived the Spanish issue internationally. Franco himself marked the end of the war in Europe, which he had managed to stay out of, with a brutal repression of his political opponents.[12] Influenced by a heavy dose of nostalgia connected to the initial conflict of 1936–39, further shaped by the seminal conflict of a generation from 1939–45, and imbued with a dynamic of its own, the "Spanish question" of the early postwar era engaged politicians, bureaucrats and the public as it had a decade earlier.

The war had been fought against fascism and Nazism, and as such it was a conflict in which "a total reordering of the globe was at stake from the very beginning."[13] Yet Francisco Franco and his regime, which included the fascist-like *Falange* party, remained in power while Hitler and Mussolini – who had put Franco in power – as well as numerous other leaders of fascist- and semi-fascist regimes had been defeated. Meanwhile, from within and without, French democrats had defended democracy and they had remade it in their own nation. They and their Allies had defeated the Vichy state and its authoritarian basis in order to reconstruct the Republic, and a "myth of national renewal, originating in national resistance" became part of the emerging political orthodoxy.[14] The myth of a nation in resistance generated by wartime experiences, and the ideals which flowed from such an image, would have relevance for both domestic and international politics, and for the intermingling of the two. Could not the lessons of wartime France be relevant for other nations? Could not a renewed France contribute to the emergence of a renewed Europe grounded in the principles of democracy and justice? In a parallel to the universalistic tone of Republicanism in the 1790s, the impact of domestic experience on international policy was profound for many who emerged from the Resistance experience in 1944. They sought to advocate for renewed democracy and republicanism in Spain as well as rebuild within France.

For individuals and groups engaged in this dialogue, the embrace of justice implied a rejection of foreign policy-making affiliated with concepts of "realpolitik". The re-drawing of maps and realignment of territories affiliated with this approach to peacemaking had clearly failed in the past.[15] Yet the concept was not at all dormant. The aftermath of the war meant that policy-makers were simultaneously developing strategy in other ways, within frameworks other than that of justice. In the case of American foreign policy, Melvyn Leffler has argued that the development of geostrategic thinking in the 1930s and 1940s resulted, by 1945, in a new concept called "national security" that gave a primary role to calculations of power, militarily, economically and otherwise.[16] This, naturally, contributed to the Cold War atmosphere but was not necessarily a product of it. Similarly, in describing the foreign policy of France's Fourth Republic, especially in the period after 1948, William I. Hitchcock has employed a concept that parallels Leffler's, arguing that a "national strategy of recovery" was pursued by French policymakers, allowing them to rejuvenate the country's economy and gain concessions from the United States on the question of German revival that also served France's national interest.[17] Certainly the idea of national security could also be applied in assessing French policy in other venues like Spain.

Moreover, the first post-Liberation governments in France did not inherit a clean slate on Spain with the removal of Vichy and the liberation of France from German occupation, and thus they had no *tabula rasa* upon which to inscribe a new, morally-based, chapter in French–Spanish relations. Non-Vichy France had had diplomatic contact with Franco's Spain since November, 1942. Such relations first developed under the auspices of the breakaway Vichy colonies in

North Africa, the French High Commission of Algiers, which later merged with General Charles de Gaulle's Free France group to form the Algiers-based *Comité Français de Libération Nationale* (CFLN) over which de Gaulle presided. Entering the post-war era, de Gaulle was willing to continue diplomatic relations with Spain that had been developed since 1942. Rather than emphasize democracy and morality, the General advocated the concept of *grandeur* as the basis upon which to rebuild the nation. National unity and national greatness were always the "imperatives" of Gaullist resistance.[18] France's reputation amongst its Allies and its international position in the world were to determine policy.[19] Foreign policy, therefore, could not always be made on the basis of morality and justice. The measurements of power had to be given significance. In North Africa, preservation of the French Empire required, in the minds of de Gaulle's aides, communication and diplomatic contact with the other colonial power in the region, Spain. Spanish colonial territory abutted Resistance territory in North Africa, and France and Spain were both parties to agreements concerning the governance of Morocco. Trade between North Africa and the Spanish mainland was significant, and necessary in order to allow the CFLN to continue to raise armies and contribute to the Allied war effort. These ideas did not disappear when the CFLN moved to Paris to become the Provisional Government in August 1944.

The divergent nature of a Resistance grounded in justice, democracy and liberation and a Gaulllist state based on realpolitik and *grandeur* would come into conflict. The dynamic of these competing visions reveal much about the transition from war to peace in the Fourth Republic. Despite being united in the war, Gaullist and colonial officials developed different plans for the post-war renewal of France in the international system than did those affiliated with the left-wing Resistance and political parties. France's transition from war to post-war was not straightforward, and this was especially true in the realm of foreign policy. For those who had conducted foreign policy from Algiers during the war, first under the High Commission and then under de Gaulle and the CFLN, and who moved to Paris as the Provisional Government, the quest for post-war *grandeur* imposed certain needs upon France. In the formation of foreign policy, France had to assess its strengths and weaknesses, seek solutions necessary for its own reconstruction and conduct political and economic diplomacy as these needs dictated. The importance of expert and professional analysis from bureaucrats who had steered non-Vichy France through the war was accepted. This was a realpolitik vision of policy-making.

The Resistance vision of renewed Republic implied a new type of politics, and this had its consequences for Spanish policy, in particular because the Spanish issue had already, in the 1930s, served as a catalyst for the debate between "new politics" and "old diplomacy." Arguments about justice had the capacity to influence debates about how to organize society and govern differently than the decision-makers of the wartime era had. While the Resistance was a varied movement, ideologically and otherwise, some generalization can be made about their approach to reconstruction. The Resistance was Republican, committed to democratic government, but a certain kind of democracy, one in which public life was ethical. This was in response not only to the authoritarianism of Vichy, but also to the perceived weakness of the Third Republic. Political machination and careerism were seen to be the abiding preoccupations of Third Republican politicians, and as the prime source of that regime's debility.[20] Renovation of French democracy meant the replacement of political elites who had dominated the Third Republic with constitutional reform, giving a greater role to the people and promoting a moralization of French politics which favored civic spirit over individual or factional interest.[21] The Spanish case fit comfortably into such a framework of political analysis. Those who were democrats should support Spanish Republicans in their efforts to remove General Franco and restore Republicanism in Iberia just as the French had removed Marshal Pétain and his Vichy regime. A democratic world system, built through the triumph of the democracies over fascism in war, would facilitate the expansion of Republican justice. Moreover, if French democrats removed elite decision-makers and had the opportunity, in a moral political arena, to express such sentiment and respond to the demands of the popular will, then their desire would prevail. Public opinion was vital here, for it was to be a new, mobilized France that embraced these principles not only internally, but universally.

Further complicating the formation of French policy was the existence, in Spain, of another policy born in war, that of France's American and British allies. The strategic requirements of these states, especially with the gradual emergence of the Cold War, led them to gradually accept Franco's regime as the best guarantee of stability in the Iberian Peninsula. France could not ignore the policies and decisions made by its Allies. Yet these two countries had also fought the war against fascism, for democracy, and expressed sentiments similar to those espoused by the French Resistance. Just as in France, the requirements of strategy and the ideals of democracy competed, but in different political contexts. The nature of those debates and the resulting policies pursued by the US and Britain inevitably complicated the debate in France.

This book is not an effort to detail France's foreign policy toward Spain in the period of the Fourth Republic. Indeed, a number of prominent issues, including the difficult question of Spain's relationship with Cold War alliances and institutions, carried into the 1950s.[22] Moreover, important relationships related to the management of each country's zone in the Protectorate in Morocco marked the period from 1945 through to the independence of Morocco in 1956.[23] What is offered here is an examination of how the idea of justice came to enter into political and public debates about the cause of Spanish

Republicanism in liberated France, and how simultaneously ideas linked to the Leffler and Hitchcock discourse on national security and realpolitik also shaped policy toward Franco's Spain. The context of "reconstruction" and "renewal" define the chronological and thematic boundaries of the book. By moving beyond the traditional documents of diplomatic history, and engaging with materials from a variety of sources, in the spirit of international and transnational history, a case study of French policy toward Spain permits us to test Judt's claim about the "lingering" impact of the war and the impact of liberation. While the documents of the Foreign Ministry, the Quai d'Orsay, remain essential in any examination of French policy toward Spain, so too are the manifestos, newspapers and tracts of a variety of Resistance and Resistance-affiliated organizations who engaged in debates over Spain. The connections forged between Spanish Republican exiles and various groups in and out of the French government also are important to examine. This transnational approach to international history encourages the examination of connections and cleavages as they relate to more universal concepts and values, in relationships between various nation-states, within nation-states, or in networks that cut across traditional national borders.[24] How justice became to be defined as a European and French value, and applied to the debate over policy toward Spain, by the government, individuals and extra-parliamentary groups inside France, as well as by Spanish Republicans exiled in France, is a fascinating story. Similarly, how the concept of realpolitik became part of the debate, and interacted with the ideal of justice, is essential to understanding the complexities inherent in the re-emergence of international politics in post-war Europe. In France, support of Spanish Republicanism and the idea of Republican restoration in Spain became identified with a "just" foreign policy while negotiations with Franco and a moderate approach to the Spanish dictatorship was seen as the rational implementation of a "realist" policy.

For many, of course, the nature of this debate was not new. During the latter part of the 1930s, France, like most of Europe, was enmeshed in a polarization that has been described as "the politics of either/or."[25] One of the consequences of such a cleavage was the formation of the Popular Front coalition of Communists, Radicals and Socialists, and its election to government under Léon Blum in June, 1936. Just as the Government was coming into office, the Spanish Civil War broke out. The Spanish Republic, also governed by a Popular Front coalition, requested French military assistance in the form of arms shipments in order to defend itself against a rightist military uprising that soon had the support of Fascist Italy and Nazi Germany. Blum reluctantly refused, and France instead promoted a policy of foreign non-intervention in the conflict. The reluctance of France's primary ally, Great Britain, to get involved in the conflict significantly influenced Blum's decision, yet the decisive factor in the decision not to aid Spain's Second Republic was the fear that such support would lead the collapse of his government and perhaps even a similar civil war between left and right within France, although now it is clear such a threat was exaggerated.[26] While Blum's decision may have saved his government for the short term, it did not end the division within France. That division was complicated by the fact that the French Left, committed to the struggle of Republican Spain, was infuriated with the Blum government for having abandoned the front line in the democratic battle against fascism. The sense of resentment did not die, nor did the Left's conviction that the fate of Republican Spain was an essential element of the fight against fascism. After the end of the Popular Front in France, Blum himself mulled over the missed opportunities for confronting fascism that had existed in Spain.[27] Popular leftist disappointment persisted beyond the war itself. As the Civil War ended, the Spanish film maker Luis Buñuel remembered that "in contrast to the French Government, that consistently refused to intervene in favor of the Republic ... the French people, and, in particular, the workers ... gave us their considerable assistance."[28]

With the onset of world war and the collapse of France in June 1940, the Spanish case, as an example of "the class war played out on an international scale"[29], was still relevant to the internal politics of France. The Right, seemingly, had triumphed across the continent. Within France, the Right not only collaborated with the German occupier, but more importantly responded to the debates of the 1930s with its own "National Revolution" – "revenge against the Popular Front more than accommodation to some Nazi blueprint."[30] Spain, now under the authoritarian regime of Franco, drew the attention of many of Vichy's political leaders.[31] The ideologues of the new regime were even more attracted to the Spanish state. Drawing parallels between Vichy, Fascist Italy and Francoist Spain, a French Foreign Ministry memo in July, 1940 contended that a Mediterranean coalition built upon "Latin and Christian solidarity" was a possible branch of the new order in Europe which could flourish.[32] Colonial competition between the two states was one factor which worked against such an alliance, and much of Franco-Spanish relations during the war consisted of rhetoric rather than policy. Yet the ideological attraction was always there, built upon the polarization of the 1930s and the legacy of the Civil War. This would inevitably have consequences for the renewed debate of the post-liberation period.

In attempting to assess the problem of Spain in the development of the Fourth Republic and its foreign policy, this work mostly adopts a chronological structure. The focus of this work is on the period from 1943 and 1948, with particular emphasis on the period up to the end of 1946. The book proceeds in three sections of two chapters each. The first section of the book sets out the framework of competing "realpolitik" and "justice" visions for French policy toward Spain. The first chapter examines the wartime experience of non-Vichy France in Spain, and the emergence of the CFLN as a partner to its British and

American allies in the implementation of policy toward General Franco. Here the basis of a realpolitik approach to Franco was laid out, and embraced by Gaullist leaders. Chapter 2 is a study of the Resistance view of Spanish policy from the Liberation in August, 1944 through 1945, outlining in particular how the concepts of democracy and justice were applied to the Spanish Republican movement. The second section examines the French Government's efforts in 1946 to forge a policy which reconciled the two approaches, seeking to satisfy domestic and Resistance opinion around the issue of justice while not isolating France from the Spanish policies of its Western Allies. Chapter 3 does this through a study of three unique policies concerning the Spanish Republicans and the cause of Spanish Republicanism, both as an exiled movement inside France and as a movement with partisans still inside Spain, policies enacted mainly during the 1944–1946 period, but that extended into 1947 in the case of contacts with the Spanish opposition. This chapter sets the parameters for what should be seen as the successful implementation of policies associated with the justice perspective. Chapter 4 examines French efforts to seek a policy that balanced realist and Resistance concerns, and to do so within the Western Alliance and later through the United Nations. The result of this effort was the decision in February 1946 to impose unilateral sanctions against Spain in the form of the closure of the Franco-Spanish border. The final section consists of Chapter 5, which assesses the public failure of France's efforts at the United Nations, and Chapter 6, which studies the Government's preparations for a retreat from any further initiative on Spain and the movement toward normalization of Franco-Spanish relations, including an end to the border closure, which came in 1948. This resulted in the end of any attempt to include 'justice' as a primary factor in French policy-making toward Spain and realpolitik acceptance of Franco's regime as a bulwark against Communism in the context of the Cold War.

The ability of Spanish Republicanism and Franco's dictatorship to engage not only Spanish partisans, but also large segments of the French political elite and the broader public, was more than a legacy of the Spanish Civil War. It also tells us something about the nature of the post-war transition inside France. The experience of war and resistance did not offer the French one single legacy. Rather, different visions of France and its role in Europe emerged, and competed, and the ensuing debate imposed constraints and limitations upon the construction of French policy. French policy and the issue of Spanish Republicanism in the immediate aftermath of war demonstrates that European renewal was a complex process that encouraged debate over ideals, perceptions and values in the international sphere as much as anywhere else.

1

The French Refugee Crisis and Econmic Warfare in Spain, 1942–1944

The one hundred thousand US troops who landed in French North Africa on 8 November 1942 in Operation Torch were taking part in a political operation as much as a military one. Its success depended upon Spain's willingness to remain uninvolved, and upon limited resistance from the French forces in North Africa, which were officially an instrument of the collaborationist Vichy regime. The likelihood of either Spain's entry into war or vigorous resistance from French forces was minimal partly because the United States and Great Britain had prepared the ground with care.[1] In the aftermath of Torch, General Francisco Franco's regime in Spain, though brought to power with the support of Fascist Italy and Nazi Germany, hedged its bets over the outcome of the war and increasingly sought *rapprochement* with the Allies.[2]

The Allied invasion also led to the formation of the *Haut Commissariat de France en Afrique Française*, or French High Commission in North Africa, with headquarters at Algiers; headed until his assassination in December 1942 by Admiral François Darlan, then by General Henri Giraud, and staffed by officials who had previously taken orders from Vichy. Its aim was partnership with the Allies. Enlarged on 12 November 1942 when the administration of the French Protectorate of Morocco accepted its legitimacy[3], the High Commission remained in power in North Africa until June 1943, when General Charles de Gaulle's Free France movement merged with the High Commission in order to create the *Comité Français de la Libération Nationale* (CFLN). The new group continued to implement the policies devised by the high commission following Torch.

The success of Torch placed France and Spain at the centre of the war in the Mediterranean.[4] Germany's response to Vichy's loss of control over France's North African territories was the decision on 11 November 1942 to occupy previously unoccupied southern France.[5] As a result, thousands of

French citizens fled across the Pyrenees into Spain, where their arrival both required, and supplied the vehicle for, new contacts between the Franco regime and the French administration in North Africa. The flow of refugees south compensated, in a small way, for the influx of Spanish Republican refugees into France in February 1939. Both groups were met by governments unsure about how to deal with them.[6] The French refugees caught the attention of all three groups who claimed to represent France: the Vichy regime that continued, after Torch, to maintain full diplomatic relations with Spain; the high commission; and later the CFLN, which inherited the high commission's diplomatic mission in Madrid in June 1943.[7] Officials that represented the two latter groups gradually displaced Vichy's as the most influential public face of France in Spain.

If the refugees supplied the vehicle for the contacts, economic and political issues shaped the relationship between French North Africa and Spain. The high commission officials posted to Spain were would-be allies of Britain and the United States, and this fact drew them into the economic strategy that underpinned the Allied relationship with Spain throughout the Second World War. The United States and Great Britain disagreed about the role the high commission and the CFLN should play in the economic war, for the British consistently argued that economic diplomacy in Madrid should remain strictly an Anglo-American affair while the United States sought to integrate French North Africa into the existing Allied policy. Thus the Allies themselves had to decide how best to facilitate relations between Spain and the entity that had emerged in Algiers. The high commission in Algiers was not a free agent in its relations with Franco.

The refugees' arrival and search for passages to North Africa obliged Spain to deal with all of the different groups who claimed to represent France. US support for the high commission was crucial during the negotiations that followed. The refugee crisis led, in turn, to discussions about French North Africa's role in the Allied economic war. Into this situation entered French officials who saw themselves as potential Allied partners, and laid the groundwork for a relationship with Franco's regime on their own, and in conjunction with Britain and the United States. The legacy of that work would go beyond the war, in the desire of the Provisional French Government, successor to the CFLN, to continue to do what it had been doing, especially in trade with Franco's Spain. Out of the experience of war came a realpolitik assessment of French needs in reconstruction, which Spain could fulfill; and, more significantly, a desire to build a role for itself in post-war relations with Spain in union with its Allies.

Crisis and Opportunity: The French Refugee Crisis in Spain, 1942–1944

The large numbers of French exiles in Spain, and their reasons for fleeing from France, entangled them in the diplomacy and strategy of the Second World War. The first group contained a substantial number of military officers who were no longer willing to serve under Vichy after southern France was occupied. They were pro-Vichy but anti-German, and wished to join the war against Germany in order to drive the occupation forces out of France. After February 1943, this elite was joined by larger numbers of French citizens fleeing the imposition of forced labor.[8] They followed the routes used by escaped prisoners of war, downed Allied airmen, Jews, Poles and other foreigners who had crossed into Spain by way of some sixty escape routes run by British intelligence and local resistance groups since 1940.[9] Most hoped to reach North Africa and to join the North African Army, which the high commission, now separated from Vichy, was organizing in preparation for joining the Allies. Thus, the overwhelming majority of Frenchmen in Spain did not think of themselves as refugees, but as potential soldiers in the crusade to liberate France from German occupation.[10] At least 8,000 had arrived by March 1943; by January 1944, their numbers had risen to 16,000.[11] Some made it as far as Barcelona or Madrid, but the Spanish authorities either imprisoned or sent refugees to the crowded and unsanitary refugee camp at Miranda del Ebro in northern Castile. On 14 January 1943, Spain closed the relatively easy route from Tetuán in Spanish Morocco to Fez in French Morocco.[12] The decision trapped most of the refugees in Spain.

The high commission had no hesitation in negotiating with Spain about the refugees, despite Spain's preference for the Axis; rather, it saw an opportunity to act with the goal of establishing international recognition for itself, an "active platform" from which it could claim legitimacy as the representative government of France.[13] Darlan and his associates aimed to obtain recognition as an alternative French government to both Vichy and the Free French primarily by committing the North African Army in the Allied war effort. Yet here was an additional opportunity, and they immediately made plans to take responsibility for the refugees before transferring them out of Spain.[14] The French consul at Tetuán, Achille Clarac, suggested that the high commission should set up an organization at Madrid to distribute funds for food and clothing among the refugee camps and prisons, help refugees with visa applications, and obtain Spain's agreement to the transfer of the refugees to French North Africa.[15] When the high commission's foreign relations secretariat took up the suggestion on 15 January 1943,[16] its goal was not solely humanitarian. The refugees and their relief offered the high commission the opportunity to present itself as the legitimate face of France.

The French Refugee Crisis and Economic Warfare in Spain, 1942–1944

The high commission was already represented at Madrid. Immediately after the German occupation of France, the air attaché at Vichy's embassy, Lt. Col. Pierre Malaise, publicly quit and declared his support for the high commission in Algiers. He fit the profile of many of the military officers who fled to Spain, and many members of the embassy staff in Madrid as well; apart from the ambassador, François Piétri, and the press attaché, Adalbert Laffon, who remained loyal to Vichy, these individuals were strongly anti-German and anglophile.[17] With the establishment of a conservative, anti-German, and non-Gaullist French regime in Algiers, officials like Malaise moved from hidden to open opposition to Vichy, although few did so publicly in the manner of Malaise. Only three colleagues from the French embassy in Madrid joined him in officially abandoning Vichy in December 1942.

Malaise was given two assignments from the high commission in Algiers: to encourage the embassy staff and French expatriates to rally to Darlan, and to persuade the Spanish and Portuguese governments to recognize the high commission in order to enable it to facilitate the movement of refugees to North Africa.[18] Yet Malaise's official position in Spain, which enabled him to carry out what he called his "hidden" mission to rescue the refugees,[19] depended upon the help of the US embassy. The high commission saw itself as a French "government" brought to power with US support.[20] In January 1943, the United States recognized the high commission as the trustee for French interests in North Africa and the United States. Although not recognizing it as the legitimate government of France yet, such action by the United States did not prohibit Algiers from trying to obtain recognition from other states.[21] In Spain, walking this diplomatic tightrope was the responsibility of the US ambassador, Carlton J. Hayes, who appointed Malaise a US attaché in name and the embassy's liaison with the high commission. The Spanish foreign minister, Count Francisco Gómez Jordana, approved the arrangement on 15 December 1942.[22] Thus Spain, without an official act, acknowledged the existence of rival French governments.

As Hayes recalled in his memoirs, US attempts to broker an agreement between the high commission and Spain about the refugees served two purposes. In the long run, any agreement would undermine Vichy's (and Germany's) influence in Spain; in the short-term it would ease the friction between Spain and France in Morocco.[23] Thus the United States too was "prompted by more than humanitarian motives."[24] Hayes helped Malaise as a way to further US and Allied political goals in Spain and the Mediterranean.

Hayes tried to tempt Jordana to advance further. He suggested on 14 January 1943 that Vichy France under German occupation was no longer an independent sovereign state, whereas French North Africa was. Therefore Spain should "at least have official relations" with the high commission, even if it continued to recognize Vichy for legal reasons.[25] Hayes used the refugee question to illustrate his point. As the extent of the French migration into Spain became clear, he wrote to the secretary of state, Cordell Hull and emphasized that it was "absolutely essential from both political and military point of view [that] we give adequate relief to these Allies of ours who cannot be expected to look to Vichy for relief."[26] At the end of January, Hayes reported not only that he had sponsored Malaise, but also that the embassy was supporting between one thousand five hundred and two thousand French refugees at a cost of ten thousand dollars per week. Hayes stressed that the refugees gave the United States the opportunity to take the lead in the Mediterranean from the British, who were critical of US desire to treat Spain with sticks as opposed to carrots. It also allowed the United States to expand its role in the region and become patron of the high commission: "I cannot over-emphasize relation of this whole problem to our war effort and desirability of not requiring the British to bear the principal burden for relieving French especially since North African campaign (sic) under our direction."[27] In response, between 27 March and 21 June 1943 the state department transferred one million dollars to the embassy for Malaise's use.[28] Thus, the US embassy not only helped to move potential troops to North Africa and obtain embryonic diplomatic recognition for the high commission, but also created a growing political role for itself on the Mediterranean front.

The British were just as aware of the geopolitical implications of the refugee crisis. The ambassador at Madrid, the former foreign secretary, Sir Samuel Hoare, recalled in his memoirs that "the work of relief and evacuation was . . . inextricably connected . . . [with] the high politics of our battle with the Germans."[29] In September 1942, the prime minister, Winston Churchill, and the president, Franklin D. Roosevelt, had divided political responsibilities in the western Mediterranean on the basis that Britain should lead in Spain and the United States in North Africa.[30] The division of responsibilities was challenged by the refugee crisis and the US decision to seek official recognition from Spain of the high commission. On 9 December 9 1942 the Foreign Office instructed the British consul general at Barcelona, Harold Farquhar, to encourage refugees who sought Britain's financial help to join the Free French, not the high commission.[31] After an inquiry from the US embassy in London as to the British policy on French refugees in Spain, the Foreign Office explained its stance to the state department on 19 December.[32] The British would encourage any French refugee that sought British assistance to support the Free French based in London, and would not assist anyone in traveling to North Africa. Unlike the United States, Great Britain believed that its strategy in the Mediterranean should remain the same as before, and the arrival of the high commission in Algiers did not change that. There was no desire in London to foster a rival French regime in Algiers, especially since there was one already established on British soil.

Hoare had told the Foreign Office on 29 November that whether the refugees joined the Free French or the high commission hardly mattered; the British should use the funds earmarked for the Free French to help any of them.³³ Hoare argued that instead of turning the refugee crisis into a debate over whether or not the high commission or de Gaulle's Free France was a better alternative to Vichy, Allied unity in Spain was more important, at least in the short-term. Allied policy worked in Madrid largely because the appearance of Anglo-American unity forced the Spaniards to negotiate on economic policy, and any sign of division might be exploited in a way that would see increased ties between Spain and Nazi Germany. Thus Allied goals in Spain obliged him to cooperate with Hayes on the refugee issue, despite Britain's suspicions of the high commission. Hoare later explained that "we alone of the Allied governments had an organization capable of dealing with the many problems created" by the refugees' arrival.³⁴ Thus almost immediately Hoare dispatched his embassy officials to visit camps in which French refugees were placed, and he authorized official complaints to the Spanish Government concerning inadequate conditions there.³⁵ For Britain as well as the United States, the fate of the refugees was tied to relations with Spain in the war, relations with Spain to the future status of the high commission, and its status to the balance of power between the Allies.

For those in London, relations with Spain seemed irrelevant, for it was the question of which French entity to support as an alternative government to Vichy that mattered. Richard Speaight of the Foreign Office wrote to Michael Creswell at the British Embassy in Madrid that "we are not prepared to see men who have opted to join de Gaulle drafted off willy-nilly to North Africa."³⁶ However, the Political and Economic Advisory Council to Allied Headquarters in North Africa agreed with Hoare that British and US officials in Spain should work out "some arrangement" that met the needs of refugees to leave Spain.³⁷ On his own, even with the Foreign Office still complaining, Hoare made an agreement in Madrid that only high military officers desiring to go join de Gaulle should be permitted to travel to Gibraltar and onto London; everyone else would be sent to North Africa under the direction of Malaise and the US Government. Hoare justified his effort as one made in order to "avoid possible friction with Col[onel] Malaise and the United States embassy."³⁸ Ultimately Hoare won out and this agreement was accepted by the Foreign Office; Britain's financial support of French refugees was provided regardless of their political affiliation and it was designed to last only as long as it took for the United States to organize enough money to take on that responsibility itself.³⁹ Despite some early interest, the Free French ultimately did not try to set up their own refugee mission at Madrid, although one of their agents, Robert Mitchell (who used the pseudonym 'Morton') joined the British embassy in February 1943.⁴⁰ However, his task was primarily to organize Free French intelligence operations in occupied France on behalf of de Gaulle's intelligence agency, the *Bureau Central des*

Renseignements et Action, and only secondarily to help the refugees who rallied to de Gaulle.[41] Unlike Malaise, he did not seek official recognition from the Spanish government.

By the end for January, money was flowing to Spain from Algiers and Washington. The high commission authorized Malaise to spend twenty-five million francs, with seventy-five percent of that dedicated to moving refugees from Spain to North Africa, twenty percent on moving them from Portugal; and only five percent for working with the British to move refugees out of Gibraltar.[42] In terms of US dollars, the total cost for refugee relief ranged from three hundred thousand dollars per month in early 1943 to five hundred thousand per month by November.[43] The inability of the high commission to convert francs to pesetas in the first half of 1943 meant the burden of the costs was borne by the United States. French contributions, made up of money from North Africa and from the profits of trade with Spain, never covered more than around forty percent of the total cost for refugee relief.[44] Nonetheless, the arrival in Spain of monies for refugee support and maintenance bought both the Americans and Malaise political influence, for as early as 15 February, Jordana told Hayes that the Spanish Red Cross would help US, British and non-Vichy French officials in looking after the refugees while they were in Spain. In addition, Spain would do all it could to help the refugees to continue their journey to North Africa.[45] He thus opened the door to negotiations about transport.

Spain, despite its recognition of Vichy as the legitimate government of France, preferred not to have to look after the refugees, and wanted to expedite their departure. This was more easily arranged with the high commission than with Vichy, as Algiers was the preferred destination of most of the refugees; to send them on was easier than to send them back. When the German ambassador, Hans Adolf von Moltke, protested Spain's willingness to negotiate with Algiers on the refugee issue, Franco replied that "notwithstanding the same friendliness towards Germany" his government maintained the Allied landings in Morocco and Algeria forced Spain to alter its stance.[46] The US pressure on behalf of Malaise played a role here, as did Spain's economic ties with French North Africa, especially Morocco. Indeed, a early as 10 December 1942, Malaise was given the first indication that the Spanish government would acknowledge him, as long as he was "discreet", owing to their need of the high commission's help in keeping North African phosphates flowing to Spain.[47]

Solving the refugee problem without repudiating Vichy proved easier for the Spaniards owing to the actions of Piétri and Malaise. In December 1942, Malaise had tried unsuccessfully to persuade Piétri to rally to Darlan, from whom he brought a personal letter. Piétri, a loyal conservative ally of Pétain, refused; he was certain that Germany would win the war.[48] Nonetheless, in mid-December, the two men made a "non-aggression" pact: Piétri would not seek Malaise's expulsion from Spain as long as Malaise did not try to persuade the French colony in Spain to take sides with the high commission; Malaise's work was to be limited to the recently arrived refugees and nothing else.[49]

In reality, Piétri made efforts to stop Malaise even when it came to refugee relief, but they proved unsuccessful. On 5 January 1943, he reminded the Spanish foreign ministry that relations between Spain and the high commission were "on the margin of regular Franco-Spanish relations" and asked it to withdraw its recognition of Malaise.[50] He also tried to maintain ties with officials in French Morocco, the source of the phosphates trade.[51] The embassy created a refugee section of its own staffed by the military attaché, Colonel Buot de l'Epine, the first secretary, Renaud Sivan, and the ecclesiastical attaché, Mgr. André Boyer-Mas, who began in early January to pay visits to refugees interned at Miranda del Ebro. By the end of the month, Boyer-Mas had organized a system of relief by which US, high commission, and (some) Vichy funds were given to the Spanish Red Cross for the relief of the refugees.[52] In fact, Boyer-Mas was working the entire time with Malaise and the US embassy on behalf of the high commission, a fact Piétri later claimed to have been aware of.[53] In Malaise's words, Boyer-Mas' role as liaison to the Spanish Red Cross was the "indispensable fiction" that enabled the Spanish foreign ministry to reconcile its recognition of Vichy with its behavior toward Malaise.[54] Piétri claims in his memoirs that the embassy took the lead in organizing aid to the refugees.[55] In fact, he allowed Malaise and Boyer-Mas to usurp his role.

Unofficial activity on behalf of the high commission became official when Boyer-Mas and most of the other embassy staff publicly resigned from Vichy's Embassy and declared their support for Algiers on 23 March. In addition to Bout de l'Épine and Sivan, they included the financial attaché, Comte Largentaye, the councilor, René Lamarle, and Roger Drouin, an economist who had been posted from Vichy in February. They immediately joined Malaise's office as representatives of the high commission in Spain. The officials at the French consulates in Barcelona, Bilbao, and Malaga also resigned and began to represent the high commission, which was accepted by the Spanish Government. Their colleagues at the consulates in Palma de Mallorca and Alicante secretly shifted their allegiance to the high commission without formally resigning from Vichy.[56] Even the *Instituts Français* at Madrid and Barcelona declared at the end of March that they had rallied to Giraud.[57] Piétri, though he knew his staff to be anti-German, was overwhelmed by the "stampede" which left him with only two subordinates at the embassy.[58] Even though Vichy replaced the consuls-general at Barcelona, Bilbao and Malaga, Piétri became a "phantom ambassador at the head of a rump embassy."[59] The high commission had become the face of France in Spain.

The day before Boyer-Mas formally resigned, on 22 March 1943, he received a letter from the high commission's secretary for foreign affairs, Jacques Tarbé de Saint-Hardouin, giving him responsibility for the relief of the refugees. Thus, he slid between the services of two French governments without changing jobs. He opened a separate office from Malaise's for refugee relief, with a staff of twenty in Madrid and others posted at the key refugee centers. He allowed Malaise to use the Red Cross liaison service as a disguise for the high commission's spies in Spain, who, in turn, made connections with Resistance networks, and carried out military reconnaissance in occupied France.[60]

The first transfer of one thousand five hundred French refugees from Cadiz to Casablanca by the high commission was agreed on 15 February: all refugees would be treated as non-belligerents and the Spanish Red Cross would hand them over to officials from the French embassy for shipment.[61] Their departure was scheduled for the night of 9–10 March. However, on the sixth, Spanish officials, prompted by von Moltke, acting on orders from Berlin, told Boyer-Mas that the high commission's ships would not be allowed to use Spanish ports, as Spain was renouncing the agreement. [62] It would only agree to issue the refugees with visas to enter Portugal, if the Portuguese government concurred. Moltke, who blamed the refugees for Germany's shortage of labor in occupied France, threatened that German submarines would sink the refugee ships if they were allowed to sail from Spanish ports. Hayes concluded that Moltke's action was, "only a part of [the] general diplomatic offensive to bring Spain into the war on [the] Axis side or exact other military concessions from Spain."[63] The decision to cancel the agreement was attributable to the debate between pro-German and pro-Allied members of the Spanish government over the direction of its foreign policy.[64] French officials concluded that the interior ministry and the police, who were markedly pro-German, had over-ruled the foreign ministry where, generally speaking, the high commission could "count on friends."[65]

Jordana told Hayes on 7 March that he was still willing to issue visas for entry to Portugal to the French refugees at Cadiz. He claimed that there was "no change in Spain's basic policy" of helping the refugees leave; the only disagreement was about the "ways and means."[66] As a result, Hayes visited Lisbon and with the Spanish ambassador, Franco's brother, Nicolás, presented an unofficial, though successful, joint request to Portugal for help.[67] The Spanish foreign ministry confirmed on 10 March that Spain would allow refugees bound for North Africa to leave Spain via Portugal.[68] In practice, visas originally permitting transit to North Africa were altered to permit transit only between Spain and Portugal. With the agreement of Portugal, the high commission began to prepare to move French refugees from Spain to Setubal, Portugal and from there to Casablanca.

Owing to Spain's prohibition of the use of the direct route to North Africa, by the end of March, one thousand two hundred and sixty five refugees were stuck at Cadiz, six thousand two hundred and sixty more in internment camps and supervised accommodation, and an additional four thousand eight hundred French refugees were in camps having declared themselves to be either Americans (eight hundred) or Canadians (four thousand).[69] With one to two hundred more crossing the border from France every day from November through June, the cost of transport was rapidly rising beyond the means of the hard-pressed high commission. Clandestine exit from Spain was expensive and dangerous, and available only to very few.[70] Nonetheless, the transit of the refugees in Cadiz by way of Setubal, which began in mid-April, gave the high commission the opportunity to bid for diplomatic recognition from Portugal,[71] and to strengthen Giraud's North African Army. For example, boats that arrived at Casablanca on 30 June 1943 brought fifty seven active and reserve army officers and eight hundred and twelve infantrymen; on 22 August, fifty four active and seventy one reserve army officers, five hundred and twenty two infantrymen, two hundred and twenty one airmen, and fifty sailors; on 25 September, fifty active and forty nine reserve army officers, one hundred forty two active and two hundred thirty four reserve infantrymen and one hundred ninety civilians who were ready to enroll.[72]

The Algiers Mission in Madrid

The refugees, despite their military value, played a more important political role. They gave the high commission the opportunity to claim to represent France, and they gave its US patrons a new weapon in the economic war being waged in Spain. From the start, Hayes had urged Malaise to behave as if the high commission was the legitimate embodiment of the French state; to seek not only provisional recognition by the Franco regime and the liberation of French refugees, but also recognition of the high commission's passports and a commercial treaty.[73] On 14 January, Hayes formally requested Spain to cease to recognize Vichy and to recognize solely the high commission.[74] Spain could not grant the request for fear of provoking Germany rather than Vichy, because Germany rightly saw the high commission as the creation of the Allies. Spain's undersecretary of state for foreign affairs, José Pan de Soraluce, reminded the high commission's officials on a number of occasions that the presence of German troops in the Pyrenees required Spain to be "prudent" lest it should provoke a German occupation.[75] Although it is now evident that Germany, bogged down in Russia, could not have diverted forces to Spain, the Spaniards could not be certain.[76] The cancellation of the agreement over the direct shipment of refugees was accompanied by the seizure of the Cherifian post office in Tetuán, an act, like Spain's occupation of Tangier in 1940, which violated agreements over Morocco dating from 1923 to which both Spain and France were parties.

Spain tried to humor both sides. As early as the end of December 1942, Pan de Soraluce told an official of the French consulate at Tetuán that Spain would be willing to receive a delegation from the high commission that would deal with subjects other the refugees.[77] In February, Hayes let Malaise approach the Spanish government directly rather than indirectly as an affiliate of the US embassy.[78] The Franco regime hoped to be able to maintain official relations with Vichy and appease Germany while obtaining the benefits from dealing with the high commission by making short-term agreements dealing with specific issues such as the refugees. As long as Malaise worked from the US embassy, and did not seek formal recognition for the high commission, the tactics were viable. The high commission, however, aimed for "*de facto* recognition of French Africa, a step preceding the necessary *de jure* recognition."[79] Thus, in February 1943 the high commission instructed the French consul-general at Tetuán, Achille Clarac, to visit Madrid to negotiate the terms of a more formal relationship with Spain.

Even if the terms of the agreement fell short of official recognition, they would give Malaise and his colleagues immunity and the right to use coded telegrams and diplomatic couriers to communicate with Algiers.[80] Clarac stressed to Pan de Soraluce that beyond refugees, the two sides shared political interests in Morocco, concern for the Spanish community who lived in Algeria (especially in the region of Oran), and mutual trade interests. He added, in proof of Giraud's goodwill, that the high commission instead of authorizing the formation of Republican organizations among Spanish refugees in North Africa was negotiating with Mexico in the hope that "red refugees" could be shipped to Latin America.[81] On 11 March, Pan de Soraluce told Clarac that Spain would allow the high commission to open its own mission with some, but not all, diplomatic privileges.[82]

Spain's decision to recognize the high commission reflected Franco's priorities in 1943: although sympathetic to the Axis cause, he sought benefits for Spain from both sides.[83] As demonstrated in the case of refugee transport, however, German pressure on the regime in Madrid remained significant. At the end of March Clarac passed along to the high commission a warning from Hayes that Franco's regime was facing a "decisive crisis" in foreign as well as domestic affairs as they fate of Spain in the war was debated.[84] Piétri attributed the privileges Malaise and his mission had won, which amounted to *de jure* recognition of the high commission, to Spain's reorientation toward a more favorable view of the Allies.[85] Over the course of the first half of 1943, this proved correct, for Spain's shift to more of a pro-Allied position was confirmed after the Allied victory in Tunisia in April. This brought immediate results for Algiers, for shortly afterwards, the head of the Spanish foreign ministry's European section, Campusano, confirmed to the high commission's first secretary in Madrid, Renaud Sivan, that Spain would make an "important modification" in its policies toward the high commission, partly owing to the Allies' success and partly to the two states' shared economic and colonial interests.[86]

Allied victory in North Africa compelled Spain to seek *rapprochement* with the Allies themselves, and with Algiers.[87] Thus Spanish officials, in meetings with Allied diplomats, cited the example of Spain's willingness to make arrangements for the transit of refugees as evidence of its neutrality.[88] By the end of May, the foreign ministry issued diplomatic passports to the high commission's officials and prepared to send its own representative to Algiers. Malaise and his colleagues moved from the US embassy into their own offices.[89] On 16 May, Giraud wrote personally to Franco to thank him for "the chivalrous spirit with which the Spanish Government has authorized the departure of many hundred French, living witnesses to the despair of their homeland." He added that the action was "the best expression of the sympathy that Spain has always shown to stricken peoples."[90]

France and Allied Economic Warfare in Spain

If the arrangements for the refugees gave the high commission its most striking opportunity to push for recognition from Spain, economic relations, if less dramatic, were more significant. Spanish agriculture depended upon North African phosphates: under agreements with Vichy, Spain received four hundred fifty thousand tons annually, mostly from Morocco, making the region Spain's largest supplier.[91] When Vichy's commercial attaché, André Pettit, resigned alongside Malaise in November 1942, Darlan appointed him the agent at Madrid for the *Office Chérifien des Phosphates* (OCP) based in Rabat. Saint-Hardouin called Moroccan phosphates "at the moment the most effective instrument of political pressure" available to the high commission.[92] He was right. In mid-December, Spain asked the OCP through unofficial channels not to cut off its supplies.[93] In response, the OCP authorized shipments as if Spain's agreements with Vichy still applied.[94]

The high commission, however, was not a free agent. The United States and Great Britain, which were waging economic war in the Iberian Peninsula, would not allow would-be allies to set their own economic goals to be reached by their own means. If the high commission aimed to expand its role in Spain, it had to contribute to Allied economic warfare policies. The Allied relationship with Spain was driven by the fear that it might join the Axis. Spain's geopolitical position at the western entrance to the Mediterranean made its decision whether to intervene in the war important to both sides.[95] Two theories are current about the benefits the Germans expected from a Spanish alliance. The first states that it would have facilitated Germany's peripheral strategy against Britain in the Mediterranean during the period when Britain stood alone, especially in 1940 when Germany contemplated an attack on Gibraltar.[96] After Italy's military failed to achieve victories in Libya and Greece, Adolf Hitler insisted in November 1940 that Spain should be forced to join the Axis, to end the war in the Mediterranean quickly.[97] The second, more recent, theory states that in 1940–41, Germany planned to use Spain as the "gateway" to French North Africa and Spain's Atlantic islands, there to set up the bases needed in the inevitable conflict with the United States.[98] Hitler wanted Spain to declare war, and Franco thought of doing so. On 12 June 1940 he changed Spain's status from neutral to non-belligerent, which was interpreted as a "first step" in the process of joining the war on the Axis side at some point in the future.[99] Spain also occupied the international city of Tangier in June 1940, and in both June and October, when he met Hitler at Hendaye, Franco offered to enter the war in return for economic and military assistance and the promise of territory in North Africa.[100] Spain's continued economic and military weakness, Germany's refusal to guarantee territorial gains for Spain, and its inability to quickly defeat Great Britain in the last part of 1940, held Franco back.[101] Spain's direct military involvement in the Second World War was limited to the dispatch of a small force, the Blue Division, to fight the Soviet Union alongside German troops in 1941.[102]

Britain, backed up by the United States after it entered the war in December 1941, aimed first at keeping Spain out of the war and second at lessening the help Spain could give to Germany under the guise of benevolent neutrality.[103] Allied officials assumed that trade with the Franco regime could be used to limit Spain's ties to Germany, deny Germany access to strategic minerals, and acquire them for the Allies.[104] Spain, of course, hoped to trade profitably with both sides, especially owing to Germany's shortage of minerals.[105] This required an assertive Allied policy that aimed to offer Spain important goods at low prices in return for purchasing Spanish strategic minerals at higher prices. As Malcolm Thomson of the British Ministry of Economic Warfare stated in February 1944, the Allies, in order to stop Spanish trade with Germany, required "both the cooperation of the Spanish Government, which we can only obtain by providing motives of self-interest, and ample purchasing power which we can only obtain by the provision of goods."[106] By 1943, Britain and the United States benefited from such trade with Spain through the acquisition of strategic minerals such as iron ore, pyrites, and wolfram, but it was a constant struggle to obtain such goods and limit Germany's purchase of the same.[107] The Allies often differed when it came to the tactics used to limit Spanish trade with Germany. Whereas Britain wished to entice Spain with Anglo-American products and by paying higher prices than the Germans paid for strategic minerals, in the hope of making Spain "economically dependent",[108] the United States, as Denis Smyth explains, saw economic warfare as "an occasion for coercion rather than an opportunity for courtship."[109]

The French Refugee Crisis and Economic Warfare in Spain, 1942–1944

The High Commission in Algiers, as an emerging ally of Britain and the US, was thrust into the debates and directives of economic warfare policy. As soon as Clarac arrived at Madrid in February, he had to deal with the question of whether or not the phosphates trade should be used as a political lever to wean Spain away from Germany. Under pressure from their own ambassador, the British had conceded that the high commission and its patron, the US Embassy, should take charge of refugee relief. However, when it came to economic matters Hoare and the Foreign Office in London were on the same page. Hoare wrote to London on 11 February 1943 that Clarac's desire to open trade talks with Madrid might give Spain the opportunity to demand certain economic concessions in return for recognizing the high commission, which "might gravely embarrass Anglo-American plans."[110] Essentially, the British assumed that by allowing trade agreements to be made independently by French North Africa, the French would pay little attention to the economic warfare goals the Allies sought through their very controlled trade with Madrid, and thus Spain would be able to achieve a greater freedom in trade, a situation that Allied economic policy sought to avoid. At the Foreign Office, one of the officers on the European desk, Horace Rumbold, agreed when he outlined the strategic problem posed by Clarac's visit:

> When Malaise established his mission, he showed signs of wanting to use the economic lever to obtain formal recognition from the Spanish Govt., and M. Clarac seems to have the same ideas. We want to prevent such a process both because the bargaining counters they might try to use might conflict with our engagement with Spain of Nov. 8th... We can't stop him from going to Madrid, and I think all we can tell Sir S. Hoare is to discourage him, in concert with his US colleague if possible, from trying to add to the status or increase the responsibility of the North African mission.[111]

The agreement Rumbold mentions underpinned the Allies' stance towards Spain in the aftermath of Torch. On 8 November 1942, Hoare and Hayes had delivered messages from Churchill and Roosevelt to Franco designed to reassure him that Allied operations in North Africa were not directed against Spain and that the Allies recognized its wish to stay out of the war. However Britain went further than the United States in promising that the war should not disrupt Anglo-Spanish trade or the Spanish economy.[112] With more victories in Tunisia in April 1943 and peace in Algeria, the British envisaged increased trade in North African products.[113] Georgianna Pouzzner of the Foreign Economic Administration in the United States agreed, writing that North African "exportable surpluses and import needs" would not only divert Spanish trade away from the Axis states to somewhere closer and more economically sound, it would also increase the amount of trade that the US and Great Britain could conduct with Spain, further reducing the "flow of strategic materials" from

Spain to the enemy.[114] From Algiers, Britain's minister resident, Harold Macmillan, echoed this sentiment, arguing that for the rest of 1943, Allied chances for weaning Spain away from Germany were best only if they promoted its trade with North Africa.[115]

The aim was clear; however, the Allies fell out over the role of the high commission in this policy. The British assumed that only British and US officials would wield the "controlling influence" in economic negotiations with the Franco regime; the high commission's mission in Madrid was acceptable only if it did not try to act independently, on its own terms, to reach its own goals.[116] The first secretary at the US Embassy in London, H. Freeman Matthews, rejected this view, calling the British, "far from helpful" for trying to exclude the high commission. As it had on the refugee question, the United States would act as a patron for the high commission on economic affairs, and thus would encourage, support, and welcome the entry of the high commission into general negotiations about the terms of trade with Spain.[117]

By the middle of April, the British agreed to support the high commission's demand for the formal recognition of its mission at Madrid, as long as more senior officials replaced Malaise and Pettit.[118] In return, Clarac conceded that any French trade negotiation with Spain had to be conducted within the framework devised by the Allies, and thus the high commission welcomed the chance to join the combined economic warfare operations of the Allies in Spain.[119] This framework centered on the purchase of wolfram and other minerals in exchange for cotton and sugar, and credits. Britain controlled its trade through the United Kingdom Commercial Corporation (UKCC), while the United States used a similar company, the United States Commercial Corporation (USCC), and private companies. Their activities were coordinated by an Anglo-American Joint Committee at Madrid that negotiated a series of short-term gentlemen's agreements with the Franco regime rather than long-term commercial treaties.[120] France now joined this committee.

The decision to allow the high commission to enter into the Joint Committee structure did not assuage Britain's doubts. As Malcolm Thomson of the Ministry of Economic Warfare explained, the French "should not be blinded, by narrow commercial considerations of price, either to the more important economic issues at stake or to the very heavy sacrifices being made by the USA and UK in pursuance of politico-economic aims in the Peninsula."[121] The Anglo-American policy of paying more for Spanish strategic goods than they were worth, in order to prevent sales to Germany, might be compromised if the French rode in looking to make a deal with Madrid. Among US officials, however, the opposite view prevailed. The entrance of French North Africa into the cross-trade system, as it was called, with Spain would not only enable the Allies to "increase [their] joint pre-emptive activities" with Franco's regime, but also reduce the burden of supplying the Allied armies in North Africa.[122] Even though some US officials wanted, like the British, to make the French trade under the auspices of the UKCC and USCC,[123] most recognized the relationship between Iberian trade, formal recognition, and acceptance of the high commission as an ally. Robert Murphy, political advisor to the Allied commander in Algiers, General Dwight D. Eisenhower, argued that the French had to be treated like other allies, for "the regime here is sensitive as regards its position and resents any approach which tends to treat North Africa as an occupied area or denies it a position of respect."[124] For Carlton Hayes, the potential of working alongside a separate and sovereign French North Africa in Spain for purposes beyond trade was immense. He wrote to Secretary of State Cordell Hull that North African trade, involving the high commission directly, "is the only bait sufficiently attractive to induce Spain to recognize French representation here. Eventually French representatives could take over French refugee problem using funds derived from such commercial transactions. They could also assist the Giraud Government in other ways and would be a valuable channel to us for military information from France."[125]

Britain's fear that the French would try to trade outside the existing allied structure was unfounded. Clarac acknowledged in April that working through the Joint Committee was indispensable both to gain Allied support and concessions from the Franco regime, even though if deprived the high commission of the opportunity to link a trade agreement with official recognition.[126] In conversation in April with the US representative to the high commission, Paul Culbertson, in Algiers, the economic affairs commissioner Joseph Bataille emphasized that the high commission was willing to give up its push for formal recognition, which Spain was unlikely to give, in return for "a prominent part" alongside US and British officials in policy-making toward Spain.[127] All that French North Africa asked for was the ability to represent themselves as an equal to the Americans and the British in trade, and thus be permitted to create their own trading enterprise comparable to that of the UKCC and USCC companies.[128]

The diplomatic, political and especially economic consolidation of the alternative face of France in Spain was furthered when France's two rivals to Vichy, de Gaulle's Free France and Giraud's high commission, combined. In March 1943, when the two men began the talks that led in June to the union of their forces in the CFLN, they agreed that the high commission mission in Madrid should represent both of them[129] The union was uneasy: de Gaulle, having "consumed" Giraud by moving many of his supporters out of key positions, first shunted him off to run the army, then off the CFLN altogether in April 1944.[130] Yet the CFLN's quest for legitimacy as an Ally, as well as its base in North Africa, ensured continuity in relations with Spain. Indeed, Saint-Hardouin's replacement by René Massigli as head of the foreign affairs secretariat in Algiers in July 1943 was preceded in June by the appointment of José Antonio

Sangróniz, a former Ambassador to Venezuela, to represent the Spanish foreign ministry to the new government in Algiers. Spanish-North African relations were growing along the lines established by Giraud's regime.

Germany and Vichy were still able to influence some of Spain's decisions; for example, the Spanish rejection in September 1943 of Armand du Chayla to replace Malaise was linked to a German protest.[131] And Gaullists and Giraudists found working together at Madrid difficult, especially in the area of intelligence operations.[132] Nonetheless, the CFLN took over the relief and transport of refugees from Boyer-Mas, and placed its representatives in most of the major cities and provinces (five in Catalonia, two in Aragon, three in Castile, four in the northwest and three in the south).[133] Most significantly, it took over from the high commission and subsequently played an important role in Allied economic war in Spain. In this manner, the CFLN oversaw the expansion of trade between Madrid and French North Africa.

André Pettit was replaced as the top French economic official in Madrid by Roger Drouin at the end of May, and he immediately took a seat on the Allied Joint Committee. In addition, the Joint Committee created a sub-committee to deal with North African-Spanish trade.[134] In August, André Audrain was appointed head of the *Office Commercial français en Espagne* that was meant to operate alongside the USCC and UKCC;[135] the Gaullist Jacques Truelle replaced Malaise at the head of the French mission in October. At the end of August, a new agreement on phosphates was reached that allowed Spain to buy three hundred sixty thousand tons of phosphates from the CFLN by 1 January 1944 in return for machinery and textiles; similar agreements followed the next April and July.[136]

More significant to the CFLN politically, the United States and Great Britain treated it as an ally in Madrid, as Massigli told the CFLN in November 1943.[137] This point was reinforced by Truelle, who constantly reminded his superiors in Algiers that it "would be [a] grave [mistake] to put ourselves in a position in which we were deprived... of the always effective and generous support offered and given by the embassies of our two friends."[138] As a result of coordinated Allied pressure, by 2 May 1944, the Franco regime gave in and signed an agreement that severely restricted the export of wolfram to Germany. In addition, Spain closed the German consulate at Tangier, withdrew its Blue Division troops fighting in the USSR and promised to expel German spies from Spain.[139] Interestingly enough, this sign of Spanish acquiescence was preceded by a Franco-Spanish accord in April, approved by Britain and the US, which allowed for a more permanent arrangement on phosphates and other trade.[140] As part of the Allied camp, then, France contributed to the overall diplomatic settlement reached with the Franco regime in 1944. From this point on, Allied policy in Spain was less about negotiating with Franco and more about ensuring that German and Spanish officials in Iberia adhered to the agreements made.[141]

France was an equal ally in this regard too, for the CFLN joined the United States and Great Britain in making demands on Spain in 1944 and 1945 to expel German agents and turn over German property to the Allies.[142]

Franco-Spanish Relations in the Immediate Aftermath of Liberation

The result of France's role as a partner in Allied economic warfare toward Spain was to create a relationship between the CFLN, which transformed itself into the Provisional Government of the French Republic (GPRF) in the midst of France's Liberation in August 1944, and Franco's Spain. The position of France's Allies was a significant factor in the creation of the relationship that emerged over the course of 1943 and 1944, as was the fact that French North Africa could contribute to economic policy in Iberia. Both factors combined to produce within the new government in Paris a desire to continue having a presence as an Allied and trading power in Spain.

Issues such as the restoration of international status for the Spanish-occupied city of Tangier were not only of interest to France, but to the Allied powers and their visions for post-war settlement.[143] Spain, wrote one official of the Quai d'Orsay in October 1944, was dependent upon the Allies for its future development and place in the world; France, therefore, could not do otherwise but decide the course of its own relations with Spain within the context of France's own position as an ally to Great Britain and the United States. Until the three western states reached an agreement amongst themselves on how to treat Spain, "the wisest counsel is no doubt not to engage the question of the future, [and] not to precipitate the development of a crisis for which the solution is not in place."[144]

In addition to continuing its role as an Allied power in Spain, the French Mission of Jacques Truelle in Madrid, aided now by the new Commercial Councillor, Jean Hugues, looked forward to planning a program of French purchases in Spain based on the need to rebuild Metropolitan France, and hoped to move from short-term buying toward a full Franco-Spanish commercial agreement.[145] Politically, the transformation of the Franco-Spanish relationship from one of wartime contingency to one that resembled a state of post-war near-normalcy was underway immediately following the Liberation of France in August 1944. Truelle wrote:

> The French Government cannot do otherwise than to continue the policy which it decided to adopt with regard to Spain, the day when a Mission, under the auspices of the Red Cross, was established in Madrid and in Algiers a Spanish Mission was set up as a Consulate for the representation of Spanish interests in all of the French Empire. Today, the Spanish Government has informed us of its

intention to go further along the road to recognition. Will we compromise ourselves in pursuing this evolution? [If we think so] it will become impossible to count any further on Spain, one of the only countries capable of assisting us in our reconstruction.[146]

In Paris, the same conclusion had already been reached, for the European section of the CFLN's Foreign Affairs Secretariat wrote to the newly appointed Secretary-Generalof the Foreign Ministry, Jean Chauvel, on 25 August that, "for however uncertain the duration of the present regime in Spain is, it is not a question for us to refuse to resume relations." The memorandum concluded that, "it is right to acknowledge that the Provisional Government welcomes without reticence, but with firmness, the openings that have been made."[147]

The two themes of coordinating Allied policy on Spain, and in seeking economic benefits for France, were the basis of an emerging realpolitik approach within the Quai d'Orsay, the French Foreign Ministry, in 1944–1945. In a note to Foreign Minister Georges Bidault's *Cabinet du Ministre* in March 1945, the European section of the Quai d'Orsay stressed:

> It is not the time, when the Americans and the British, without any preoccupation over the past attitude of General Franco's Government, deploy all their efforts to open in Spain new markets and secure certain provisions, to think ourselves able to break relations with a Spain that, according to our Commercial Councilor in Madrid, is disposed to send to France the primary materials necessary for the resumption of our industry.[148]

Following the Liberation of France in 1944, and throughout 1945, Spanish foodstuffs proved vital to France's reconstruction, with 20% of all French fruit coming from across the Pyrenees.[149] The Quai achieved what it had long sought from Spain with the signature of the Franco-Spanish commercial treaty in September, 1945, an agreement which reaffirmed the processes and procedures of the 1940 trade accord between Franco and the Third Republic as the best way to organize Franco-Spanish trading relations for the future.[150] Maurice Dejean, who had been involved in the final negotiations, held that such arrangements with Spain did not "give any political advantage" to the Francoist regime; instead, it was France that received economic and other advantages, and the French Government welcomed this, especially as the only other option was to "leave the field open to our competitors like Great Britain and the United States."[151]

In the immediate post-war period, as Fernando Guirao has argued, the Spanish Government positioned itself to appear to the West in a positive light, especially concerning its potential commercial role in European reconstruction.[152] And certainly these arguments were met with receptive ears amongst Britain, French and American officials contemplating economic renewal as well as the continuation of the conflict with Nazi Germany, at least in the short term. However, the Spanish position was also interpreted by the West in an affirmative manner because of the relationships built up in the years of Allied economic warfare. This was especially so in the French case.

Summary

Francisco Franco's Spanish regime, while certainly not powerful economically or militarily, did play a role of "international significance" for both Nazi Germany and the Allied powers as it debated whether or not to enter the Second World War in 1940–1941, and then proceeded to test the goodwill of the United States and Great Britain by continuing to offer the Nazis significant assistance through 1944–1945.[153] Spain's potential to shift the geostrategic advantage in the Mediterranean to the Axis led to the economic warfare policies of the Allies, which combined coercion and a desire to control Spain's trade with the promise of material benefits if the Axis was abandoned. The complex nature of Allied diplomacy in Spain created many challenges for the United States and Great Britain, and indeed Allied policy was not always consistent in facing these. Arguably, the impact of Operation Torch and the creation of an Allied French entity in North Africa, combined with the German occupation of Vichy France in response, created one of the most significant obstacles to a clearly defined and smoothly implemented Allied policy in Spain.

More significantly for this study, the movement of refugees from France to Spain, and their desire to join the emerging army of the French high commission in Algiers, created the pretext for Spanish-Algiers relations. Due to the continued existence of Vichy France, however, the Spanish Government was not completely free to deal with French North African high commission in the open. Only the support of the Allies, in particular the United States, allowed French North Africa and Spain to negotiate with one another, first indirectly, then bilaterally. The success of this opening would encourage the high commission, and its successor, the Algiers-based Committee of General Charles de Gaulle, to expand on relations with Madrid, partly in order to stake a claim as the legitimate representative of France in the world. The Spanish decision in March 1944 to pass over its trusteeship of German interests in North Africa to the International Red Cross was, for Spanish representative in Algiers José Antonio Sangróniz, equivalent to Franco's *de facto* recognition of the CFLN as the legitimate government of France.[154]

These openings represented the basis for a realpolitik approach to Franco's Spain in the aftermath of Liberation and the CFLN's transformation into the Provisional Government of the French Republic. France had good reasons, especially economically, to continue to work with Franco. Moreover, the realpolitik approach to Spain was linked to France's emergence as an ally of Great Britain and the United States. Having entered the diplomatic world of Madrid with Allied support, France could only continue as a member of the Allied front as the post-war status of Franco's regime was contemplated. In short, economic motivations and Allied policy, both of which had been essential in wartime, further served to reinforce the status quo. While it was conceded that no French citizen viewing Spain from the other side of Liberation "had any reason to favor the maintenance in power of a regime that was imposed, five years ago, only with the support of Italian tanks and German air planes, at the price of the expulsion and persecution of the liberal and democratic class which France counts as its true friends,"[155] such sentiment could not be the motivating factor behind policy. National self-interest and alliance politics required France to continue developing its position in Iberia as it had been during the war, through diplomacy, economics and consultation with the western Allies. This was the basis of France's realpolitik approach to Franco in the immediate aftermath of France's own Liberation.

2

The Resistance and Spanish Republicanism in Liberated France, 1944–1945

While writing about the "Vichy Syndrome", Henry Rousso took time to comment on its cousin, the "resitancialist myth."[1] Constructed by both Gaullists and Communists in the period immediately after French Liberation, the image of a nation opposed to Nazi occupation and Vichy collaboration provoked representations of moral choice, deep-rooted democratic impulses and an idealistic cause. Of course, this was over-stated, but its pervasiveness and the extent of propaganda associated with such imagery in the aftermath of French Liberation seemed to hearken the beginning of a "new politics", one symbolized by centre-left coalition governments which conceived of issues as "moral engagements."[2] Yet despite the prevalence of the "Resistance myth" and its imagery, both Rousso and Jean-Pierre Rioux argue that it did not change politics, citing, for instance, the fact that a new "Party of the Resistance" was unable to be created.[3] In Rousso's words, "the post-war citizen clung to the reassuring image of a resisting France, but the desire for a return to normalcy and the wish to forget the exceptional circumstances of the Occupation stood in the way of any real consecration of the Resistance."[4] The historiography of the Fourth Republic has been grounded in tales of failed revolution and missed opportunity and arguments that the continuity of elites and political parties represented a lack of imagination and vigor in political life and the process of reconstruction. The result was that by early 1945, "it was clear that the utopian hopes of an alternative legitimacy emerging from the Resistance had been dashed."[5]

Yet there remains the fact that from late 1944 through 1945 and into 1946, French popular sentiment increasingly favored removing Franco from power and restoring Spain's pre-Civil War Republic. How does the renewed debate over Spain fit with such conclusions about a new era of politics? Previous studies have demonstrated the importance of the Spanish question in French politics immediately following the Liberation.[6] While Spain always attracted liberal and left-wing coverage in the United States and Great Britain, Jill Edwards is quick to remind us that the Spanish Question was, in these countries, never more than a "side-show."[7] By contrast, John Young has emphasized that in France left-wing politicians in the Constituent National Assembly saw the Spanish question "almost as *the* most vital question in foreign affairs."[8] However, the significance of this focus on Spain for the larger debate about France's role in the world has been neglected. Anti-Franco sentiment was especially strong among the parties and movements of the internal French Resistance that had, they argued, revived French republicanism through the defeat of the collaborationist Vichy regime. These groups desired to use the idea of universalistic republicanism as the basis for a reconstructed Europe, and the argument in Franco's case was particularly strong because not only was Spain an authoritarian state, but during the Second World War the Spanish regime was "repeatedly at the edge" of a decision to join the Axis in war.[9] Thus many individuals in France believed that removing Franco from power was a justifiable war aim whose achievement could lay the groundwork for a new foreign policy in the post-war period. Justice was to be served by pursuing such a policy.

This chapter examines the propaganda, press coverage and actions of various Resistance organizations, political parties and newly-formed groups such as the *Association France–Espagne* when it came to the question of Spain. Such propaganda concerning Spain and the cause of Spanish Republicanism drew upon links, both real and imagined, between the French Resistance and the Spanish opposition, much of which was exiled inside France during this time, and advocated that France pursue the end of the Franco regime as a policy goal. The concept of justice as a motivation for international change dominated the discourse. In addition to articulating a rationale for support of the cause of Spanish Republicanism, many with ties to the Resistance proved to be supportive of Spanish Republican activism along the border with Spain, despite concerns of the government in Paris about the impact such activity could have on relations with Madrid. In these ways, then, the argument for justice and the preferred policy of isolating Franco with the intent of facilitating his exit from power were made, in opposition to any idea of realpolitik.

The Resistance and Foreign Policy

The makers of policy toward Spain before Liberation, the representatives of Algiers, whether in the name of General Giraud or General de Gaulle, were elites, with ties to the military and the Third Republic, who had broken from Vichy. They were only part of the French Resistance. The larger internal

Resistance, and the mass of the French public, had been unable, under German occupation, to play a role in the formation of French North Africa's international policy. The Spanish issue, as it had in the 1930s, would serve as a lightning rod for those on the Left not directly involved in the formation of policy. With the move of de Gaulle's Provisional Government back to France itself, the interests of the broader Resistance movement and the general public would have to be considered by those who had made policy solely from Algiers and Madrid. As Jacques Truelle predicted in conversation with the Spanish Foreign Minister, the next stage of French–Spanish relations would be "decisive."[10]

The division of the Resistance between internal and external groups only became more complicated after Liberation, as newspapers, reorganized political parties, and other veterans' and ex-Resistance groups joined the political fray. Such diversity makes it impossible to write of a "Resistance vision" that was coherent. Yet even in the divided experience of war, there were important continuities. While the internal resistance produced documents calling for a new politics, General Charles de Gaulle "used the word renewal rather than revolution, [but] his meaning appeared none the less radical."[11] By broadly categorizing the Resistance not as a single movement, but rather as a loose coalition of traditional left-wing political parties, independent Resistance movements and veterans' associations, newspapers, intellectuals, and pressure groups it becomes easier to trace the influence of the Resistance on Fourth Republic policy. Those with Resistance ties who became involved in the French debate about diplomatic relations with Franco's Spain can be divided into three groups, none of whose members were necessarily exclusive. First, there were the non-party resistance organizations themselves. One example would be the *Mouvement de Libération Nationale* (MLN), formerly known as the *Mouvement Unifié de Résistance* (MUR). This organization was represented in Paris by its daily newspaper, *Franc-Tireur*. In the region of Toulouse, where a majority of Spanish Republican exiles lived and where the Spanish issue was most lively, the MLN published the daily *La République du Sud-Ouest* and also assisted an umbrella organization of Spanish exiles, the *Junta Espanola de Liberación*, with the publication of a French language newspaper dedicated to the Republican cause, *l'Espagne Républicaine*. The second set of Resistance groups consisted of the political parties: Communists (PCF), Socialists (SFIO) and Christian Democrats (organized in the newly formed *Mouvement Républicaine Populaire*, or MRP), as well as Radicals and others. Finally, new associations concerned solely with the Spanish question sprung up, the most important of which was the *Association France-Espagne*, a multi-party pressure group organized at departmental and national levels.

The involvement of these groups in the debate about relations with Franco's Spain was evident in the debates of the Constituent National Assembly, in organizational congresses and most especially in the press, primarily through newspapers which they owned and secondarily via the production and distribution of pamphlets and other literature. Indeed, the most visible expression of the "new society" that the Resistance hoped to forge came in the proliferation of newspapers, most born clandestinely and which, from 1944–5, took over the presses of those newspapers associated with Vichy.[12] Until 1947, socialist and communist newspapers were over-represented amongst those being published, and the right was decidedly under-represented.[13] A number of newspapers associated with non-party Resistance organizations also appeared. Through this medium, it seemed that the images and rhetoric of the "Resistance myth" would manifest themselves in editorials and commentary that advocated political change and new policy directions.

In terms of particular policies to be followed internationally, the Resistance emphasized the principle of democratic policy-making and democratic goals above all. In contrast to General Charles de Gaulle's desire to return to France a place of *grandeur* on the world stage as one of the Great Powers, Resistance ideas of foreign policy saw greatness as a result of "proclaiming democratic principles and international solidarity, and supporting all initiatives with the aim of applying these principles . . . "[14] Moreover, France's own history reinforced recent experience and suggested the broad outline of a foreign policy based on principle. Writing in the Socialist *Populaire de Paris*, Charles Dumas emphasized that:

> because [France] has so suffered and because French civilization is made of moderation, wisdom, justice and humanity, and also revolutionary boldness, she can ask of others to sacrifice sovereignty, to renounce ambitions of dominance or national egotism, and tell them that humanity disturbed by an unparalleled storm is not able any longer to delay in these ruts . . . [15]

The Resistance and Spanish Republicanism

To apply such rhetoric to the Spanish case was easy enough. The war had been fought to liberate France and other European nations from fascism, to replace fascism and Nazism with democracy. In Spain there remained a government with ties, direct and indirect, to the Axis states. Even before France's liberation, as the CFLN established itself in Algiers, the Spanish Government protested the inclusion of Spanish Republicans in public celebrations of the French Resistance, writing in November 1943 that such activities constituted "a dangerous precedent."[16] Within weeks of the liberation, these fears were realized as a broad campaign to end the reign of Francisco Franco began. On 7 September 1944, *Combat's* lead editorial reminded readers, "This European war that began in Spain, eight years ago, cannot end without Spain."[17] In *Le*

Populaire de Paris, Marcel Bidoux wrote that as "the daughter of Italian fascism and German Nazism, [Spain] will fall with them."[18] After the war ended in Europe with the final defeat of Nazi Germany in May 1945, the call to deal with Franco arose with renewed vigor. It was a "paradox" that Franco continued to rule while his Fascist and Nazi patrons had been defeated.[19] In Toulouse, the MLN daily *La République du Sud-Ouest* wrote that the Franco regime was "a monstrous anachronism in a world liberated from fascism."[20] At the end of May, 1945, the Foreign Affairs Commission of the Assembly voted unanimously to pass a resolution which called for France to end diplomatic relations with Franco. The Chair of the Committee, Socialist Vincent Auriol, underlined that "the goal of the Allied victory was to establish democracy in Europe. Therefore, fascism must disappear in Spain."[21] The resolution was renewed in August.[22]

Such calls for action against Spain were evident in amongst liberal and leftist opinion in the United States and the United Kingdom as well. In January 1945, a large demonstration in favor of a Republican Spain was held at Madison Square Garden in New York City, where the call went out that "Hitler must go, Franco must go!"[23] In Britain, the *New Statesman* advocated that the Labour Government elected in July 1945 work for "the restoration of Spanish democracy", and Labour Party Chairman Harold Laski agreed.[24] At the founding conference of the United Nations in San Francisco, all three Western powers supported a resolution excluding Spain from membership in the world body, an appeal repeated by the Big Three powers at Potsdam in August, 1945.

Yet there was never a point in 1945 at which the Anglo-Americans moved beyond rhetorical condemnation of the Spanish regime. They took no active steps to force General Franco to leave power. Strategic considerations and economic motives compelled Great Britain and the United States to look beyond their antagonism toward the Spanish regime.[25] France did likewise. Jacques Truelle had been in Madrid since the autumn of 1943 acting as the official diplomatic representative for the CFLN, negotiating trade agreements and, along with the American and British ambassadors, keeping Spanish neutrality as advantageous to the Allies as possible. Republican France, then, was well placed to build a broader relationship with Franco when, on 9 August 1944, Truelle reported that Spain would soon end its recognition of Vichy as the legitimate government of France just as de Gaulle planned his move from Algiers to Paris in order to take up leadership of a new Provisional Government of the French Republic.[26] Within the next year, in September 1945, a new Franco-Spanish trade agreement was signed at San Sebastian.[27] Foreign Minister Georges Bidault and the Quai d'Orsay ignored the May and August 1945 resolutions of the National Assembly which called for a diplomatic break with Spain, and a Foreign Ministry official dismissed such measures, stating to an American official that they were simply "electoral maneuvers" on the part of the left and that France's position remained unchanged – "it is preferable to continue the status quo."[28] The French Foreign Ministry not only believed that a relationship with Spain gave them economic benefit, but also that France alone could not remove General Franco through sanctions – only a joint Allied policy could do that, and clearly the western allies had little interest in taking such an active step.[29] Thus, both for self-interest and for practical effect, French policy towards Spain as developed by the Quai paralleled that of its Allies.

Yet the context in which the French Government tried to maintain this policy was very different than that of its allies. The real difference between French and Anglo-American anti-Franco activists was in the ability of French anti-Franco activists to draw upon images and themes unique to France. It was through this appeal that the French Resistance made its mark on France's postwar policy toward the Franco regime, for the Government and the Quai d'Orsay was forced to adopt a different policy from that of the United States and Great Britain. The ultimate message found in France's anti-Franco campaign was that the French Resistance and the Spanish Republican cause had a direct connection unshared by others.

In the Resistance press of 1945, two points were stressed again and again in order to express the close association of Resistant France and Republican Spain. First, the common history and heritage shared by the neighboring states was stressed. On one level, this was simply a call to Latin brotherhood. The more powerful appeal, however, was related to the Republican culture in both states, and the fact that recent history in both states was dominated by successful attacks on these traditions. Indeed, here the image of the resistant nation, what now is referred to as the "Resistance myth" in French historiography, was seen to be re-occurring in Spain. Second, there was a connection of debt. This debt was initially built upon the residual guilt of the French centre-left that "abandoned" Republican Spain in the 1930s; in the post-Liberation it was expressed most prominently by the paying of homage to the many Spanish Republican exiles that had fought alongside French partisans in the liberation of France itself.

The first element of the anti-Franco campaign that was aimed to appeal directly to French citizens was the common Republican history of the two Latin states. The rhetoric and imagery associated with this aspect of the campaign consistently sought to portray the Franco regime in Spain as the close relative of the Vichy state led by Marshal Philippe Pétain that had only recently been removed from France. The logical conclusion of such an argument was that just as Pétain and the Vichy regime represented for the Resistance an imposition and an aberration of the French Republican state, so too was Franco's government for the Spanish state. The subtext of this argument went further, and drew parallels with the essence of the Resistance myth. If Spain, like France, was naturally a Republican state, then the Spanish people, like the French, were quietly opposed to the regime and were simply awaiting the opportunity to greet the end of the regime with a return to Republican legitimacy as had so recently occurred in post-Liberation France. These arguments, which were designed to stress the French experience, and align the French *nation des résistants* with the Spanish cause, were repeatedly apparent in the leftist and Resistance press from autumn 1944 through 1945 and 1946.

The means of making these particular points were varied. In Toulouse, the Communist *Voix du Midi* simply stated that Franco's attitude in war, described as "neutral collaboration . . . evoked the position of the 'Marshal'." In *Franc-Tireur*, Pétain was cast as "this 'Franco of France' and Franco 'this Pétain of Spain'." Readers were reminded of the Marshal's stint as the Third Republic's Ambassador to Spain in 1939, just prior to the collapse of 1940, and his "spiritual ties" to the Caudillo; "the same traits of political *tartuffery*, of bloody cunning, of pseudo-social weasel-facedness . . . the same absurd tendencies toward corporatism, supported by bands, *falange*, legion or *milice*."[30]

The Resistance drew parallels not only in the nature of the two regimes, Franco's and Pétain's, but also in their manner of coming to power. In essence, the claim was made that both France and Spain were by nature and popular will Republics, and thus it was only due to outside pressures that the anti-Republican regimes of Vichy and Franco were brought to power. This assertion went to the heart of the Resistance myth, that France in fact was a nation of resisters who suffered under Pétain and his German allies, and that the Spanish people were in exactly the same situation. For the *Franc-Tireur*, both dictators had "delivered their people to the enemy."[31]

The most explicit use of the "brotherly Republics" line of argument came in the Toulouse weekly *L'Espagne Républicaine*. This paper actually ran a column entitled "Parallels" written by François Donnez, and his column in the initial issue, 30 June 1945, was entitled "Franco-Pétain: Blanc Bonnet ou Bonnet Blanc ("Six of one and one half dozen of the other")." Donnez wrote that not only were Spain and France "two Latin sisters" aligned by race and blood, but by "a series of calamities and trials"; "Franco, Pétain, two names which will remain coupled because they are the same and they evoke similar nightmares," Donnez wrote, recalling anti-Republican statements by both made in 1936.[32]

Donnez also made a point in his column to remind voters, during the 1945 French elections, that no party represented Pétain's policies, which demonstrated that he never represented the French people, just as Franco did not represent the Spanish people.[33] He was imposed upon the Spanish nation just as according to the Resistance myth Pétain had been imposed upon France. Other "Parallel" columns were entitled "Two Republics to be Remade" and "Francoists Equal Francophobes, Republicans equal Francophiles."[34] The conclusion meant to be drawn from such use of the mirror image was clear. If Franco was Spain's Pétain, then it was only a question of time before the Spanish people, like their French counterparts, rose up and reclaimed their nation as a

Republic. Even papers like the Socialist *Le Populaire de Paris*, which preferred not to mention Pétain, and instead spoke of the Occupation as a German one alone, still insisted that it was wise not to forget the French experience of the wartime repression because it was the same as what continued in Spain under Franco and the *Falange*.[35] The Spanish people, it insisted as the war in Asia came to an end, were "quasi-unanimously" in favor of a Republic.[36]

The fact of Republican solidarity and historical experience led to the conclusion that the destinies of the two states were inextricably intertwined. Therefore, France was compelled to do all it could to support Republican Spain. This was the spirit behind the Constituent National Assembly's motions that called for diplomatic rupture with Spain. It was echoed in the press. Jean Cassou, one of de Gaulle's original appointees as Republican Commissioner in Toulouse until wounded during the Liberation, and a prominent intellectual, was also President of the *Association France-Espagne*. He wrote in December 1944 that France's recent past, combined with its longstanding Republican tradition, meant that "at the moment when France emerges from its own humiliation, and recovers its shape, it understands that this shape will be unable to have all its significance if it does not correspond to the situation in other nations" like Spain.[37] Albert Camus in *Combat* wrote that "passion [will] join reason and truth" if France constructed its post-Liberation foreign policy on the basis of international democracy and acknowledged that the Republic was in fact the legal form of government in Spain.[38] The implication was that France would take measures to make it so.

If these themes of shared experience and common political history were persistent and consistent throughout 1945, they were overshadowed by that second element to the Resistance's anti-Franco campaign: debt. Debt extended back to the French experience of the Spanish Civil War, and the perception that the French Left, in power during the Popular Front, had let down its Spanish comrades. The sense of regret, shame and debt remained palatable in 1945. Jean Cassou recalled that during the Civil War, while visiting the front, Spanish Republican President Manuel Azaña had exclaimed, "That is your front, your own front, Frenchman!" Cassou, in December 1944, acknowledged that now every French citizen understood that "it was us that Hitler attacked on the Madrid front."[39] An editorialist in *Combat* confessed that "many of us, since 1938, have been unable to this of this fraternal country without a secret shame ... we must not recommit the same errors."[40] At the end of 1945, in an interview with *L'Espagne Républicaine*, Albert Camus said that, "for nine years men of my generation have lived the life of Spain. It is like a wound that will not close."[41]

This debt was of course one shared by many on the left in Europe and elsewhere. What extended the debt in France was the legacy of the aftermath of the Spanish Civil War. While Spanish immigrants and refugees had come to France throughout the nineteenth and early twentieth centuries, it was the aftermath of the Spanish Civil War that truly began the era of the Spanish political refugee that sought haven in neighboring France. The large scale flight of Republicans from Spain followed the course of military events in the Spanish Civil War: after the Basque campaign of autumn 1936, after the victory in the North by Franco's Nationalist troops in the summer of 1937, after the end of the Aragon campaign in April 1938.[42] By mid-June 1938, it has been estimated that forty to forty five thousand Spanish Republican refugees were in France.[43] In January and February 1939, however, the situation completely changed with the fall of Catalonia to Nationalist troops and the realization that Franco was going to win the war. In this period, roughly five hundred thousand Spanish refugees came into France, including at least two hundred thousand Republican soldiers.[44]

These Republican refugees were to experience a variety of difficult circumstances over the next few years. Most were housed in harsh internment camps upon their arrival. After the start of war in September 1939, many joined the French military and fought unsuccessfully against the German Army or else worked in industry. The arrival of the Vichy government under Marshal Philippe Pétain, who had once fought alongside Franco in North African colonial wars, raised the specter of forced repatriation as Francoist Spain and Vichy France began to develop close relations, symbolized by the Franco-Pétain summit at Montpellier in February 1941.[45] While some eight hundred Republican leaders were sent back to imprisonment and death in Spain, both Vichy authorities and German authorities in occupied France saw the Spanish refugees as a potential workforce, and most were organized into work groups or sent to German forced labor camps; from 1942–4, somewhere between forty and sixty two thousand Spanish exiles worked in either the Todt Labor Organization in France or were sent to German factories.[46]

As the Resistance movement in France began to develop in 1942, Spanish Republican refugees played an important role. Leadership of the Spanish movement was taken up by the *Partido Communista Española* (Spanish Communist Party or PCE), which formed the *Union Nacional Española* (UNE). This coalition included leftist and centrist republicans, socialists and anarchists, but the PCE remained the sole organizing force.[47] Created at the 'Grenoble Conference' in November 1942, the UNE, later called the *Agrupación de Guerrilleros españoles* (AGE), was based in the southwest and became part of the French Resistance organization *Franc Tireurs et Partisans (FTP)- Main d'Oeuvre Immigrant (MOI)*.[48] Other Spanish guerrillas were also organized in occupied France under the MOI divisions. Anarchist fighters remained outside any formal organization, but cooperated with the *Forces Francaises de l'Interieur* (FFI), the overall military structure for the French Resistance. In May of 1944, the French Resistance reorganized itself into the *Comité de Libération National* (CLN) and all Spanish guerrillas were grouped together in six divisions through the AGE. Many others were arrested and placed in concentration camps, or aided the Resistance in less obvious ways. While the exact numbers of Spanish exiles in the UNE forces affiliated with the FFI in the southwest were around seven and a half thousand by autumn 1944, it is impossible to delineate exact numbers across France; the best that can be said is that a "significant percentage" of Republican exiles chose to affiliate with the French Resistance.[49] Spanish forces liberated in whole or in part numerous towns, cities and departments in the southwest, and the French Resistance leader Pierre Bertaux concluded that in the Pyrenean zone of France, Spanish fighters played "a very important part – I believe, the most important."[50]

This unique situation would prove to form the basis of the most effective anti-Franco propaganda used by the Resistance and the leftist political parties in France. On 7 September 1944, the Resistance newspaper *Combat* included an article entitled "Our Spanish Brothers" which provoked a complaint from the Spanish Consul in Paris.[51] The writer mentioned that France had shamed the Spanish Republicans twice, once in the civil war with a policy of non-intervention, and once in 1939 with the creation of inhumane and prison-like refugee camps.[52] In his study of press attitudes toward Italians and Spaniards, Antoine Bechelloni has concluded that regardless of the nature of the newspaper or journal – political party paper, committee of liberation or resistance journal, national or local weekly or daily – the issue of relations with Spain in the three months following Liberation was accorded an important place.[53]

As early as mid-September 1944, a press conference held by UNE *guerrillero* leaders in Toulouse prompted the MLN's *La République du Sud Ouest* to celebrate the Spanish *maquis* for their "service to France" and reminded readers that, "for them the battle is not finished."[54] Reviewing France's non-intervention in the Spanish Civil War and the internment of Spanish refugees in 1939, *La Voix du Midi* remarked with awe that after the defeat of France the Spanish refugees "rose, in the thousands, forgetting the past, without rifles" just as the French people had, and "with us, they fought, and they were killed when necessary, with us."[55] François Donnez in *L'Espagne Républicaine* described Spanish participation in the Resistance as "instinct, because they come from a people always taken with liberty and always oppressed; they joined with Frenchmen who wanted to reconquer their country and with [French] Republicans who wanted to reconquer their Republic."[56] What did such a debt mean for France? How was it to be repaid? From Toulouse, the Communist daily *La Voix du Midi* reported that "the hour of [Spanish] liberation will sound; the UNE asks the French people to give a fraternal hand and France gives its heart, knowing that its own liberation will not be definitive until the last Hitlerian has been chased off."[57] There was never any thought of military support, or active French intervention in Spain. From Paris, *Combat* editorialized:

> We have no intention of intervening in Spain. We are also of the feeling that the Republicans must wait for the right moment to move with certainty. But we know that it will be necessary for Allied diplomatic pressure to guarantee the fall of Franco and to avoid the flow of the most generous blood in Europe.[58]

In the face of government arguments for continued diplomatic relations and trade with the Franco regime, the Resistance asserted that indebtedness superseded such concerns and required France to make a sacrifice as Spanish Republicans had done:

> Witness to such sacrifice and courage cannot permit France to forget what it owes to the sons of free Spain. This debt engages our country with the Spanish Republic. It forces us to aid it in its rebirth. It does not permit us, under the egotistic pretext of immediate advantage, to contribute to the consolidation of the Francoist tyranny.[59]

Crisis Along the Pyrenees

The participation of Spaniards, particularly leftist Republicans, in the French Resistance was no surprise. Yet it was only a start for many of them. They saw the struggle against Hitler as a necessary precursor to the renewed battle against Franco within Spain itself. In June 1944, the UNE newspaper *Reconquista de Espana* stated that Spanish Republicans must work with the Allies and the FFI first and foremost, but that such Resistance was ultimately only a precursor to the goal of removing Franco from power in Spain.[60] A member of the British Special Forces who parachuted into the region of Perpignan on 17 August 1944 reported back to the British military attaché in Madrid that "the expulsion of the Germans and the liberation of this section of France constituted only a beginning for them [Spanish maquis], and that their main object was to make trouble for the present Spanish regime."[61] As most of southwest France became liberated over the course of August 1944, Spanish guerrillas in southwestern France turned their thoughts toward the "reconquest" of Spain. Their campaign for Republican Spain took shape initially through the occupation of Francoist consulates-general located in the major towns and cities of the southwest. By the end of August 1944, the Spanish Government reported that the Consul at Pau had been arrested and the Consulate occupied; the Consul at Toulouse had been assassinated and the Consulate occupied; similarly, the Republican flag was flew over the Spanish Consulate in Perpignan.[62] Throughout August and September, Republican exiles would occupy many other properties owned or operated by the Spanish Government. In December 1944, the Quai d'Orsay was able to conclude that of fifteen Spanish consulates in France, only five remained open.[63] Meanwhile, arms that Spanish guerrillas had used and stored in the fight for France's Liberation began to move closer to the Spanish border in the Pyrenees. In late September, it was reported that a group of Spanish guerrillas had crossed the border into Spain near Puigcerda and stolen arms from the Spanish border patrol there.[64] In the eastern area of the Pyrenees, there were reports that twenty to forty armed men per day were crossing the border near Auzat and laying the groundwork for a revolt on the Spanish side. Numerous other incidents involving border crossings and skirmishes with Spanish troops were reported throughout September, October and November 1944.[65] In short, there was a crisis along the Pyrenees.

The fact that the Spanish guerrillas were able to advance at all was due to the chaotic situation on the ground in liberated southwestern France. The Provisional Government did not have complete control of the situation on the ground. As France gradually became liberated over the course of August 1944, the various troops of the FFI were transformed on the spot into the army and border patrol of the GPRF; the majority of the regular French Army, itself composed mainly of Resistance fighters and the remnants of de Gaulle's North African army, was still fighting the Germans in eastern France and the Low Countries. In the southwest, Spanish guerrillas were a major component of the region's FFI forces. The reality, at least initially, was that in various parts of the Pyrenean region, the Government in Paris had little or no direct control of FFI troops, especially Spanish ones, who now seemed intent on occupying consulates and preparing border incursions. A French officer responsible for border security admitted in early October that in many regions France's ability to control its own side of the Pyrenean border was "extremely weak", and that the Government could not expect to impose its decisions on the Spanish *maquis*.[66] In the eastern Pyrenees especially, Spanish guerillas generally outnumbered the French FFI soldiers: in the department of Pyrénées-Orientales, there were one thousand five hundred Spaniards and only five to six hundred French amongst the FFI contingent as of 1 October 1944.[67] The Prefect of Pyrénées-Orientales acknowledged that the situation was potentially explosive, with possible international repercussions, but that as much as he found the situation "distasteful", he was "powerless" to change it until regular Army troops arrived.[68] In autumn 1944, despite objections from the Minister of War, André Diethelm, the regional military commander in the southwest, General Collet, had agreed with General Luis Fernandez of the UNE that the roughly seven thousand five hundred UNE troops should remain armed and part of the FFI in the short-term.[69]

This was thought to be just one part of a potential guerilla movement. French intelligence reports called the total number of armed Republican exiles, "a veritable Spanish Republican army", consisting of anywhere from twenty to thirty thousand men. The Spanish *maquis* had trucks, armored vehicles, rifles, handguns, mortars and canons as well.[70] A document by a *guerrillero* member put the actual number of Spanish *maquis* organized into eleven battalions throughout the southwest at twelve thousand.[71] They faced an estimated sixteen Spanish divisions, or two hundred and thirty thousand troops, based between the River Ebro and the border.[72] The American Military Attaché in Madrid reported that if France and its Allies did not respond politically and diplomatically to quell the Spanish exiles, the Spanish General Staff was prepared to consider taking "matters into its own hands to eliminate these disturbing elements."[73] The head of the Office of Strategic Services in the United States, William J. Donovan, assessed the situation at that time as "not presently acute, but delicate with impossibility of determining which way events will turn."[74]

It was clear that the leadership of the UNE, as well as of many other Spanish Republican groups, viewed the armed invasion of Spain as the next step, after French Liberation, in the war against fascism.[75] The most significant attempt to instigate a new phase in the political history of Spain came when Spanish guerrillas invaded the Val d'Aran on 19 October 1944. This valley juts northward into France west of Andorra and was separated from Spain by mountains that remained impassable in winter. The decision to invade, in the hopes of provoking a general uprising against Franco, was made by the leadership of the PCE in France.[76] The night of 18–19 October 1944, some three thousand five hundred to four thousand members of seven UNE divisions crossed into the valley and, between 19 October and 28 October, some seven thousand Spanish Republicans were in the Aran at various times fighting with forces from the Spanish Army. They retreated only when it was clear that the national revolution they hoped to provoke was not forthcoming.[77]

Beyond the activism of Spanish guerrillas and a lack of control over their own borders, policy-makers in Paris were faced with a variety of situations in which the French public and, more troubling, FFI forces and their commanders in the Pyrenean region championed and/or actively supported the Spaniards' actions. In this manner, the cause of justice and Spanish Republicanism was served in more ways than simply through advocacy of a different French policy. In the southwest of France, incidents of consulate occupations and sporadic guerrilla attacks were vocally supported by the newspaper *La Republique du Sud-Ouest* and many shared the point of view that Franco's Spain must be dealt with in the short term. Vincent Auriol was a French Socialist Deputy who would in late 1944 become the President of the new Consultative Assembly. Prior to the war, he had also been a deputy and chaired the Socialist Committee of Parliamentarians that exposed the inhumane conditions of the refugee internment camps in the southwest in 1939.[78] Auriol spoke at the Congress of the Spanish Socialist Party (PSOE) in exile at Toulouse in September 1944 and stated that "my presence here . . . is equivalent to recognition of the Spanish Republic."[79] Later, he would write to Foreign Minister Georges Bidault and

Allied Headquarters in order to ensure that Spaniards found in German work camps and factories not be forcibly returned to Spain.[80]

Vocal support for the Republican cause was augmented by the revelation that many in the French Resistance, now responsible for security in the border region were either condoning or actively assisting the activities of the Spanish *maquis* against the Franco regime. In the middle of October 1944, the Montpellier Resistance newspaper *Le Midi Libre* reported that in April 1944 an agreement between the UNE and the regional *Mouvement de la Libération Nationale* (MLN *Zone Sud*) had been reached which committed both organizations to the same goal, the defeat of international fascism. Moreover, it was reported that each group would aid the other, the UNE in the battle for French Liberation and the French in return giving the UNE "what assistance it could" for the battle against Franco inside Spain.[81] The Quai d'Orsay's closest representative to the situation in southern France was Jean Coiffard, the French Consul in Barcelona. He met with Col. Gilbert Carrel, the FFI Commander in Montpellier in early October 1944, who confirmed the existence of this agreement and added that since the Spaniards had kept up their half of the bargain, "It is impossible for us not to hold to the contracted agreement." He added, "we will make all effort to liberate Spain."[82]

The situation was most tense in Toulouse. The strength of Communist and other leftist elements in the Toulousian resistance and their placement in leadership positions upon liberation gave the city a reputation amongst officials in Paris as '*La République rouge de Toulouse*'.[83] Spanish activists were part of this movement. The Resistance's *Radio Toulouse* continued to broadcast Catalan language programs across the border well into the autumn of 1944, an activity that provoked complaints from British intelligence to the French Ambassador in London, René Massigli.[84] Ravenal, the local commander of the FFI, worked closely with the Spanish *maquis* in the region, giving them major responsibilities for policing. Ravenal reportedly worked without making a great effort to receive appropriate orders from Paris nor did he seem to express any concern about this.[85] The Spanish later insisted that Ravenal had contributed greatly to the activities of the armed Republican movement at this time.[86] Pierre Bertaux, de Gaulle's Republican Commissioner in Toulouse immediately following Liberation, forged many contacts with Spaniards during the war, and he acknowledged not only their value, but also their strength in the aftermath of Toulouse's Liberation. As Commissioner, he took the opportunity on more than one occasion to help Spanish forces move their cache of arms to storage areas closer to the border. Working without the knowledge of Paris, Bertaux felt that such an arrangement was not only the most honorable approach, but that it also had the added benefit of eliminating any number of conflicts which could arise within Toulouse if he had antagonized the Spaniards.[87]

The strongest French supporter of the UNE was the French Communist

Party (PCF). It was well known that the Spanish Communist Party, and thus the UNE, was funded almost entirely by the PCF.[88] As indicated, the connection had been forged in the Resistance, when UNE guerrillas were part of the Communist FTP-MOI *maquis*. Notable French Communists such as André Marty worked closely with the UNE.[89] Having said that, the UNE did not actually expect that French Communists would accompany them in any invasion of Spain, but it was understood that support, moral and otherwise, was necessary in order for the PCE and the UNE to carry out their plans for Spain's liberation.[90]

The Government Response

The crisis on the Pyrenean border, then, was a serious one that presented the French Government with a number of risks. First, the border situation threatened to compromise growing Franco-Spanish relations desired by the Government in Paris. Throughout 1944 and into 1945, the situation along the border would appear to Truelle to be the main stumbling block for a normalization of French–Spanish relations, and he wrote that while clearly no admirer of Franco and his "military caste", he came to regard the UNE and other Republican groups as "intellectual elites [who] . . . dispersed in exile have lost contact with the masses."[91] Indeed, Truelle complained to his American colleague in Madrid, Ambassador Carlton Hayes, that the activism of French FFI and even the occasional American OSS agent in favor of the Spanish *maquis* meant much of his time in Madrid was spent trying to "avoid trouble" with the Franco government by explaining away such incidents.[92] As early as 2 September 1944, the Spanish Government had complained to the British Government about the influence and activities of Spanish Republican units on the French side of the Pyrenees.[93] Later, the Spanish Government emphasized the inactivity of local French authorities in ten different cities where consulates were attacked and/or occupied, and an internal Spanish Foreign Ministry document stressed that the situation as a whole revealed "the peculiar way in which the French Government understands and applies traditional principles that have governed relations between our states and that have been universally accepted as part of international law."[94]

Second, while there was general agreement that the Franco regime was not worthy of support on ideological grounds, there also was a reluctance to precipitate a Spanish crisis or renewed civil war; neither France nor its Allies wanted this. Thus the best policy was to maintain economic and diplomatic contact with Franco; such contact not only continued, but flourished in the period immediately after the war, building on relations established during the conflict. Naturally, the existence of the Spanish guerrillas and various border incursions in the Pyrenean region over the course of the last few months of 1944 threatened the general direction of Allied policy that was developing. France was required to act in a manner that pre-empted the expansion of any crisis. France's inability to act in the first few months after Liberation prompted American and British military attachés in Madrid to discuss the possibility of regular Spanish forces crossing into France in pursuit of Spanish *maquis* and prepare an Allied response to such action.[95] In short, the threat the Spanish *maquis* presented to general Allied policy, and in particular French-Allied relations concerning Spain, was present if not immediate.

Finally, there was the potential that the Spanish case would have a significant impact on domestic politics. Within the government, there was a fear that attitude taken by local French authorities toward Spanish exiles would have perhaps greater import at home, and threaten the new Provisional Government.[96] The powerful moral cause of the Republicans against the semi-fascist regime of General Franco risked dividing the already fragile coalition of the Provisional Government and the FFI. Indeed, tensions were readily apparent. Jean Coiffard was compelled to remind Carrel, the FFI commander in Montpellier, that it was the Foreign Ministry, and not the FFI, that made foreign policy.[97] This was exactly the sort of attitude that the French Resistance believed it had fought to get rid of. In Madrid, Jacques Truelle concluded that the Communists and others in the southwest who made policy on the ground had "almost openly broken with de Gaulle" and were acting "according to their own beliefs or prejudices," instead of in the national interest.[98] For his part, Bertaux's opinion of the policy-makers in Paris was that they were "ignorant, pretentious and finally useless" when it came to dealing with the Spanish situation.[99]

The first step in any Government policy was to gain control of the border situation. As Foreign Ministry official Maurice Dejean put it, if France had no particular reason to support Franco, it equally had no reason "to allow the establishment on its border a source of chronic troubles."[100] Col. Noetinger, the French Military Affairs Commander in Toulouse, insisted that the need for regular French troops, or even American troops from the north of France, was urgent.[101] As a result, on 6 September 1944, General Bertin of the French Army ordered all FFI troops to withdraw from the Pyrenean frontier and established the principle that no Spanish troops (armed or not) should be in a fixed position within forty kilometers of the border. In reality, this was impossible to enforce, especially in the many mountainous and isolated corners of the Pyrenees.[102] An additional step was taken in October 1944 when, on orders from the Council of Ministers, French military intelligence created a special body under General Cailles in October 1944, the *Commandement Militaire de la Frontière*.[103] The organization was given authority over Gendarmerie, FFI and Mobile Guard troops in order to facilitate the disarmament of Spanish *guerrilleros*. Such power was warranted, stated the official decree, given the "state of siege" that existed in southwestern France.[104]

The Government, however, did not rely on local French forces alone. The American military dispatched a small mission to the region to coordinate border patrols by as many regular troops as possible.[105] Most significantly, through either the *Commandement Militaire* or through the use of Spanish-based French officials, multiple contacts with Franco's Government were made in order to control the border situation. Lt. Col. Richard of the *Commandement Militaire*, who became known for his intelligence contacts with the Franco regime,[106] had many meetings in San Sebastian with Spanish military commanders, and with the Civil Governor of Girona. These Spanish officials requested increased deployment of French troops along the border and even offered to sell Spanish side arms to the French army; weapons that Richard noted were "of superior quality to the arms parachuted in to us by the Americans."[107] Jean Coiffard in Barcelona met regularly with regional military commanders in order to pinpoint exact locations of Spanish Republican border crossings which he then forwarded to French authorities to enable them to intervene and disarm guerillas. Similarly, any increases in Spanish border fortifications were outlined to Coiffard in order that the French military not be alarmed.[108] With sixteen divisions and over two hundred thousand troops in the Pyrenean region, the Spanish Army was able to regularly arrest those who continued to cross the border after October, generally in small groups of ten or fewer.[109] Despite this, through November, the Spanish Foreign Ministry continued to complain about armed groups in the border region and especially of the tolerance many French officials gave those groups.[110] Yet the reality was that by the end of November, de Gaulle's Commissioner in Bayonne could report that the majority of Spanish FFI troops were out of the immediate border area and order had been restored along the frontier.[111]

Similarly, many of the Republican occupations of Spanish Consulates-General in France were resolved over the course of the autumn. Still, activism existed amongst many exile groups and continued to play an important role in forcing French government action. In December 1944, a group of Spanish Republican businessmen occupied the Spanish Chamber of Commerce in Paris. They argued that the Chamber was not a government organization, but an association of Spanish businessmen in Paris, and thus that they and not the Franco Government ran the building. This provoked an immediate complaint from the Spanish Consulate-General in Paris (Embassy status had not yet been given) to the Quai d'Orsay.[112] Police and Interior Ministry officials attempted to negotiate with those occupying the building, but by January 1945 there had been no resolution to the situation. At this point, the Spanish Government took its first aggressive step and threatened to close the French Chamber of Commerce in Madrid and in Barcelona; in the opinion of Jacques Truelle, the threat was entirely serious: "if we want to avoid grave consequences for commercial relations between our two countries and for the continued protection of important

French interests that we possess in Spain, the situation [in Paris] must be brought to a quick resolution."[113] This warning prompted Bidault to write directly to the Interior Minister, the Socialist Adrien Tixier, in order to expedite the evacuation of the building.[114] Spanish Minister in Paris Miguel Mateu noted that the pro-Republican press coverage of the incident and the desire to keep the Republican Chamber open on the part of many French Cabinet Ministers, including Tixier himself, threatened to split the French Government. Bidault won out, however, and the Republican occupation ended on 16 January 1945 when the French Government shut down the building. Mateu concluded that the retreat of Spanish Republican exiles in the face of French Government pressure had "important consequences" for the general direction of Franco-Spanish relations as it revealed that Paris was not in sympathy with those supporting the occupiers.[115]

Soon enough, however, the crisis re-emerged when Spanish Republican businessmen proceeded to open a separate "Republican Chamber of Commerce." The Spanish Government not only requested that the Republican Chamber be shut down, but also demanded that the original building seized by the French Government be turned over to Spain so that its "official" nature would once again be recognized and in order that trade relations between the two countries not be interrupted.[116] This challenge was reiterated to Truelle in Madrid by the Spanish Foreign Ministry's Economics Officer; current French–Spanish agreements dealing with a variety of traded products, such as pyrites, would not be affected, but the beginning of talks for a commercial treaty between France and Spain would be postponed until the Chamber of Commerce had Spanish-appointed officials in the building.[117] Spanish Foreign Minister Jose Lequerica considered French tolerance of the rebel Chamber leaders "an inadmissible act of violence" and demanded that the Chamber's restoration to the Spanish Government and its appointees was a "minimum" in order to restore normalcy to Franco-Spanish affairs.[118] By the end of February, the Spanish Government again had possession of the building and the renegade Chamber was effectively shut down.

A Challenge to the Government

The outcome of incidents like the Chamber affair, and the Quai d'Orsay's continued general relations with Spain, meant that the anti-Franco campaign evident amongst Resistance organizations and their press did not let up. The primacy of the Spanish question was indeed a feature of the frequent meetings of the Assembly's Foreign Affairs Committee. The subject of Spain came up at the very first session of the Committee at which Bidault appeared, in November 1944.[119] In February 1945, relations with Spain were the subject of an intense debate. Florimond Bonte of the Communist Party stated outright that he and his colleagues believed the Government should immediately end diplomatic relations with Franco. Pierre Cot recalled Spanish–German talks in 1940 about Francoist expansion into French Morocco, and gave his opinion that the policy of the Government, which had continued relations with Spain, was "in opposition to the sentiment of the Assembly."[120] Socialist Jules Moch was wary about opposing the Government while the war was still ongoing, but agreed fully with Cot's appraisal of the situation. In the end, a delegation of representatives was sent to see Bidault and express the views of the Commission.[121] Outside of the Assembly, other French officials affiliated with a variety of Resistance organizations spoke out on the Spanish question. In one case, the Sub-Prefect of Bayonne stated in January 1945 that Nazi Germany was continuing the war against France by sending fascist agents over the Pyrenees from Spain, thus demonstrating Spain's continued commitment to fascism.[122]

There was also practical evidence that these views, and the propaganda campaign ongoing in the French press, reflected, to some degree, the popular mood. In Toulouse, there were widespread protests in March and April 1945 when a new Spanish Consul-General arrived, including a rally that the local Communist press claimed attracted twenty five thousand.[123] Similar protests occurred in Pau, Perpignan and Bayonne.[124] On 15 June 1945 a train of Spaniards returning from labor service in Nazi Germany was attacked in Chambéry (Haute Savoie) when rumors circulated that the train actually held members of Franco's Blue Division that had fought alongside Nazi troops in the Soviet Union. This attack represented, at least partly, the mood of political activists toward Spain, and toward the French Government's decision to continue diplomatic relations with Spain. More particularly, the incident underlined the importance of the Spanish question to a Resistance vision of France and French politics, even if in this case its retributive aspect was most prominent, for it was Resistance figures that were the main provocateurs in Chambéry.[125]

While Chambéry may have been a dramatic moment, the antagonism towards seemingly pro-Franco Spaniards that the incident represents appears to have been widespread especially on the part of local French officials. Defying the official government position that Spaniards in France were free to return to Spain, many officials did what they could to block the transit of such individuals, especially those, like the Chambéry group, who were crossing France en route to Spain from Germany, where they had been wartime laborers. Tomás Suñer, the Spanish Consul in Paris, noted as early as May 1945 that official documents provided to Spanish laborers did not indicate their citizenship, thus were impossible to be used as a border-crossing document. Moreover, he noted that assistance with paperwork for Spanish workers seemed to be taken over from the Government by the *Ligue des Droits des Hommes*, which had an anti-Franco position, as well as by Resistance leaders, like General Riquelme in Toulouse, who were close to Republican Spanish exiles.[126] The result was, in the eyes of the Spanish Government, official French meddling in the attempt by Spaniards scattered across post-war Europe to return home. In the files of the Spanish Consulate General in Paris, there are numerous reports of individual cases of such obstruction. A typical one tells of three men returning from labor service in Germany who, upon reaching the border, were refused exit from France by French border guards. They then tried to cross clandestinely, were stopped, and taken to Perpignan to be interrogated by the French Fifth Bureau (the 'Political Information' arm of French intelligence). When released, they were forced to join an obligatory work group from which they escaped and made it back into Spain.[127]

Summary

With the end of the war in Europe, the campaign against Franco in the French Resistance press only increased. The leading newspaper of the MLN, *Franc-Tireur,* criticized the government's decision to apologize to Spain after Chambéry, writing that "is this the spectacle that a France of the Resistance wants to show to the democratic world?"[128] Later, the paper published a picture of Franco, Pétain and Mussolini together with the caption, "has Franco forgotten that he is ... Franco? ... the Allies have also seemed to forget, and our Government almost as well."[129] The Communist *Voix du Midi* called the Government's agreement to allow the train to enter France an example of the "deplorable policy of flirting with Franco."[130]

It would be wrong to assume that all of the French press, or even all of the Resistance press, covered the Spanish question in the same way. Indeed, some notable exceptions existed. The official organ of Bidault's own party, the MRP, echoed many of the same themes as other papers concerning Spain, yet it never went beyond Bidault's own policy and never called for a unilateral diplomatic rupture on the part of France. To the contrary, it reported the Quai d'Orsay point of view in some detail. On 11 December 1945, *L'Aube* reported on a speech the Foreign Minister made in Saint-Etienne. Bidault stated that the Spanish case had produced "many useless emotions" and that the various press campaigns encouraging government action were the political equivalent of "setting fire under the trees in the hope of ripening the fruit faster."[131] In the National Assembly, André Mutter of the right-wing *Parti Républicain de la Liberté* (PRL), a veteran of de Gaulle's Fighting France and the CNR during the war, consistently spoke out against any French involvement in Spain's internal affairs, once stating "We are not in Spain."[132]

Yet Resistance imagery was conspicuous when it came to the Spanish question. Built upon the images associated with France's own Resistance myth, applied to the Spanish case in a way that linked the fates of Republican France and Republican Spain, this imagery could not be ignored by the foreign policy elites of the Quai d'Orsay. A member of the British Foreign Office privately expressed sympathy with his colleagues in the Quai d'Orsay, writing, "It is too much to expect them to be able to restrain French public opinion."[133]

The Spanish case brought to the surface the very different visions for "restored" France. The veterans of the internal Resistance held that their experience gave them the authority to remake the nation, and they would do so from the ground up, supporting democracy and practicing it at the same time. By contrast, those who had spent the war in Algiers making policy, and perhaps in Vichy before that, did not qualify as true *résistants*. The Spanish question, as a debate between the advocates of justice and realism, had the potential to act as catalyst for a division between France and Spain, between France and the Allies, and between the Government of Charles de Gaulle, which when in Algiers had developed relations with Franco's Spain, and much of the internal Resistance, which had fought for the liberation of France alongside Spanish Republicans dedicated to overthrowing Franco. Throughout 1944 and 1945, the argument for a foreign policy grounded in morality and justice seemed as strong as ever.

3

French Politics and the Cause of Spanish Republicanism, 1944–1947

Georges Bidault, in his first appearance before the Foreign Affairs Commission of the French Constituent National Assembly in Paris in November 1944, reminded legislators that "we are not at war with Spain" and that the "relatively explosive situation" that existed in the Pyrenean border region had to be handled "with some caution."[1] A response to the border crisis and the general anti-Franco attitude prevalent in Republican France that served French goals, the first and foremost of which was to maintain open relations between Paris and Madrid in the context of normalized "international life and diplomacy", had to be found, and this became the focus of policy-making in the immediate aftermath of Liberation. At the same time, however, Bidault did not contest the ideological goals of the Spanish Republicans, and indeed welcomed them, stating that it was only right for France to send the message to Spanish exiles that a Republican future for Spain was "not just envisioned, but prepared for."[2] In making this statement, the Foreign Minister acknowledged the power that the idea of Spanish Republicanism had inside Liberated France.

In the case of Spain, a realpolitik approach already existed within France, one grounded in the experience of war, as Chapter 1 demonstrated, and tied very closely with French views of its goals within the emerging Western Alliance. The Quai d'Orsay consistently evaluated the Spanish issue not in relation to a Resistance point of view, but rather as one of the peripheral issues related to European reconstruction that had to be assessed on the basis of its significance to the emerging Western alliance. Aware of the fact that unilateral action in one arena might threaten France's goals in another, French officials actively demonstrated the ability to think broadly of a "national strategy" aimed at recovering French leadership within the Alliance, and subsequently they imposed limits on themselves and their reach concerning Franco's Spain. There was never any question, in 1945, of ending diplomatic and economic relations with Francisco

Franco. Indeed, for most of 1945 and into 1946, France attempted to forge a Spanish policy that mirrored that of its allies the United States and Great Britain, especially in the area of trade where a significant commercial agreement with Spain was signed in September 1945.[3]

Yet at the same time, as Bidault's comments suggest, there was a level of shared sympathy with the cause of Spanish Republicanism and with anti-Franco activists within the French political sphere. The war, after all, was fought for democracy and justice. Government bureaucrats, politicians and journalists were products of the Resistance experience, just as they were also leaders who saw the importance of alliance politics and a national strategy for French recovery in world affairs. How to balance shared sympathy and cause with an awareness of the broader international picture in post-war Europe was difficult, and in this sense was part of a much broader debate occurring inside France concerning the proper role for Paris to take in the world. The Resistance vision of a more interventionist, democratic foreign policy was not completely rejected by those within Government, for they too had come through the war and rejected Vichy.

This chapter will demonstrate that in the effort to appease Spanish Republican exiles and their domestic supporters, the French Government often found itself becoming more and more drawn into the politics of the Spanish resistance and took more assertive positions *vis-à-vis* Franco's domestic policies. The result was a set of policies – a special statute for Spanish Republicans inside France, a commitment to defend Republican political prisoners inside Spain, and a series of relationships between the French Government and the broad Spanish opposition to Franco – that clearly marked France as the most assertive member within the Western Alliance in terms of its support for the cause of Spanish Republicanism and a foreign policy driven by the rhetoric of justice.

France's International Refugee Statue for Republican Exiles

In dealing with Republican exiles, resolving the crisis caused by the presence of armed *guerrilleros* was the most pressing matter facing the French Government in the immediate aftermath of Liberation. By the end of 1944, all agreed that there was little chance of foreign military intervention against Franco or of foreign support for the *guerrilleros*. Moreover, those who continued to cross into Spain posed less and less of a serious threat. Many, indeed, questioned the utility of the guerrilla warfare strategy in the weeks after the failure of the Val d'Aran invasion, which had indicated that the prospects for launching a revolt inside Spain were virtually nil. As David Wingeate Pike has observed, "it was a mistake to imagine that the Resistance in France could serve as a model for the

Resistance in Spain, and that the Spanish people burned with a desire to rise against their oppressors."[4] With the exception of the PCF, most individuals, parties and movements associated with the French Resistance were far more comfortable, from autumn 1944 onward, to rally around the call for a new Spanish government without actively preparing or supporting an actual armed movement to facilitate such a change in regime. Indeed, after Val d'Aran, the majority of the Spanish Resistance in France chose to abandon the UNE and its emphasis on guerrilla tactics. On 23 October 1944, less than two months after the Liberation of Toulouse, the Socialists (and their trade union, the UGT), anarcho-syndicalists (and their trade union, the CNT) and the smaller left-of-center Republican parties had left the UNE and formed the rival *Junta Española de Liberación* (JEL), also known in various places as the *Agrupación Democrática Española*. This group was quick to announce that it had no intention of becoming involved in French politics and that it opposed the preparation of any "reconquest" of Spain from French territory.[5] Local French officials found it easier to deal with the non-violent approach of the JEL/*Agrupación*, and expressed relief that the UNE militants were being surpassed by this group.[6] The decline of the UNE and its guerilla activities contributed greatly to the dissipation of the crisis atmosphere along the Pyrenees. Inter-Republican debates had weakened the Spanish Government in the civil war against Franco, but had been somewhat patched over in the French Resistance, for initially the UNE included all Spanish Republican groups except for the anarchists. Now they returned, albeit in relation to a very different debate about tactics.

Nonetheless, pressure still existed from these new exile groups who increasingly advocated the idea of international economic and other sanctions against the regime, and looked to France, their country of exile, as a potential leader in this initiative. Most importantly, within France domestic support for action supporting Spanish Republicans in general had not dissipated. Increasingly, over the course of 1945, the French Left and Resistance overlooked the dissection of the Spanish opposition movement into various groups and instead continued to emphasize France's debt to the exiles as a whole. Thus the French Government could not ignore the exile community in Spain nor its French allies, even after the number of cross-border incidents declined. Short of breaking relations with Spain, which was not an option, France had to find ways to appease critics and embrace Spanish Republicanism while continuing to trade with Franco.

The socioeconomic and political situation of the Spanish exile community played an important role in suggesting possible avenues for the French Government to pursue. As Geneviève Dreyfus-Armand has emphasized, most exiles simply wanted steady employment and an end to relying on social assistance provided by aid organizations like the American Unitarian Service Committee that had been working with Spanish exiles in France since 1938.

While it was undeniable that most refugees had made it into Spain with Republican affiliations, not all were political activists or intellectuals. Indeed, many exiles consisted of the same types of individuals who made up the traditional Spanish immigrants to France, namely agricultural and industrial workers.[7] As one prefect reported, the demobilization of *guerrillero* groups from the end of 1944 greatly assisted in the reduction of local tensions and the movement of Spanish exiles into local economies and local community life.[8] While the size and diversity of the intellectual leadership was an important fact that could not be ignored, neither could the fact that some refugees might be content with a relatively non-political gesture on the part of France.

One of the first policies pursued by the French Government in relation to the Republican exile community was its advocacy of international protection and aid for Spanish refugees in France. Such a policy sought to provide economic security for the majority of refugees who simply wanted some form of normality while at the same time satisfying the activist exiles and their French supporters that the Government was indeed a supporter of Spanish Republicanism. Foreign Minister Georges Bidault made the proposal for refugee protection in the midst of the border crisis in October 1944. Bidault wrote to Interior Minister Adrien Tixier with the idea that the French Government could grant Spanish Republican refugees a statute of protection that would provide them with work status and aid but do so in a manner that would avoid raising protests from the Spanish government.[9] Bidault's plan centered on international, rather than French-mandated, protection; with international support, the cost to the French Government would be minimal and the Spanish Government would have fewer grounds upon which to protest.

The precedent for such assistance to refugees came through the League of Nations. The 1920 and 1928 Geneva Accords on refugees had placed White Russian and Armenian refugees under the protection of the League instead of their respective national consulates, due to the fact that their governments had refused, for political reasons, to recognize them as citizens. In the case of White Russians and Armenians, the national governments of the Soviet Union and Turkey, respectively, had no interest in representing individuals from groups they considered political and/or ethnic enemies of the state. These refugees were commonly known as Nansen refugees, after Frederick Nansen, the Norwegian who had established the League program. The Nansen Program began with legal protection, but by the time of the 1933 Convention on Refugees, it had extended to include the distribution of benefits to refugees as well.[10]

Within France, offices that provided aid and identity papers to Russian and Armenian exiles were established and run by the League with some French Government input. In 1936, the system was extended to refugees from the Saar, although in this case France bore the brunt of the costs associated with assistance.¹¹ A similar model was proposed by Bidault in the case of Spanish refugees, who, it was argued, should not be forced to seek representation from consulates occupied by Franco's appointees. As with the earlier programs, he too looked to the League of Nations to step in, for the League was still, barely, alive in the days before the creation of the United Nations in 1945. The program would be run by the League's High Commission on Refugees, with a committee composed of French Government representatives and representatives from various Spanish Republican groups established in France since the end of the Civil War in 1939, including the UNE, UGT, CNT, Catalan and Basque Nationalist groups.¹² The League of Nations High Commission for Refugees representative in France, Lester, was brought into the French planning by mid-October 1944.¹³ The former President of the Spanish Republic, Juan Negrín, also welcomed the French policy initiative.¹⁴

The effort to appease the majority of exiles, and encourage their settlement into everyday life, combined with an action meant to underline the special status of Republican refugees, seemed on course. However, even though the French goal was not to demonstrate open support for the Republican goal of removing the Franco regime, a number of problems existed in getting an agreement for international support. The weakness of the League of Nations was perhaps the greatest challenge. The League was by 1944 a skeleton body being run out of the British Foreign Office. René Massigli, the French Ambassador in London, was in charge of getting the League – and thus the British – to agree to such a program. Second, in contrast to the White Russian and Armenian cases where the respective governments had publicly stated their desire not to represent political refugees, the Spanish Government had said no such thing concerning exiles in France, and this raised concerns for many, especially within the British Government. Third, rather than introduce an entirely new regime of protection based on the Republican nature of the exiles, and thus explicitly support the goal of returning Republican government to Spain, the actual legislation proposed and enacted by France was seen in large part as a gesture meant to calm down refugees rather than press for a particular cause.

The weakness of the League of Nations in its dying days was demonstrated by the fact that the League's Assembly and Council, which ran its affairs, were not meeting; instead an interim Control Commission had decision-making authority, and it was not at full strength itself, for all of its funding came from the British Government.¹⁵ The League's High Commissioner on Refugees, Herbert Emerson, could not spend any additional money without the approval of British Foreign Office. If the structural and administrative weakness of the League risked compromising the proposal, the involvement of the British, and their desire not to antagonize the Franco government, added a second concern. From day one, the British opposed the French proposal in large part because of their fear was that Spain would protest that action of the League; such a protest just might lead to an international outcry over Franco's continued existence in power, which would have consequences far beyond the refugee issue.[16] The French Government repeatedly attempted to ensure the British that the Spanish Consulate had raised no fundamental objections to the plan when it was informed in January 1945.[17] Indeed, Spanish documents reveal that in meetings with Spanish representatives, members of the Quai d'Orsay emphasized that the only motivation behind the policy was to deal with an "internal security problem" that the refugees represented and that France had "no desire" to intervene in domestic politics with the proposal.[18] The British, however, were not convinced, and rejected the proposal in April 1945: "we . . . have not been able to satisfy ourselves that the Spanish Government have formally disinterested themselves in the fate of these refugees."[19]

The British response eventually led the League's Secretariat to suggest that the French abandon the League of Nations, but instead approach the Intergovernmental Committee on Refugees (IGC) with a Nansen-like proposal. The IGC was a body of Allied states created in 1938 to negotiate with Nazi Germany and possible receiving states in order to move Jewish and other refugees out of Germany. In this it largely failed, but was revived in 1943 to open talks with neutral states in order to find safe receptions for wartime refugees.[20] There was a fear by many still involved with the League that if Spanish refugees successfully used the League for aid, then many emerging governments hoping to establish themselves as legitimate after the war, such as the Communist Lublin government in Poland that competed with the prewar Government in exile, would also seek refugee protection for more political reasons, and thus cause any number of international problems.[21] The practical aspect of working through the IGC also appealed to the British, for under all IGC programs, money was distributed to refugees not through international or national bodies, but rather through private charitable organizations. In the case of France, many of these groups were already working with Spanish refugees (as they had been since the Civil War era), and simply would use IGC and French Government funds to supplement existing programs. The implication was that relief, not international recognition of the Republican cause, was the main motivation behind the effort to internationalize assistance. Members of the IGC on the ground in France, led by the IGC Chief Representative Valentin-Smith, supported such a proposal with the argument that the creation of "reception centers" for Spanish refugees would more easily move them away from the activity of guerilla warfare and consulate occupations.[22] The idea of appeasing and calming down refugees was equally a goal of the French, especially in light of the ferment that occurred along the border in the last part of 1944. Indeed, by using the League of Nations model of consulting with exiled groups, Georges Bidault expressed the hope that what would result was not only refugee assistance but also the ability of the

French government "to exercise an influence over the Spanish colony that we lack at the present."²³

A third problem with the refugee proposal was the reaction of the more political elements of the Republican exile community. The intention of the French Government to limit this package to assistance rather than open support of Republicanism was apparent to many leaders. The Spanish Socialist trade union, the UGT, was based in Toulouse, France, while in exile and had a representative on the exile committee that worked with the French Government in crafting the legislation and later in administering it. The UGT did not protest the implementation of the French initiative, but did note its nature as a "token" gesture and underlined that the actual working rights given to refugees under the statute were not much different from those granted to Spaniards under the 1862 Franco-Spanish agreement that enabled Spanish workers to more easily find jobs in France.²⁴ While acceptable to the activists in the exile community, it was not sufficient to stand in as a replacement for an overtly pro-Republican policy that sought to encourage the removal of Franco from power.

The French statute for protection of Spanish Refugees was issued in March 1945 and was subsequently given international status through the IGC in June. The *Office Central des Réfugies Espagnols* was created under IGC authority and was advised by both the French Government and the exile community in France. From March 1945 through November 1946, over forty thousand work-related documents were issued by the Office.²⁵ Recently arrived refugees who crossed the Pyrenees clandestinely were welcomed alongside those who had been in France since the Civil War. Only in 1950 was a more restrictive policy enforced that limited assistance to "established" exiles.²⁶

The Spanish Government protested mildly after the French Government issued its decree, but there were no economic or other threats made, such as those that had been issued at the time of the Paris Spanish Chamber of Commerce episode.²⁷ In March 1945, Miguel Mateu, the Spanish Minister in Paris, collected reports from all the Spanish Consuls-General in France on the subject of Spanish refuges, asking for numbers, the number deemed "repatriatible" vs. "political", and their responses to the proposed French statute.²⁸ While most Spanish Consuls-General saw the statute as a French concession to local Communists and the UNE, they did not object to it since in their opinion most of the Spanish exiles were politically motivated and therefore un-repatriatible.²⁹ By contrast, a French Police report declared that approximately two hundred and fifty thousand of the approximately three hundred and four thousand Spanish refugees in France had to be considered "apolitical" or at the very least, content to settle in France for the foreseeable future.³⁰ In any event, the Refugee Statute was enacted and work permits issued. France successfully "calmed down" the Spanish exiles without fully committing to pressing for a regime change in Madrid. Yet as time went on, the linkage Spanish officials saw, between supporting political exiles and assisting in advancing their ultimate goal, would be more and more difficult to avoid.

French Intervention in Cases of Political Prisoners in Spain

As noted, after the UNE's failed invasion of the Val d'Aran in October 1944, most Spanish Republicans dismissed major armed interventions in Spain as a viable method of overthrowing Franco. Yet clandestine border crossings continued on a much smaller and much less organized scale. A typical example was one near Tolosa, Spain, in April 1945 when twenty Republicans encountered a Spanish army patrol and two were killed.[31] More likely than not, Spanish Republicans were not killed but arrested in the course of such crossings. Thus many Spanish veterans of the French Resistance found themselves political prisoners under Franco. One of the most direct ways in which France repaid its debt to Spanish Republicans was through its involvement in the cases of such individuals who had been part of the French Resistance, had subsequently returned clandestinely to Spain, and were arrested and facing death sentences there. Intervention in an effort to commute death sentences in Spain became a sustained, important, and overlooked government policy, one that responded to the public demand that post-war France make foreign policy more democratic, more humanitarian, and more republican. Moreover, in the implementation of this policy, it became clear that more than appeasement of Spanish exile activists and their French supporters was at work here. While this motivation was not absent in the construction of French policy, the involvement of French officials in Spanish Republican prisoner cases also reveals real shared sympathy with the Republican cause and with the notion that an activist, interventionist, and moral foreign policy was an important part of France's post-war recovery.

Repression under General Francisco Franco was not new. As Michael Richards has written, immediately following the end of the Spanish Civil War in 1939, repression had an important place in Spain as part of Franco's victorious "purification" of the nation and related installation of military, authoritarian and autarchic culture in place of more humane ideas of political economy.[32] Between 1939 and 1944, almost two hundred thousand people were executed in Spain by the Franco regime; those targeted by the state first and foremost were those deemed incompatible with Franco's conception of the Nation as nationalistic, militaristic, and Catholic, namely Republicans, unionists and freemasons.[33] Franco's systematic repression of opponents never ended, lasting well into the last days of his regime in the 1970s. Yet the changes in the course of the Second World War in France mark an important moment in the history of this repression. In late 1944, as small groups of armed Spanish Republicans entered Spain from the relative safety of liberated France, authoritarianism in the hands of the Spanish police was reinvigorated. The Spanish fascist party, the Falange, in its organ *Arriba*, wrote that France had lost control of its borders to Spanish "Reds" and that the Spanish Army would respond if necessary.[34] French authorities based in Bordeaux learned that previously released political prisoners in Spain were being re-arrested in the aftermath of French liberation, as well as those who had crossed the border from France.[35] France was gradually drawn in due to the circumstances of this particular round of repression inside Spain.

The question of political prisoners inside Spain, especially those with ties to France, was not new for the activists trying to get the French Government to adopt a firmer line toward the Franco regime. The *Comité France-Espagne* had been formed in Toulouse, in 1944, with one of its primary activities defined as pressuring French and Allied governments to do all they could in order to prevent executions of Spanish Republicans.[36] The growth of similar local and regional committees across France led to the creation of a national *Association France-Espagne* by June 1945. As demonstrated, there were many groups in France, and especially in the French press, that advocated a different approach to Franco's Spain than that taken by the Government in Paris. The importance of the *Association France-Espagne* was that while it shared the general belief that France should rupture all diplomatic ties to Spain, it largely dedicated itself to advocating that France use the ties it had in Spain to press for the commutation of death sentences imposed on Spanish Republicans with ties to France. Led by the academic Jean Cassou, this organization initiated public petitions and held rallies opposing the imposition and execution of death sentences inside Spain, created a commission of jurists to review such cases in order to demonstrate the lack of a rule of law in Spain, involved other groups such as the *Ligue des Droits de l'Homme* in the cause, and urged French and Allied intervention. The Association also published a memoir of a former political prisoner in Spain, Ramon Via.[37] From these non-governmental efforts emerged an activist and Resistance-inspired government policy.

The *Association* was successful in getting the Government to intervene for a number of reasons. Naturally enough, its advocacy of intervention picked up on the general arguments made by those who wanted France to adopt a firm anti-Franco policy, and thus increased pressure on the Government. Moreover, the *Association* had significant membership amongst members in the Constituent National Assembly, one that crossed party lines. Vice Presidents of the organization included Madelaine Braun, a member of the Communist Party and Deputy Speaker in the Assembly, as well as Charles d'Aragon, a member of Foreign Minister Bidault's Christian Democratic movement, the MRP.

The March 1945 announcement of the execution of sixteen political prisoners by the Franco government led to the first major petition campaign, based in Toulouse, in April. The petition sent to President Charles de Gaulle by the local *Comité France-Espagne* condemned the executions for targeting those who merely wanted to "make a democratic Republic in Spain to be a friend of liberated France" and demanded that the French Government urge Franco to end the executions and allow French delegations to visit prisons inside Spain. It was signed by a number of prominent Toulousians, including the former Resistance General Riquelme, as well as by the editors of every newspaper in the city.[38]

This was followed by the first significant intervention by the French Mission in Madrid, also in April 1945. That month José Vitini, a former FFI commander with three years of wartime service, was executed in Madrid. Protests and petitions aimed at President de Gaulle followed, and in Toulouse every newspaper again condemned the execution and demanded France action.[39] On 29 April 1945, the head of the French Mission in Madrid, Jacques Truelle, was directed by the Foreign Ministry to personally approach the Spanish Foreign Minister in order to forcefully emphasize that the execution of the Resistance hero Vitini was an "unfriendly gesture" toward France that "risked seriously affecting" French–Spanish relations.[40]

The second major case to gain significant publicity in France was that of FFI veterans and Spanish Communist Party leaders Santiago Alvarez and Sebastián Zapirain who were given death sentences in September 1945. Both the French Socialist Party (SFIO) and the *Conseil National de la Resistance* made requests to the Quai d'Orsay to intervene with the Franco government and demand commutation.[41] A Paris rally in favor of commutation that featured exiled Spanish Communist Dolores Iaburruri was the subject of a counter-protest by the Spanish Mission in France that threatened French–Spanish relations if the French Government 'persisted in their lamentable attitudes towards such public meetings.'[42] Yet by October, reports existed that *Radio Madrid* (official radio of Franco) suggested that the two might be released if they found another country willing to take them in; the French Government was willing to investigate this but could not confirm it as late as November 1945.[43]

The *Association France-Espagne* and its parliamentary members met with Foreign Minister Georges Bidault on 26 November 1945 to ask for his assistance in a number of cases, including Alvarez and Zapirain, former FFI member Ventura Marquez (who had a French wife), 22 trade union members held in Cadiz, and five former FFI veterans held in Barcelona, including Cristino García, a former FFI commander. Bidault agreed that France had an obligation to intervene in these cases on principle.[44] The same group had met with Spanish Minister in Paris Miguel Mateu in early November, at which point he dismissed them as using the cases of political prisoners as simply "a new pretext in order to attack Spain." However, by the time of Bidault's meeting with them, Mateu was concerned enough to report to Madrid that while no one in the French Government had yet taken a "grave position" the possibility that such activity could lead to a French break in diplomatic relations with Spain was present.[45]

By the end of 1945, French interventions were a regular feature of the diplomatic activity of French Minister in Madrid Bernard Hardion. The campaign within France continued to expand so that by 1946, requests for intervention to the Government involved multiple organizations. One representative example, made in December 1946 in the case of Agustin Zoroa Sànchez, came at the request of the Federation of Spaniards in France, the Spanish Communist Party in exile, the Veterans of the FFI Resistance, the National Association of Deportees the French Socialist Party, the CGT trade union, the Union of French Women and the Communist Party of France. Later, a number of members of the National Assembly, including the leaders of the *Association France-Espagne*, added their concerns in this case to the Government.[46]

From Madrid, Hardion insisted in each case of speaking directly with Spanish Foreign Minister Martín Artajo, seen by many as a moderate within the Franco regime. Despite the fact that by the end of November 1945 both French and Spanish officials welcomed a sharp decrease in armed border crossings and incidents likely to lead to arrest[47], French officials did not stop their observance of the Spanish legal system when it came to political prisoners. In addition to intervening in specific cases, French representatives in Spain kept a close watch in the Franco Government's supposed amnesty program for political prisoners returning from exile. As early as June 1945, the French Consul in Barcelona, Jacques Coiffard, reported that the amnesty was more rhetorical than real; after two to three weeks of relative freedom, most exiles returned from France found themselves in prison for additional interrogations and eventual charges.[48] Between April 1945 and January 1946, Bernard Hardion intervened in sixty-two cases. The demand for interventions came from the Foreign Ministry in Paris, from groups like the *Association France-Espagne* via the Foreign Ministry, or directly to Hardion from families of the accused. Hardion emphasized that even in cases where a French intervention had not resulted in a death sentence commutation, it had bought time for the accused, as none of the individuals the French had spoken for had yet been executed.[49] A sense of success, then, contributed to the longevity of the policy of intervention. Undoubtedly, however, the values behind such a policy were most significant.

Eventually, the record of French interventions and the injustice of Franco's regime led the Madrid Mission to expand its efforts beyond assistance to those Spanish Republicans who had direct ties to the French Resistance. At a trial in Alcala de Henares in December 1945, fifteen of twenty five Republican activists found guilty of political crimes received death sentences. Families of the accused visited Hardion and pleaded for a French intervention. Hardion, although noting these individuals had no ties to France, responded that "I did not believe that I could refuse that which struck my most elemental humanitarian sentiments."⁵⁰ The French delegation did indeed intervene in the weeks following the sentences and successfully obtained the commutation of nine death sentences. Similarly, at the request of the Spanish Socialist Party in exile (PSOE), an observer from the French Mission in Madrid attended the February 1946 trial of 37 Socialists in Alcala de Henares. Their crime had been to try and re-establish the PSOE as an underground organization. Despite a lack of ties to France, the French Mission decided to intervene in this case with the Foreign Ministry as well as send observers to attend the trial, and the result was a series of relatively moderate sentences, ranging from six months to twelve years in jail. The PSOE credited France's involvement as a major factor in the outcome.⁵¹ Of the sixty-two cases France was involved in by January 1946, only about half had some connection to France and the French Resistance.⁵² In Barcelona, the clandestine lodge of the Freemasons (heavily persecuted by the Franco regime) contacted French Consul Jean Coiffard and asked that French diplomatic mail be used to allow the Masons to report on conditions inside Spain to Spanish exile groups in France and French Masons as well. This was subsequently done, as it was for a series of clandestine Catalan groups and the Spanish Human Rights League.⁵³

Activism extended beyond the individuals based in Madrid such as Bernard Hardion. Thanks to press reports, the petitions of groups like the *Association France-Espagne*, and ties the Government had with the Spanish exile community in France, officials at the Quai d'Orsay in Paris regularly made inquiries to their Mission in Madrid about particular cases and about the Francoist justice system generally.⁵⁴ In the autumn of 1946, Hardion made interventions in six specific cases brought to his attention by officials in Paris. In these instances, Hardion underlined the value of research done in Paris to authenticate direct ties to the French Resistance, arguing that his rate of success was greater if a French role could be undeniably demonstrated.⁵⁵ Thus the importance of cooperation between the Mission in Madrid and government officials in Paris was made clear. Moreover, Spanish groups in France began to regularly contact the Quai d'Orsay in order to thank the French Government for interventions, raise awareness of new political trials, and make the connection among France's efforts, a general commitment to justice, and the cause of Spanish Republicanism.⁵⁶ In one specific case, Georges Bidault even arranged for a French lawyer to represent one Republican detainee and the Government went to work in order to facilitate his entry to Spain.⁵⁷

What arguably is most striking about the intervention policy was in fact the consistency of language used by Spanish Republicans, by their supporters from the French Resistance, and by officials within the Foreign Ministry. Government officials who did not want to see an end to French–Spanish relations surprisingly echoed the language of the exile and Resistance press in France. Writing of his efforts to help the families of political prisoners with no ties to France, Bernard Hardion stated that their approach to him was "witness to the confidence certain sectors of the Spanish people put in our country and of the radiance beyond our borders of our liberal and humane traditions."[58] Hardion underlined that he never intervened as part of a diplomatic negotiation or bargaining ploy; his actions and words were always motivated "strictly by humanitarianism."[59] Foreign Minister Georges Bidault, in December 1945 testimony to the Foreign Affairs Commission of the Constituent National Assembly, called the question of interventions in Spanish trials as one of his Ministry's "most passionate" issues.[60]

In short, the motivation behind French action was more than simply the need to respond to public pressure, even if that was most evident in the early days of the intervention policy. There was clearly a sense of justice seen in the words of the French Government officials involved. Although inspired by the Resistance and the left as part of a general policy that advocated an end to relations with Spain, those in the Government who maintained that relations with Spain should not be broken because of ideology shared the sentiments behind such action. The ideals of justice in the republican and liberal sense inspired this policy once it was entered into. In that sense, the attitudes of officials and those of Resistance veterans and the left-wing press were remarkably similar, and in this we have evidence, arguably, for a Resistance vision of a new foreign policy being put into action.

French Support for the Anti-Franco Opposition

A strategy meant to give voice to Resistance and left-wing critics at home and offer a response to their concerns about policy toward Spain ultimately had to grapple with the preferred policy choice of the left: open support for a potential democratic alternative to the existing regime in Madrid. Mateu's fears that official contacts with Spanish political exiles and their French supporters could lead to more were justified. Yet while clearly sharing sympathy with the cause, French officials were far more cautious in approaching the question of facilitating the creation of a potential alternative government than they were in creating the refugee statute or in intervening in political prisoner cases. Thus when domestic politics demanded a more overt anti-Franco position, Christian Democrat and Gaullist officials in the French Foreign Ministry, the Quai d'Orsay, turned to the *raison d'etat* model of Napoleon III at Plombiéres rather than a more aggressive interventionist commitment to building republican democracy. In this instance, what emerged was a French policy that sought to respond to critics within the structures of the emerging Western Alliance French officials preferred to work from.

France encouraged the development of a Spanish opposition movement not inspired by France's own liberation and subsequent republican form of government, but rather one that had a chance of success in removing Franco and one that also would have the support of the entire Western Alliance. In 1946–7, this meant support for an alternative regime closely linked to the Spanish Pretender Don Juan, not support for a regime based upon pre-Civil War Republican structures. Spanish monarchists were seen to be more stable than the divided republican movement and France made a more positive assessment of the potential support a monarchical regime would be able to receive. Moreover, a government involving monarchists was the preferred option of the British and, eventually, the United States, when these governments thought about removing Franco from power.

As with Spanish Republican exiles and political prisoners, the development of a comprehensive French policy toward the opposition to Franco demonstrates that the emergent Fourth Republic did not simply turn its back on revolutionary politics; yet when it came to foreign policy it also did not embrace such politics to the detriment of France's position in the world. Resistance idealism and practical politics came together rather awkwardly in the case of Fourth Republic policy toward Spain. For Foreign Ministry policy-makers, domestic pressure to restore republicanism in Spain was to be appeased only as necessary for political survival. When it came to conceiving of an alternative regime to Franco's, alliance politics trumped Resistance ideals.

Spanish exiles in favor of a regime change in Madrid organized themselves around the JEL in the aftermath of the Val d'Aran failure. At the United Nations founding conference in San Francisco, the JEL presented the French delegation with a detailed critique of Franco's relationship to the Axis powers. By doing so, it demonstrated the regime's fundamental incompatibility with the emerging world order of the United Nations.[61] France, along with the United States and Great Britain, supported a Mexican resolution against Spanish admission to the UN. Yet all three states also continued to maintain diplomatic relations with Spain and negotiated trade and other agreements with the Franco regime over the course of 1945. The JEL was not recognized as a government-in-exile.

However, a series of analyses undertaken immediately following the conference by the French Foreign Ministry concerning the Spanish opposition movement suggests that a debate about the value of working with the various movements opposed to Franco was beginning. While the Foreign Ministry did not support the establishment of a government-in-exile on French soil, it did not dismiss the anti-Franco opposition entirely. France began a process that ultimately allowed for the development of an official relationship with the JEL. The intent was not to overthrow Franco or even to encourage such action, but rather prepare for a future Spanish regime should the *Caudillo*'s disappear.

The Franco regime, a Foreign Ministry official wrote, "lacked roots within the country, and its situation was far from being solid and assured." On the opposition side, multiple divisions between extreme left, moderate left, extreme right, moderate right, and the army were troublesome as well, and those revolutionary forces based in France were clearly insufficient to overthrow the government. A leftist government would only take power with external support and the likelihood of civil war, a situation that would be "catastrophic not only for Spain but for all of Europe." However, a monarchical restoration might be able to rally moderate Republicans, the army, and the "neutral masses" around a single solution and lead to a peaceful transition to a more moderate Spanish regime. Moreover, although Great Britain and the United States had done little to foster a change in Spain's government, it was evident that the incompatibility of Franco's regime with the Allied world order would soon change the Anglo-American attitude toward Franco as well. The report concluded that "the fall of General Franco is a certain fact, the only doubtful point being whether or not his regime will be liquefied in blood and anarchy or through a formula of pacification and stability that will assure Spain a place in the reconstruction of the world."[62]

This memorandum was significant for a number of reasons. First, although it did not seek to change French policy in the sense of ending diplomatic and economic relations with Franco, which in the summer of 1945 were improving, it did acknowledge that France must be prepared for an end to the Franco regime and could help, in a small way, to foster that end. Second, it demonstrated that despite the supposed unity of French and Spanish Republican ideology, the Quai d'Orsay feared that the divisions among various Republican parties were too deep for a Republican restoration in Spain to be feasible. Instead, the Quai proposed that a moderate monarchical restoration, with some Republican support, was an option that could succeed and to which France could contribute. Third, it argued that both the United States and Great Britain would likely adopt a similar approach to the Spanish question. While well aware of domestic rumblings, French policy toward Spain was to be made largely within the context of its relationship to the US and Britain.

A history of Allied contact with the Spanish opposition, particularly in its democratic manifestations, republican and monarchist, existed since the Second World War.[63] There were different perspectives as to the viability of certain options. The British had long considered the monarchy as an appropriate alternative in Spain; the Spanish pretender, Don Juan, was a grandson of Queen Victoria, and a careful cultivation of pro-monarchist elements within Spain occurred throughout 1945.[64] The United States, meanwhile, generally believed that restoration was almost as incompatible with the post-war world as was Franco's regime.[65] In fact, the Allies were not as divided as it might seem, for the matter was not seen as a pressing one in any of the three capitals, despite the revival of the monarchical option when Don Juan released his Lausanne Manifesto in March 1945, proclaiming his desire to serve as King of Spain.[66]

Nonetheless, the issue was percolating and as in Paris, the question of which alternative best offered the chance for a successful and peaceful transition to democracy confronted policy-makers in London and Washington.

Like the Americans and the British, French officials believed that the Allies could trade with Franco and avoid internal intervention in Spanish affairs while simultaneously indicating to opposition figures "in a clear and definitive manner that Franco could not continue in his current position."[67] Thus a potential French and Allied move toward the Spanish opposition slowly emerged over the summer of 1945. Such an approach emphasized the creation of a united and moderate alternative regime before any action to remove Franco was taken. It drew upon the relations with Army generals, non-Communist Republicans, and monarchist politicians that France and its Allies had maintained since the war. This effort also built upon actions being taken by Spanish opposition figures themselves. The non-Communist left inside Spain, united in the *Alianza Nacional de Fuerzas Democráticas* (ANFD) led by the anarchist José Luque Argente, opened talks with monarchist generals in Madrid that were closely followed by the Embassies of the three Western allies.[68] An Allied approach that seemed to favor such a broad-based regime thus emerged, and news of a successful verbal agreement between the ANFD and leading monarchists in November 1945 was greeted as "sound" by Great Britain and the United States.[69]

The discussions of 1945, however, did not involve the Republican-government-in-exile that was formed out of the JEL group. In August 1945 the JEL succeeded in reconstituting the Spanish Republican parliament, the *Cortes*, in Mexico and elected a government-in-exile under the leadership of José Giral Pereira. The new foreign minister, Fernando de los Ríos, immediately contacted the French Government requesting official recognition.[70] There was absolutely no chance that France would consider official recognition and thus end its relations with the Franco Government. As emphasized earlier, relations with the Spanish opposition were a secondary strategy, preparing the ground for relations when Franco did finally leave power. Moreover, the French Foreign Ministry did not consider Giral's government representative of the opposition because it consisted of left republican and socialist parties only, and thus had no ties to left socialists like former Republican Premier Juan Negrín, no Communist involvement, and no contact with monarchists and moderate right-wingers such as José Gil Robles, former leader of the conservative party in the Spanish Republic. The Quai d'Orsay's European Director, François Coulet, told British Ambassador to France Duff Cooper that the exiles in Mexico "appeared to have completely lost touch with their own country" and the more moderate opposition elements there.[71] American and British sentiment was much the same.[72]

However hesitant the Western powers were about Giral's government-in-exile, they did not rule out some role for these Republicans in a future Spanish regime. The United States and France were particularly eager to discuss the possibility of trying to move Giral closer to the moderates in order to create the broadest coalition possible.[73] All agreed that the Quai d'Orsay was best positioned to maintain contact with this group without formally recognizing them as a government.[74] A number of factors combined to place France in a position that made it best suited to deal with Giral as part of a general effort to encourage the Spanish opposition. A majority of the ministers in the cabinet-in-exile sought entry into France from Mexico in order to be closer to their fellow refugees. Even if the Republican Government-in-exile itself could not be granted official status, France would not deny these politicians entry as individuals. Bidault hoped that such individual immigration would lead to a more or less "official" unofficial relationship between the Giral Government and the Quai d'Orsay.[75] In addition, anti-Francoist sentiment among political parties, press, and other organizations within France sparked a strong expression of pro-Giral Government feeling that the Quai d'Orsay could not ignore. Such support has led one historian to comment that by the end of 1945, British and French views of Spanish Republicans were "diametrically opposed", with the French being strongly in favor.[76] In reality, contact with Giral was not meant to be exclusive, but rather was to be used in order to foster a broader strategy of opposition to Franco.

José Giral himself followed a number of his ministers into France in February 1946. The French claim that he entered the country merely as an individual and not due to his status as the head of a Spanish Republican government-in-exile was rejected by Madrid out of hand.[77] Indeed, Giral's Foreign Minister, Fernando de los Ríos, attempted to negotiate with the French Government in order to obtain de facto diplomatic immunity and semi-legal consular offices for Giral government ministers residing in France.[78] These demands were rejected as being incompatible with the fact that there was no formal recognition of the Giral government.[79] Yet contact was not ended. The desire of Bidault to maintain ties with Giral as part of a broader Spanish strategy won out, not only in relation to a debate within the Foreign Ministry, but also against the opposition of de Gaulle.[80]

France's decision to act as a bridge between the Giral Government and the Allies, and between the Giral Government and more moderate elements of the Spanish opposition, would have been insignificant if there was not a belief, held by all parties that an alternative regime that could prevent renewed civil war was likely to develop. Although the JEL, Giral, and other Republicans, on the one hand, and the monarchists, Don Juan, and the army on the other, had acted fairly independently from one another, the evidence suggested that since autumn 1945 these groups were coming to see the need for cooperation if they were to have any success. As noted, a verbal agreement on cooperation between the ANFD and leading monarchists was reached in November 1945. Their goal at this point was to find common ground in order to form a provisional government under Don Juan that would seek to replace Franco and hold a plebiscite to determine Spain's political future.[81] By January 1946, the British Foreign Office considered the rapprochement to be "growing steadily" and believed that all three Western allies should "encourage the Spaniards to set their own house in order" when it came to thinking of an alternative regime to Franco's.[82] In February 1946, British Foreign Secretary Ernest Bevin proposed that the Allies think of the transition to a post-Franco regime as a two-stage process. The first stage consisted of Franco's removal and his replacement with a provisional government, presumably broadly-based. Only during the second stage would they consider whether the new regime should be a monarchy or a republic.[83]

As the Western powers slowly drifted away from a strict interpretation of non-intervention in Spain, the Spanish issue began to dominate domestic French politics. In February 1946, that pressure from the public and the parties in the National Assembly forced the French Government to close its border with Spain.[84] A joint statement of France, Britain, and the United States opposing the continued existence of an authoritarian Spain on 4 March 1946 followed this unilateral action. The Tripartite Note made explicit the hopes of the Western Allies with regard to the creation of a broad-based anti-Franco coalition. The note emphasized Allied non-intervention in Spanish internal affairs while at the same time it called for the Spanish people to form a "provisional government" that would prepare for elections that would allow Spanish citizens to "define the type of government they desire."[85]

Both the Giral Government and Republicans within Spain considered the Allied statement to be less than ideal.[86] Nonetheless, the Republican Government-in-exile realized that it needed to expand its base of support in order to have a chance at gaining more explicit support from other governments. By the end of March, the Giral Government was joined by the Spanish Communist Party with the appointment of PCE member Santiago Carrillo to the Cabinet.[87] Yet the more significant issue for Giral and his Cabinet concerned their relationship with the ANFD inside Spain and in particular with its strategy of holding talks with moderate monarchists and generals. As late as January 1946 the Spanish Socialist Party in France officially rejected the idea of talks with Don Juan as well as the creation of any regime that was not explicitly republican.[88] Within the Republican government-in-exile, however, there were elements that believed a "democratic monarchy" might have a better chance of success than a simple restoration of the pre-Civil War Spanish Republic, and thus contact was established between these members of Giral's Cabinet and the ANFD in Madrid.[89]

The anarcho-syndicalists organized in the MLE-CNT movement were the strongest advocates of pursuing talks with monarchists and the Spanish Army. In March 1946, the congress of the MLE/CNT-in-exile met in Toulouse and decided that rather than formulate its policy from France, it would submit to the authority of the clandestine movement in Spain, which already was vocal in its support of negotiations with moderates and monarchists.⁹⁰ By May 1946, the Secretary-General of the clandestine CNT, Vicente Santamaría, became the Secretary-General of the ANFD as well, and launched a new stage in the effort to unite the Spanish opposition. In France, the leading CNT minister within Giral's government, José Leiva, promoted a strategy that sought to affiliate the Republican government-in-exile to Santamaría's efforts inside Spain. Leiva argued that reconciliation with the internal Spanish opposition was necessary to win external support as well as improve the chances of removing Franco. Increasingly, many Socialists in the Giral Cabinet, led by Trifón Gómez, were convinced that this was indeed the case, and supported such a move.⁹¹ By May 1946 the PSOE-in-exile, meeting at Toulouse, softened its January position and encouraged finding "another formula" besides strict republicanism in the search for an alternative to Franco.⁹²

While Giral himself was suspicious of the discussions being held in Spain and fearful that the British were encouraging such talks in order to restore the monarchy permanently, others wanted to move forward.⁹³ France was thus forced to choose between its desire to bring Spanish Republicans into the broader anti-Franco framework that was developing and its support of Giral. The leader of the Republican-Government-in-exile was abandoned, but the desire to unite the Spanish opposition was not.

Vicente Santamaría contacted the French Mission in Madrid in April 1946 in order to express his interest in working with those members of the Giral Government in France who supported the idea of a broad-based opposition movement. Santamaría requested French support in maintaining communication between the ANFD and these individuals, especially José Leiva of the CNT.⁹⁴ As a result, the French Government increasingly developed contacts with CNT and Socialist leaders who supported the ANFD approach, supported their position in talks with other Republicans in exile, and facilitated communications between these individuals and the ANFD in Spain that was conducting negotiations with Spanish monarchists and generals. Eventually, the French Mission in Madrid and the Quai d'Orsay in Paris assisted in those negotiations. From Santamaría's initial contact developed a whole range of relationships between members of the anti-Franco opposition in France and Madrid and the French Government.

The primary contact was made by the French Mission in Madrid, with the knowledge and support of the mission's head, Bernard Hardion, and in particular by an unnamed member of the staff there.⁹⁵ This official, referred to in documents as 'Monsieur X', primarily dealt with CNT representatives in Madrid, most notably the Secretary-General of the CNT and ANFD, Santamaría.⁹⁶ He also served as a conduit between CNT members inside Spain and those in France, often using the French diplomatic pouch to transmit Spanish opposition material back and forth between the capitals.[97] Hardion made it a regular practice to read this correspondence and report to Paris on developments within the ANFD camp.[98] The CNT had made similar contacts with the British Embassy in Madrid, but the Secretary-General confided to 'Monsieur X' that he trusted the French more in terms of their support for a strong Republican role in any alternative Spanish regime.[99] In addition, French intelligence agents maintained important contacts with the other side of the talks in Madrid, monarchist members of the Spanish military.[100]

A series of meetings between Santamaría and the General Juan Beigbeder (later joined by General Antonio Aranda) began in May 1946. By mid-August, the Quai d'Orsay decided that talks were progressing well, and it informed Leiva that France now definitely supported a transition-type regime and that it desired ANFD participation in such a regime rather than continuing its support of the Giral Government even if Giral expanded his Cabinet to include monarchists, the military leadership, and Catholic parties.[101] The original goal of bridging the gap between Giral and the internal opposition was officially abandoned as France looked to support other Republicans who were willing to work within the framework of the Tripartite Note and achieve a real agreement with Spanish generals and monarchists.

The broad lines of what an alternative regime would look like – three generals, four to seven monarchists, and between four and seven republicans – were agreed to by both sides by the end of August.[102] As negotiations moved from a general framework to a more specific agreement, French involvement increased. Jean Chauvel, Secretary-General of the Quai d'Orsay, coordinated the government's support for the role undertaken in negotiations by Vicente Santamaría, the Secretary-General of the ANFD, as did Fourcaud of French Intelligence.[103] Chauvel later informed the British Embassy that his personal authority over the French Government's efforts was done with the approval in principle of Bidault, but without the knowledge of the European section of the Quai d'Orsay or the French Council of Ministers.[104] Santamaría emphasized to Chauvel that the ANFD desire to reach an agreement with Spanish monarchists was in direct response to the Allied Tripartite Statement on the subject of a broad transitional regime in Spain.[105] Chauvel later stated that he believed the work of French intelligence in Spain that had focused on the development of contacts with both monarchists and the CNT was done in order to "bring together inside Spain the various elements capable of bringing about a change of regime." France's interference in the internal affairs of its southern neighbor was justified by the desire to act as an "honest broker" in a process that the Spaniards themselves were in charge of.[106] On 7 October 1946, Bidault, acting in his capacity as Foreign Minister and Prime Minister of the Republic, met for over an hour with Santamaría, encouraging him to reach an agreement with

Generals Beigbeider and Aranda as well as other representatives of Don Juan. As Bidault put it, "I can do no better than to remind you of the words Napoleon III said to Cavour at Plombières: Make it so, but make it so quickly."[107]

Santamaría spent the month of October meeting in Paris, London, and Lisbon with monarchists and internal opposition figures, Socialists, anarchists, and members of other exiled political groups. One of the most important of these meetings facilitated by the French government was held in Paris between Santamaría, Trifón Gómez, a representative of Don Juan's secretariat, Vegas Latapié, and Julio Lopez Oliván, an associate of the monarchist politician Gil Robles.[108] An ANFD-Don Juan agreement in principle was reached at Estoril, Portugal, in October 1946 and Santamaría expressed his satisfaction for France's role in facilitating his ability to negotiate.[109] However, the implementation of the agreement was delayed until Santamaría could return to Madrid in order to sell it to all members of the Alliance. The delay was not without risks, for there was a significant chance that the monarchists either would decide they were strong enough to go it alone or that Franco might approach Don Juan and discuss the possibility of a more conservative restoration.[110]

Such pessimism was well founded. The CNT, Socialist and Republican parties involved in the Alliance all disagreed with one aspect of the proposed pact, that which allowed Don Juan to reserve his right to act freely if the situation changed. In other words, if Franco agreed to a restoration, or a military coup developed, then Don Juan could break the agreement without further negotiation, leaving the ANFD to accept the fact that it was agreeing to the possibility that a right-wing conservative regime might emerge instead of a left-leaning republican one.[111] Santamaría was told to renegotiate this aspect of the accord, which required not only new assent from Don Juan, but from the monarchist generals in Madrid as well.[112] Such a mission was unlikely to succeed, to say the least. During November 1946, more talks occurred between the two sides. However, the ANFD concluded that it was impossible to reach an agreement with Don Juan. Vicente Santamaría, in whom Bidault and Chauvel had invested their support, resigned from the organization.

In Madrid, the French Embassy scrambled to save the Estoril agreement. Bernard Hardion did all he could to get Santamaría to withdraw his resignation; he contacted other ANFD members in order to emphasize to them, "with force", that the rejection of the accord negotiated by Santamaría was also considered an insult to France and its anti-Franco efforts.[113] Hardion also met with the other side of the negotiation, the leading monarchist in Spain, General Antonion Aranda, in order to encourage him to continue talks with the ANFD, which the latter duly promised he would do.[114] Yet those who wanted to abandon any future talks with Don Juan, led by CNT members José Luque and Enrique Marco Nadal, now held the upper hand within the ANFD.[115] Ironically, Marco Nadal was a Spaniard who had been involved in the French Resistance and whom French intelligence had helped return to Spain clandestinely in October 1945.[116] Hardion was directly involved on behalf of France in the complex world of intrigue and division that marked the politics of the internal Spanish opposition. At Hardion's request, 'Monsieur X' held two meetings with Marco Nadal and Luque, in order to ensure that negotiations did not completely break off with Don Juan.[117] However, by 7 January 1947, negotiations had failed to move Don Juan away from the contentious point that allowed him to maintain his freedom of action, and the ANFD voted to break off talks with the monarchists for good.[118] In early January, Franco's police arrested both Aranda and numerous leaders of the ANFD, thus making impossible any future talks.[119]

Due to the influence of the new French Premier, Léon Blum, who greatly regretted his inaction *vis-à-vis* the Spanish Republic during the Spanish Civil War, a relationship with the Republican government-in-exile was reinvigorated in January 1947.[120] Lionel Vasse, the Quai d'Orsay official responsible for immigration, became the official French contact with the government-in-exile in Paris, now headed by Rodolfo Llopis after Giral resigned due to criticism of his foreign policy and his refusal to deal with the variety of anti-Franco elements within Spain.[121] In contrast to Giral, Llopis initiated talks in Paris with a monarchist representative, Lopez Oliván.[122] France again encouraged these discussions, and went so far as to allow Llopis to meet with both French Premier Paul Ramadier and Georges Bidault in March 1947.[123] Moreover, within Spain, French intelligence continued to foster negotiations between ANFD representatives and those who supported Don Juan.[124] Yet soon enough, the debate about whether or not to deal with the monarchists again surfaced within the Llopis Cabinet. Communist members of the Government-in-exile charged, correctly, that the CNT was more committed to the ANFD than to Llopis. Two competing claimants to the position of Republican government-in-exile would harm any negotiations, and the situation was worsened when a third Republican government-in-exile was created in Mexico hoping to reassert Giral's insistence that any new regime be strictly Republican.[125] In addition to the growing divisions amongst Republicans, monarchist demands that the Estoril accord of 1946 was the only basis upon which to move forward did little to promote any chance success in negotiations.[126] In June 1947, the Quai d'Orsay declared that "the course of the Spanish question had led to yet another dead end."[127]

Surprisingly, the last French initiatives in the spring of 1947 coincided with a sense of hope for an alternative Spanish government amongst officials in Washington and London. In April 1947, American Undersecretary of State Dean Acheson became involved in a project to create a "positive" Anglo-American policy in Spain through encouragement of the opposition to unite against Franco.[128] Acheson's idea for a new effort was simultaneously echoed in London where a new Minister of State in Clement Attlee's Government, Hector McNeil, proposed that Britain, France, and the United States make another effort to approach all of the anti-Francoist groups, inside and outside Spain, as well as Franco, to encourage the formation of a new Spanish government.[129] Ultimately Foreign Secretary Bevin, acting upon the advice of the former Ambassador to Spain, Sir Victor Mallet, and the Permanent Undersecretary of State, Sir Orme Sargent, dismissed the proposal as too dangerous to risk.[130] With no support, the Republican government-in-exile became even weaker with the resignation of Llopis in August, and the ANFD collapsed shortly thereafter.[131] Only one initiative to revive republican-monarchist discussions was left, that of Indalecito Prieto, mandated by the PSOE in July 1947 and welcomed by supporters of Don Juan who had rejected Franco's Law of Succession, announced in March 1947 that gave the dictator the right to nominate a future monarch.[132] Prieto's mission led to a final "stir of encouragement" in the autumn of 1947, when he and the monarchist Gil Robles met in London, a meeting facilitated by the British Foreign Office. However, no results came of this.[133]

Summary

For the Left and those who emerged from the French Resistance, the Spanish question was part of the larger post-war debate about what a renewed France represented, not only at home but abroad as well. The notion of a democratic and just foreign policy, made by the people for the purpose of exporting republicanism beyond the *Métropole*, led to support for the Republicans of Spain, many who found themselves exiled in France, and a small minority of whom became militarily active in the *guerrillero* movement that attempted to foment a rebellion against Franco using southern France as a base. Wary of breaking relations with Franco's regime and committed to constructing Spanish policy within the framework of the emerging western alliance, as they had during the war, French Foreign Ministry officials were nonetheless not immune to these sentiments. Policies concerning Spanish Republicans and their cause reflected the desire of the Government to appease public opinion while not necessarily legitimizing the primary goal of taking direct action to precipitate Franco's fall. Yet these same policies also betrayed sympathy toward Spanish Republicans and their ultimate goal that cannot be dismissed. Without rupturing relations with Franco, the Quai d'Orsay seemingly embraced the idea of assisting democratic Spain. Officials shared with French anti-Franco activists and with Spanish exiles the ideal of universal republicanism, reminiscent of the Revolutionary era. As 'Monsieur X' wrote of efforts to aid the anti-Franco opposition:

> Concerning France, if we must regret the fact that our country was not, in the aftermath of V-E Day, in a position to take the initiative that would allow for the

emergence of democracy in Spain, a diplomatic success which would re-establish our prestige in Europe . . . since the spring of 1946, despite accumulative obstacles and deep traps, and without compromising the French Mission [in Madrid] with the regime, the presence of Republican France amongst those Spaniards taken with the idea of liberty has been maintained, according to instructions received [from Paris]. France's position alongside the opposition in the storms of clandestinity . . . will not fail – we have all the right to think – to reveal its value, the day when fortune will change sides.[134]

In dealing with exiles on French soil, with political prisoners in Spain, or with the anti-Franco opposition, while Government actions fell short of breaking significant economic and political relations with Franco's regime, they nonetheless demonstrated the ability of the "justice model" of foreign policy-making to influence the French Government in the aftermath of Liberation. No cause was as powerful as that of Spanish Republicanism when it came to applying such a model to the international scene. Moreover, once such policies were initiated, government officials pursued them energetically, even to some extent echoing the moral themes of the Spanish question originally raised by Resistance and other activists; this was especially the case in the context of the political prisoner cases and in the attitudes exhibited by 'Monsieur X' in his dealings with the anti-Franco opposition. The result was a sustained if quiet effort that combined support for Spanish Republicanism with efforts to internationalize the issue of the incompatibility of Franco's dictatorship with a new, democratically reconstructed Europe.

4

French Initiatives on Spain, 1945–1946

On 12 December 1945, the French Foreign Ministry approached the British and American Embassies in Paris with a *Note verbale* that proposed opening a tripartite discussion on the possibility of a change of policy toward Spain. The French note to London and Washington emphasized the growing public dissatisfaction with Franco's actions and attitude during the war. Furthermore, it noted that such reaction was particularly strong in France. Yet at the same time, Franco was in a fundamentally strong position, and the risk for France to act alone was great. The note, thus, proposed that one avenue of action was open if the intention was in fact to topple Franco: a joint diplomatic rupture with Spain on the part of France, Great Britain and the United States. The French were willing to consider this immediately, and requested a meeting of foreign ministers or high officials.[1]

This initiative, coming as it did in conjunction with a series of pro-Republican policies implemented by the French Government, marked a new stage in efforts to reconcile the demands of the public for an aggressive anti-Franco policy with a desire to work within the western Alliance. The proposal was thus motivated by the success of the Resistance and Resistance-affiliated individuals and organizations to mobilize French opinion around the concept of justice and foreign policy as applied to the Franco dictatorship. Yet it was also born from a desire within the Foreign Ministry to apply a realist view towards France's position in the world and consequently to prioritize policy-making in Europe within the alliance. If earlier initiatives with regard to Spanish Republicans responded to the calls for a just and democratic foreign policy, they did not directly confront the Franco regime with sanctions or ultimatums. Yet for the Foreign Ministry and Georges Bidault, the Foreign Minister, the risk of acting unilaterally was to threaten France's place in the alliance and to fail in changing Spain. Thus the note of December 1945 was a more transparent effort to balance domestic concerns with those of the Quai d'Orsay. It was not meant to be a new direction, simply a new effort. To the Foreign Affairs Commission of the National Assembly, Bidault reinforced the cautious tone of the French Note. "The policy of the French government," he said, "is a bit of a policy of *attentisme*... It is from the French Government and me that the proposition of rupture with Franco came. We will see what the other [powers] do."[2] An internal memo prepared for Bidault confirms that the French hopes were exactly as he expressed: the possibility of a rupture or other sanction was accepted, but only if the other western powers agreed; the note of 12 December represented "a polling" of France's allies, and nothing more.[3]

This initiative, to further build on policies initiated by France in the name of Spanish Republicanism, combined the boldness of potential sanctions with the caution of Bidault's comments. It also underlines the complexity of France's search for an international role in the post-war world. William I. Hitchcock has asserted that France, rather than resisting adherence to divided Germany and the emerging Western Alliance, successfully influenced alliance policies in the remaking of Western Europe economically, militarily and politically as it pursued a "national strategy" to reclaim a leadership role in the world.[4] Hitchcock underlines the importance of chronology, arguing that from the decision to move toward West German sovereignty through to Germany's entrance into NATO, France won a series of "decisive victories" in inter-alliance debates and thus fundamentally shaped Western policy in Europe.[5] Others have also applied such concepts of realpolitik to French foreign policy after the Second World War, and argued that the groundwork for this successful period of influence was laid as early as 1945, amidst many other pressing concerns, including the political and social tensions that arose from the Resistance experience and reorganization of the constitution.[6] No one concedes that the path to success was easy. Indeed, Michael Creswell and Marc Trachtenberg argue that domestic politics, and especially the strength of the French Communist Party (PCF), did not allow for a public display of such pro-alliance sentiment that was apparent within the Government in the immediate post-war era.[7] France's influence, then, was felt behind the scenes.

The French Note on Spain could clearly fit into this analysis, for it entailed the pursuit of a policy balanced between the demands of domestic opinion and calls for justice with the realism of the Quai d'Orsay and France's Allies. There are certainly parallels to what many historians have concluded concerning French ingenuity in shaping Allied policy towards Germany, which Charles Cogan has written resulted in "more winning than losing."[8] How far would this go, however? Were there limits to the ability to be creative and achieve what the Quai wanted? In the case of Spain, the gamble taken by the Quai d'Orsay with the December note was that some gesture involving the Great Britain and the United States, taken with other policies toward Spanish Republicanism, would enable France to craft a foreign policy that combined the calls for universalistic republicanism and international justice while at the same time keeping France aligned with its western partners on this issue. Would the practical realities of international politics be able to accommodate the calls for justice in France?

Background to the December Note

As stated in the previous chapter, for most of 1945, the policy of the French Government was to pursue a trade agreement with Franco's Spain in order to exploit the possibility of trading for goods needed in the process of reconstruction. A series of short-term credit arrangements were made from September 1944 through April 1945.[9] Some pacification of Spain was required in order to carry this out. In February 1945, on the orders of General de Gaulle, the French Government banned Spanish language newspapers from being printed inside France, a measure which forced the JEL exile group to produce their newspaper, *L'Espagne Républicaine*, in French.[10] Despite a series of policies aimed at benefiting Spanish Republican exiles and Spanish Republicanism generally, the Quai d'Orsay persisted in its pursuit to reach long-term agreements with the Franco Government. Indeed, the reappearance of divisions within the Republican ranks both weakened the Republican cause and increased the likelihood that Franco would remain in power.[11] Upon news of trade negotiations between France and Spain underway in San Sebastian in August and with Spain prepared to join Allied talks on the international status of the city of Tangier, the press increasingly condemned France for acting as a willing participant in the Allied "double game" with Spain: rhetorical condemnation but working relations.[12] Once the trade agreement was signed in September at San Sebastian, the British Embassy in Paris reported to London that the left wing press in France was "furious".[13] In Madrid, Bernard Hardion told Spanish Foreign Minister Martín Artajo that anti-Spanish hostility in France could be overcome.[14] Indeed, it has been argued that the juxtaposition of the Refugee Protection Statute with the Commercial Accord was full of consequences for the refugees inside France, demonstrating to them the real position of the French Government towards their situation.[15]

However, the French Government, recalled Jean Chauvel in his memoirs, could not escape the fact that "the Spanish Civil War left its traces within French public opinion to the extent that any Spanish issue . . . reawakened strong and contradictory emotions."[16] The Resistance and the Left had pressed the Government and received some results, but they continued to argue that diplomatic rupture and sanction against Franco's regime was the only policy a Republican regime in Paris could adopt toward Madrid. The October 1945 elections strengthened those political parties most associated with an aggressive anti-Spanish policy, notably the Communists. The agreement between Charles De Gaulle, the Socialist SFIO, Communist PCF and Christian Democratic MRP of 21 November 1945 that formed the basis for a new government of national unity included a clause guaranteeing a reconsideration of France's relations with Spain.[17] Beyond the governing parties, other groups within the National Assembly had reason to re-open the file on Spain. In late November, Emmanuel d'Astier de la Vigérie of the *Mouvement unifié de la Résistance* (MUR) proposed a new discussion on the possibility of a diplomatic rupture with Spain in light of the fact that Foreign Minister Georges Bidault had ignored the earlier May and August Foreign Affairs Committee motions on the matter.[18] By December, the Spanish question became a subject of discussion at the Council of Ministers.[19] It was evident that sooner or later, a policy on Spain that was more appealing to the parties and the Resistance would have to emerge.

The Foreign Minister did not relish the challenge, but the reality of politics meant that he was not yet finished with formulating new policies toward the Franco regime. By the end of 1945, a further effort was made to assess the relationship between the Provisional Government of the Republic and its authoritarian neighbor to the south. A series of analyses were produced by the Foreign Ministry's European section in an effort to re-evaluate France's position on Spain. These documents effectively served to defend and further justify the Quai's policy to date. Since the Liberation, France had been content to ally itself with Great Britain and the United States in their approach to Spain's government under General Francisco Franco. Like the Anglo-Americans, French officials acknowledged that the Franco regime was incompatible with the emerging democratic order in the west, and that the *Generalissimo* had clearly favored the Axis powers for most of the war. For these reasons, France agreed with its western allies that the regime should be morally condemned and excluded from the United Nations. From this perspective, many of the policies toward Spanish Republicans described in Chapter 3 developed. However, despite the defeat of Nazi Germany and Fascist Italy, Franco remained in power, and was essentially unchallenged at home. Since the end of the war in Europe, the French Mission in Madrid, under Jacques Truelle and then Bernard Hardion, had renewed commercial relations with Spain, defended French citizens living in Spain, and had actually helped Spanish Republicans by being in a position to intervene for the commutation of death sentences imposed on them by Franco's tribunals.[20] As Britain and the United States were similarly pursuing political and economic advantage within Spain and rhetorical condemnation without, there was little reason for France to act differently.[21] Therefore, 'official' France had consistently concluded that sanctions against the Franco regime, as demanded by many of the Resistance organizations, would be meaningless. Within the French Foreign Ministry, its European and Economic sections and amongst French diplomats in Madrid, moreover, there remained a belief that continued diplomatic and economic relations with Spain were in the national interest.[22]

Such views made it impossible to consider a flip-flop on French policy toward Spain. However, faced with the desire of the coalition government's political parties and the Council of Ministers to become involved in policy-making, officials at the Quai d'Orsay had to go further. From the point of view of the European Section, a change to its position on Spain had to address three concerns. First, a new policy had to respond to the domestic antagonism towards the continuation of Franco in power, an antagonism that expressed itself through demands for a more aggressive policy than the current Allied moral condemnation of Spain. Second, it had to accept the fact that in order to encourage a change of regime, only a concerted western policy, in conjunction with Great Britain and the United States, had any chance of success. As the Ministry's European section concluded, it was advisable "not to risk the inconveniences of rupture since it could only have a decisive influence on the evolution of the situation in Spain if it was accompanied by a similar measure on the part of the United States and Great Britain."[23] Third, and related to the second concern, the policy could not hurt France disproportionately as compared to its Anglo-American competitors in the Spanish economy. As Chauvel emphasized to American Ambassador Jefferson Caffrey, the Quai d'Orsay desired an outcome that reconciled domestic political exigencies and international realities.[24] The note of 12 December 1945 was the official initiative meant to do just that.

American and British Responses to France

Initial reaction in Washington and London to the French note of December 1945 seemed to bode well for France's desire to seek a new policy within the Alliance. In both the United States and Great Britain, it seemed that domestic criticism of existing Western policy on Spain was growing as it was inside France. Organizations such as the Joint Anti-Fascist Refugee Committee and Friends of the Spanish Republic, trade union confederations like the AFL-CIO, and periodicals like the *Nation* were all active in promoting the cause of Spanish Republicanism.[25] Anti-Francoist sentiments were prominent among elected officials such as Congressman John Coffee of Washington.[26] In an article published in France in August, British Labour Party Chairman Harold Laski wrote that Labour was committed to ending Franco's rule in Spain, even though British Foreign Secretary Ernest Bevin in Parliament repeated the traditional British warning against intervention.[27] Most significantly, there were signs from the United States that the State Department was fundamentally dissatisfied with the current situation of non-intervention. Twice in the last quarter of 1945, there were reports from both French and British sources that the United States was considering delivering an ultimatum to Franco.[28] In Madrid, retiring US

Ambassador Norman Armour met with Foreign Minister Martín Artajo and spoke of ways to force Franco's resignation to a military or civilian *junta*, and soon after the US confirmed that it would replace Armour with a representative at the rank of Chargé d'Affaires[29] The downgrade in rank of the Madrid appointment implied a less than normal diplomatic relationship, and one that was deteriorating.

The French initiative of 12 December thus drew upon what seemed to be a growing international and domestic consensus that action had to be taken against Franco and his regime. Rumors of all sorts flew around the Embassies of Madrid, including one that suggested that that the Spanish issue could be raised at the upcoming Council of Foreign Ministers (CFM) meeting in Moscow.[30] James Dunn of the State Department's European division was initially in favor of considering the possibility of a diplomatic breach, although British Chargé d'Affaires Douglas Howard told Bernard Hardion in Madrid that the British, while critical of Franco, still believed in a "policy of presence" in Spain.[31] Whatever differences existed, it was clear that, like the French, the American and British governments were willing to explore options solely within the context of inter-alliance relations.

Not surprisingly, this was not the interpretation of many within France who had been involved in the Spanish question for some time. Communist and Socialist members of the government who had promoted a more aggressive policy interpreted the origins of the French initiative differently, and saw the 12 December note as a demonstration of France's unique role as a western leader, autonomous from the Anglo-Americans.[32] Within the Foreign Affairs Commission of the National Assembly, a motion was passed on 19 December that encouraged the French Government to "prepare and realize" its own diplomatic rupture, regardless of the Allied response.[33] Albert Camus expressed his opinion that it was not a time for the "realists" to reign, but rather that France, aligned with Spanish Republicans, had a task to "show to the Americans especially, to the English and to all other realists of any country that the only order in Spain is . . . the Republican order."[34] The possibility of a rupture within the Alliance over Spain was seen by critics as something to relish. In the case of Spain, then, one can engage with Mark S. Sheetz's question of whether or not French obstructionism within the Alliance, when it appeared, was "just a stratagem to deflect domestic political pressure" by simultaneously considering if in some cases it could impose real constraints on policy-makers and force a break that was not desired.[35]

In December 1945, there was no premonition that anything quite as dramatic as a divided Allied policy on Spain would occur. Officials in Paris did not consider anti-Francoism to be a vital part of the construction of post-war French international policy. For them, the issue of diplomatic rupture or sanction against Spain was solely one that could be pursued within the confines of the Anglo-American-French relationship. Jean Chauvel, for one, felt that if any risk was inherent in the Quai's strategy, it was not that France would abandon its Allies over Spain because of different priorities, but rather that domestic and party opinion inside France would not diminish in its expression of anti-Francoist attitudes and could in turn reject the Quai's pursuit of a balance between internal politics and external alliance, forcing some sort of parliamentary showdown.[36] Thus as France "polled" its Allies, it simultaneously continued economic trade with Spain. In response, the Resistance and party press was left to ask, "What game is the Quai d'Orsay playing?"[37] Only in more moderate papers such as *Le Monde* and *Le Figaro*, and in the MRP's own paper, *l'Aube*, was there cautious support for the Government, and a belief that Anglo-American support was necessary; in other words, support for the French proposal exactly as Bidault cast it.[38]

The sense that France finally would act, and that France could act with or without its western Allies, also permeated the Spanish Republican exile community. One of Giral's ministers in France, Nicolau d'Olwer, stated that the anti-Franco campaign of newspapers like *Franc-Tireur* had been largely responsible for the Government action, and he concluded that the Spanish people were now counting on France to follow through with its threat of rupture.[39] The Spanish Socialists (PSOE) also welcomed the government initiative, and attributed it to the Socialist and Communist gains in the October elections. Furthermore, the PSOE urged its members inside France to press their local and Departmental SFIO sections to ensure that the French Government would move forward and ultimately break diplomatic relations with Franco.[40]

British and American responses to the French note of 12 December 1945 were in line with Bidault's initial caution and again conformed to precedent. The British Foreign Office was quite content with the current policy of rhetorical condemnation and political non-intervention, and opposed the idea of consultation as suggested by France. Non-intervention had the support of Foreign Secretary Ernest Bevin, who in August, 1945 spoke in the House of Commons about his dislike of the Franco regime while reaffirming his and his Government's desire to avoid renewed civil war in Spain. British policy rejected any sort of military, political or economic sanction.[41] Despite agitation by Harold Laski and others on the Labour Left, and despite Prime Minister Clement Attlee's own anti-Francoist views, held during the Civil War and after, the Cabinet supported the position of Bevin and his Foreign Office advisors.[42] For example, in October 1945, the Cabinet agreed to support Bevin's recommendation to ban only the trade of weapons and semi-military equipment with Spain, and not enforce a broader ban on all equipment that could later be converted to military use.[43] Douglas Howard of the British Embassy in Madrid approached French representative Bernard Hardion and stated that the issue was not one of replacing Franco but rather one of altering the regime and its political system to conform more closely to Western ideas.[44]

The fear of renewed civil war in Spain, and the potential for a Communist victory and thus Soviet influence over the western Mediterranean, dominated British thinking and colored British reaction to the French note. Ambassador Sir Victor Mallet wrote on 3 December 1945 that while it was "idiotic to attempt to prophesy exactly how and when Franco will disappear," it was clear that "no new regime wants to be born of a fresh insurrection and blood bath." He continued, "There has been enough killing for one generation, even in bloodthirsty Spain; and thus it is that fear of this operates so strongly in favor of not disturbing the dreary status quo."[45] As 1945 came to an end, the left-wing of the Labour Party continued to hound Bevin about Spain, but he and the Foreign Office remained confident that British Mediterranean interests required tolerance, if not overt support, for the current regime, in order to maintain a regional balance of power and continued peace.[46]

In their response to the French note, the British underlined that they were not convinced that rupture would lead to a replacement of Franco by a "solid, representative and stable regime." In fact, they argued that there was a "serious danger that civil disorder would then break out in Spain, in view of the absence of any alternative administration which could at once assume power." Worse, the British feared that the bulk of the moderate Spanish population, fearful of renewed civil war, would rally behind Franco. The Foreign Office believed that the course towards evolution should be allowed to "develop spontaneously without external interference."[47] For this reason, the British rejected Bidault's suggestion for a consultation among the three Western allies and preferred to continue as things were.

The United States was more receptive to the French idea of holding a discussion among the three powers. While the State Department continued to share the concerns of the British regarding a renewal of civil conflict in Spain, they also believed that the West could move beyond the current policy of moral condemnation.[48] The French proposal for a meeting of high officials to discuss the Spanish question gave United States policy-makers an opportunity to consider their options. The fact that United States policy toward Franco's Spain was in flux before the arrival of the French note was evident with the decision by Washington not to replace its Ambassador in Madrid with another official of equivalent status. In the aftermath of receiving the French note, evidence that the American government was willing to seriously consider moving in the general direction which the French proposed was provided by Assistant Secretary of State James Dunn, who informed the Spanish Ambassador in Washington, Francisco de Cárdenas, of the following:

> . . . official relations between the two Governments were bad, and as they were

becoming increasingly worse and were not even remaining in the same state but deteriorating progressively, I saw no other outcome of such a progressive deterioration than the final rupture of diplomatic relations . . .[49]

Again, on 20 December 1945, Dunn told Fernando de los Ríos, the Foreign Minister of the Spanish Republican Government-in-exile, that the United States welcomed the French initiative and that the US was prepared to discuss "every aspect" of the question with France and Great Britain, including the possibility of diplomatic rupture.[50]

The primary American position on the Spanish question, as originally articulated by President Franklin D. Roosevelt in March 1945, had relied on the politics of pressure, not direct intervention. However, it did not dismiss the possibility of sanctions of some sort against the regime and, under President Truman, this approach remained predominant. In response to the French note of 12 December, the US Ambassador in Paris, Jefferson Caffrey, was instructed to emphasize that the American policy was, for the moment, consistent with Roosevelt's letter to Armour and that the US welcomed tripartite consultations amongst the Western Allies as those "most directly interested" in Spain.[51] While there was no question of military intervention, the elements of what constituted ostracism were under debate within the State Department.

The United States was equally aware, however, of the need to coordinate its action with the British before any meeting with the French occurred. A harmonization of policies and approaches, although often difficult, had been the basis of both American and British policy-making on Spain since 1940, and this was not about to change. Aware of the British hesitation regarding any new approach to Spain, John Hickerson of the State Department's Office of European Affairs informed British Ambassador in Washington Lord Halifax that the United States did not, in fact, contemplate diplomatic rupture with Spain, but did seek a tripartite meeting, if only to coordinate policy and ensure that the French Government "did not jump guns."[52] At the same time, cognizance of British opposition to France's proposed meeting did not mean that the US was prepared to stand pat. For instance, Undersecretary of State Dean Acheson, who was given the task of working out with the British a common position *vis-à-vis* France, was a firm believer in extending Roosevelt's policy to include more coercive measures against Spain, possibly including sanctions of some sort. The Undersecretary of State sought to manage the transition to a more "positive", or aggressive policy on Spain that went beyond rhetorical condemnation but stayed within the bounds on non-intervention.[53]

On 18 January 1946, Acheson met with British Minister in Washington John Balfour to discuss the issue of coordination. He stressed that the French initiative, combined with the support it had received in the French press and public opinion, "reinforced the thesis which he himself entertained, that it now devolved upon our three governments, if possible acting in concert, to have made some positive new movement in relation to the Spanish problem."[54] Balfour expressed the British belief that things in Spain should be left to develop independently, and that therefore no meeting of the three Western powers should occur. If views had to be exchanged, they should be done through diplomatic channels only. Acheson disagreed, for he "did not feel that we could go on indefinitely with mere statements of our dislike for Franco but that we would be obliged to take some action." He proposed a meeting of the three foreign ministers that would result in a statement on Spain. Such a statement would repeat the moral condemnation of General Franco's regime, as the earlier San Francisco and Potsdam declarations had, but might also encourage the Spanish people to take measures themselves for change.[55] Acheson concluded by stating that such a step would "give heart" to opposition elements within Spain; would meet the demands of growing pressure for action on Spain from pressure groups within the United States; and would help move the French Government away from a formal rupture of diplomatic relations while addressing the similar concerns of public opinion there.[56] The question of sanctions did not even arise, as Acheson was searching for a workable policy, not merely an aggressive one.[57] The Acheson proposal foreshadowed the March 1946 Tripartite Statement on Spain, although, as will be seen, this document did not achieve the results he envisaged.

The National Assembly Debate

Acheson's concern with French opinion, as expressed to Balfour, came only a day after the conclusion of a remarkable three-day debate in the French Constituent Assembly which clearly revealed the current atmosphere of the French political arena with regard to Spain. The motion under discussion in the Assembly emerged from the all-party Commission on Foreign Affairs. It congratulated the Government on the December initiative and called for a break of diplomatic relations with Francoist Spain. The leading speakers for each of the main political movements- Daniel Mayer (SFIO), André Marty (PCF), Gilbert de Chambrun (MLN) and Charles D'Aragon (MRP) – all had proven records of support for the Spanish Republican cause.[58]

Daniel Mayer opened the debate on Spain for the Socialist Party, and argued that France should take further initiative on the Spanish question and give asylum to Spanish democrats.[59] André Marty reviewed Franco's position during the Second World War, spoke of the continued tolerance for former Nazis and Vichy collaborators living in Spain, and complained about the constant presence inside France of Francoist spies. Casting his argument as one of French national security, Marty stated, "It is clear that Franco, enemy of

France before the war, during the war and after the war, remains and will remain the enemy of France, both him and his regime." He then concluded with a challenge, for he asked how France should treat such an enemy. In answer to his own question, Marty criticized earlier inaction and the French–Spanish commercial treaty of September 1945, but welcomed the Government's December initiative and urged France to continue to lead on the Spanish issue by ending diplomatic and commercial relations with Francoist Spain.[60] Fellow Communist deputy Jacques Duclos echoed Marty's comments and criticism. He called on France to live up to its democratic heritage, and attacked Bidault's approach to date, stating that the Spanish issue was the Foreign Minister's "worst file" and concluded with his hope that the motion on the floor brought with it an opportunity for change.[61] Only Georges Bidault's own party, the Christian Democratic MRP, offered a straightforward defense of the Foreign Ministry's approach. Deputy Charles D'Aragon began his speech by casting the Government's note to the United States and Great Britain as a direct consequence of the unanimous motion of the Assembly's Foreign Affairs Commission that called for rupture. He cast Bidault as a leader of French opinion against Spain, conveniently overlooking the fact that Bidault had felt confident enough to ignore such motions in May and August 1945. The sole dissent against action on the Spanish issue came from Jules Ramarony and Andre Mutter of the right-wing *Parti Républicain de la Liberté* (PRL).[62]

The debate in the Constituent National Assembly seemed to give credence to the Quai's fears that pressure for a more confrontational policy toward General Franco might endanger its efforts to pursue a balanced policy which took account of both public and alliance opinion. While all speakers praised the Government's initiative of 12 December 1945, they also attacked Georges Bidault and the French Foreign Ministry for their attempts in 1945 to maintain a relationship with the Spanish Government. Resistance deputy Gilbert de Chambrun was typical, for he criticized the Quai d'Orsay for not taking any action prior to December, especially as in the course of various election campaigns the majority of members in the Assembly had been moved by public opinion to take a stand against Franco.[63] He went on to criticize the very bases of Western policy thus far, namely the fear of renewed disorder within Spain, the fear of division amongst anti-Franco Spaniards, and the fear that Franco would benefit from defending his country against external intervention. It was clear, concluded de Chambrun, that only by taking "principled positions with perfect confidence that our country can recover its radiance in the world and the means of French *grandeur* to which we attach great importance . . . and it is through this that our country can permit the great Spanish nation to reclaim the course to its proper destiny, one that conforms with the interests of France and of humanity."[64]

Gilbert de Chambrun's speech reinforced the tone of the debate that the Spanish question had taken since Liberation in August 1944. What was at stake was nothing less than the construction of French international policy, the idea of the French state in the world, in the aftermath of conquest, occupation, resistance, invasion and liberation. De Chambrun and his colleagues from the Resistance and the Left saw *grandeur* for France not as a partner among Great Power dealmakers, but as state which rejected the realism of the emerging international order in favor of a policy based on ideals. Charles de Gaulle and his Foreign Minister, Georges Bidault, saw themselves as seeking international status in 1945 for a weakened yet important power. In conjunction with the United States and Great Britain, France had the possibility of influencing the course of western policy. Yet in order to influence, one had to be at the table. The French Note of December 1945 was an attempt by Bidault to appease domestic critics while at the same time maintaining a common allied position on Spain. In actual fact, it provoked an even greater intensity of debate within France concerning Francoist Spain and increased the likelihood that the Assembly might demand something more aggressive from the French Government before its Allies were ready to move.

Despite the general tone, the French Government realized some victories of its own in the parliamentary debate. Prior to the opening of debate, the wording of the motion being considered was changed in one important respect. The motion on the floor had developed from Emmanuel d'Astier de la Vigérie's proposal in the Foreign Affairs Commission which had called upon the Government to "prepare and carry out" a break in diplomatic relations with Spain. The implication of d'Astier's initial motion was clear – the Commission was in fact calling for action on the part of France regardless of what came of discussions with the other western allies. Thus, France might have to break off relations with Spain unilaterally if the motion carried. This outcome would be entirely unpalatable to the Quai d'Orsay, whose policy was, above all, based on coordination with the Allies and balance between domestic and alliance concerns. The Council of Ministers, in January 1946, supported the Quai's position. Most significant in their support were the Communist ministers. In fact, they had played a key role in managing the Assembly debate by using their parliamentary power to moderate the phrasing of the motion under debate. Within the Foreign Affairs Committee of the Assembly, the original motion called for France to "prepare and carry out the severance of diplomatic relations," with Franco's Spain. By the time the motion appeared on the floor of the Assembly, it resolved that France only "prepare" for a diplomatic rupture.[65] Bidault was able, for a time at least, to separate the Communist ministers from the rhetoric of their supporters, and their party propaganda. The issue of Spain was not yet as important as to risk the break-up of the coalition government; on that point, the Foreign Minister and his colleagues agreed.

Bidault himself spoke to the motion on 17 January. To great applause, he stated that France would not forget Franco's attitude during the Civil War and World War; that France was indebted to the many Spanish Republican exiles who had fought for its liberation; and that the Government, the Assembly and the nation were united in the effort to see the Spanish people again free. However, he quickly moved on, justifying the approach of the Foreign Ministry to date. He believed that he and his advisors had gone a long way toward compromise with the parties and public opinion through their note, and desired an acknowledgment, on the part of the Assembly, that they accepted this. He claimed that France, through its note to Washington and London, had gone further than any other country in pressing the Spanish issue in accordance with the rhetoric of the Yalta Declaration on Liberated Europe. Yet he argued against going further still without Allied support and participation; an isolated action, he claimed, would not lead to significant change in Spain and would, in fact, go against the spirit of Yalta Declaration which had specifically called for joint Allied action.[66] This was, in essence, an articulation of the Quai d'Orsay's reasoning for the December initiative, and for a policy based on reconciling the power of domestic emotion with the requirements of France's international situation and alliance obligations. Georges Bidault concluded with an earnest and forceful plea: "Give me a good domestic politics, and I will give you a good foreign policy."[67]

The Constituent National Assembly later that day, 17 January 1946, unanimously passed a motion congratulating the Government on its December note to the United States and Great Britain and asking the Government to "prepare for" the rupture of diplomatic relations with Franco's Spain.[68] Foreign Ministry officials in Paris were pleased that the Assembly did not yet force France to break off diplomatic relations with Spain on its own; the Government could "prepare" for rupture through continued consultation with the United States and Great Britain. Quai d'Orsay officials were quick to point out to the US Embassy that France's policy had not changed. France, they maintained, continued to seek a tripartite solution. They emphasized that even the French Communist Party understood this policy and they did not foresee any change in party tactics that would cause Communist deputies to exert immediate pressure upon Bidault or the Council of Ministers for a change.[69] In the United Nations General Assembly a few days later, Bidault demonstrated exactly that point by voting, alongside his Western allies, for a declaration which reiterated the San Francisco ban on Spanish membership in the United Nations, and called upon member states to take the spirit of this action into consideration when formulating policy toward Spain. In his speech to the General Assembly, Bidault would only concede that French policy was different from that of its Allies to the extent that the existence of the Franco dictatorship in Spain was a "matter of deeper and keener regret for France" than for any other state.[70]

Evidence was abundant, however, that the optimism of Quai d'Orsay officials was misplaced. While it was true that Communist ministers within the Government had accepted Bidault's compromise plan since December, the expansion of the anti-Franco campaign in the press and amongst the public since the French note suggested that the issue of relations with the *Generalissimo* was not going to become a simple one any time soon. In its coverage of the parliamentary debate, the Socialist newspaper *Le Populaire de Paris* editorialized that France need not concern itself with Great Power alignment, but rather that it should align itself with "its great liberal and democratic traditions and the thought of these most noble sentiments."[71] Moreover, the Communist daily *L'Humanité* had been running a series of articles in the weeks leading up to the debate concerning the implementation of the Franco-Spanish commercial treaty, providing readers with frequent reports about potato deliveries to Spain.[72] Only Bidault's own party paper, *l'Aube*, defended the Minister's "excellent formula" of not mixing internal and foreign policy.[73]

In his speech 17 January, Bidault could not limit his comments to a mere defense of the Foreign Ministry's note to Great Britain and the United States. Specifically referring to Communist criticism of the Government's trade agreement with Spain, he defended the latter instrument, claiming it to be a continuation of pre-war agreements, and a necessary part of France's own reconstruction. Furthermore, he went into detail about potato and other deliveries made to Spain. This only prompted shouts and jeers from the Communist benches.[74] While PCF Ministers supported the Government initiative on Spain, clearly there was support within the party for a more aggressive policy. Bidault's comments implied that a policy based on emotion and ideology alone was not a choice preferred by his Ministry, which felt confident following the Assembly debate. However, the response to his speech, and the general strength of the anti-Franco campaign in the press, foreshadowed the potential which emotion and ideology had concerning the Spanish question.

There were fears that the French Constituent National Assembly's motion would not help the Allies in Madrid. British Ambassador Sir Victor Mallet complained to Bernard Hardion that the strength of support for the motion could only produce a "stiffening" of Francoism within Spain, not any political liberalization.[75] Whether the population regarded the French motion as another expression of historic French anti-Spanish sentiment or as a Communist-inspired attack on Spain, Mallet claimed the result would be growing support for Franco as a defender of the nation.[76] Of greater concern, however, were Allied fears of what might occur in France. An observer of the Assembly debate, US Embassy official Gordon Wright, noted that Bidault's comments on trade with Spain were received "coolly" by the Communists and Socialists.[77] From the Foreign Office in London, R. Sloan recorded on 24 January that the very fact that all political parties in France seemed to agree on the need for a harder line on Spain meant that the outlook for future policy was "dangerous."[78]

The García Case and France's Unilateral Sanctions against Spain

Indeed, events soon conspired against the carefully calculated approach of the Foreign Minister. French public and party opinion simply was not as patient as the Quai d'Orsay and the Minister would have liked. Although the French Assembly had passed a motion which supported the government's policy, pressure from the Left, Spanish Republicans and others only intensified from the end of January and into the month of February 1946. The resignation of Charles de Gaulle from the head of the French Government on 20 January 1946 complicated matters and his government gave way to a coalition government of the MRP, PCF and SFIO under Socialist Félix Gouin. The issue of Franco's Spain played a direct role in the formation of this government, as the accord of the three parties clearly stated their intention to implement the resolutions of the National Assembly on Spain hitherto ignored by the Quai d'Orsay, resolutions which called for an end to diplomatic relations.[79] The noted historian of the Fourth Republic Georgette Elgey highlights the significance of the coalition accord on France's foreign policy, for instead of analyzing issues in light of international realism, they were now conceived of in terms of "moral engagements". The question of relations with an ideologically semi-fascist Spain was primary in any such principled reformulation of diplomatic priorities.[80] Moreover, the Spanish Socialist trade union confederation in exile, the UGT, took advantage of the change in government and approached the umbrella group for French labor, the Communist-dominated *Conféderation Generale de Travail* (CGT), on 25 January 1946. The UGT requested a renewed effort on the part of the CGT to work for a French break in diplomatic relations with Franco's Spain, which the CGT agreed to do, in addition to aiding the clandestine efforts of the UGT inside Spain.[81]

The fear that the proposed meeting of Western powers would not arrive in time to appease the French parties increasingly worried Georges Bidault after de Gaulle's departure. Bidault told the British Foreign Secretary on 1 February that domestic pressure could force France to unilaterally break off relations with Spain at any time. France's Spanish policy, he told Bevin, was predicated on the hope that a coordinated tripartite gesture would assuage the "impatience" of the French people for unilateral action, and he asked for a positive sign from Britain that a meeting of the three Western allies could be held soon.[82] Officials in the Spanish Government told American officials that an increased role for parties of the left in the new French Government concerned them, but that they hoped Bidault's continued presence would temper in practice the anti-Francoism of those who called for a formal break.[83]

It was not the General's departure, however, that emboldened the French Left and Center to demand more from Bidault. Rather, it was the death sentence imposed by Spain on twelve captured Spanish guerilla leaders, one of whom was Cristino García, who had played a major role in the French Resistance. García was a veteran of the Republican side in the Spanish Civil War who had joined the *Mouvement d'Ouvriers Immigrés* (MOI), a section of the French Communist resistance organization *Francs Tireurs et Partisans* (FTP) during Second World War. He soon rose to become a commander of a group of Spanish *maquis* in the Departments of the Gard, Lozère and the Ardeche, and organized a major prison break in Nîmes in February 1944. At the moment of French Liberation, he was named a commander of the FFI. From there, García quickly moved to join Spanish *guerrilleros* in France making clandestine border-crossings into Spain.[84] It was on one of these missions, while allegedly robbing a bank in Madrid, that García was arrested. His death sentence, imposed at the end of January 1946, was met with a public outcry inside France. Both the *Association France-Espagne* and the Young Socialists of the Gard brought the García case to the attention of the Foreign Ministry, which intervened in Madrid on more than one occasion seeking commutation of the death sentence imposed by the Spanish courts.[85] García was not the first Spaniard with FFI ties to be executed in Spain despite French intervention. In the growing anti-Franco mood of the French Assembly and public, however, his execution on 21 February 1946 was a catalyst for an outpouring of public opinion that made the Spanish issue, arguably, the most important in France for a number of weeks

The García case first came to the public's attention due primarily to the efforts of the Communist Party, for Garcia was a member of the Spanish Communist Party (PCE). The PCF's main organ, *L'Humanité*, was the major force in organizing opinion concerning the García case. From 31 January until 10–11 March 1946, there was not one issue that did not have a front-page story about Spain, and the majority of these dealt with the García case. The Communist organ reminded its readers that García, "a Spanish patriot, is equally, we know, a soldier in the liberation of our own country", a man who embodied the comprehensive "spirit of sacrifice required in the antifascist war for democracy."[86] The newspaper reported in detail the vast number of CGT sections, local PCF cadres and other groups which held meetings and passed resolutions calling for Government intervention in the García case and diplomatic rupture and trade sanctions against Spain.[87] Other groups were also involved, most notably the multi-party *Association France-Espagne* which distributed five hundred thousand pamphlets concerning García.[88]

Once García was executed, the call for action became almost universal. The pressure to take a diplomatic initiative against Franco out of debt to Garcia was now elevated because his execution was seen as a sign of Franco's defiance toward France and its ideals. "It is the last card", wrote Charles Dumas in *Le Populaire de Paris*.⁸⁹ In *Franc-Tireur*, the event of García's execution was used once again to cast the Spanish question in terms of its parallels to the fight for French liberation, most especially in terms of the debt owed by France to Spanish Republicans involved in that battle:

> Have we forgotten that fascism exists at our border? Was it not against all fascisms that Cristino García and thousands of our Spanish brothers fought with us on our soil? Did they not fall beside us, as at the Eysses prisons, under the same Nazi bullets, for France? And today will we disown their sacrifice, their blood and their martyrdom because the fight against fascism has moved to the other side of the Pyrenees? No, thank you!⁹⁰

Reaction to the news of García's death sentence was particularly strong in the south-west of France, and, as it had nationally, the Communist Party and its affiliates took the lead in calling for a diplomatic breach with Franco's Spain. *La Voix du Midi* exclaimed that "France must avenge this affront... it is an act of defiance against the civilized world. It is before anything a slap in the fact to France, who especially intervened for these artists of its own liberation."⁹¹ Editorialist Georges Fournial criticized the "two-faced policy" of the Allies, who morally condemned Franco's actions whilst continuing to trade with him. He went on to express support for a speech that André Marty had given in Toulouse, in which the latter repeated a theme which he had first articulated in the Assembly debate, namely that France's national security was at risk as long as Franco, or even a monarchist replacement, was in power.⁹² In Sète, Spanish Republican exiles and the CGT, PCF and SFIO protested the García execution in front of the Spanish Consulate-General on 27 February. The building was occupied, and the Consul fled. Similarly in Auch, Spanish Republican exiles involved in a protest sponsored by French leftist parties attacked the home of the Spanish Vice Consul.⁹³ The veterans of the FTP in the region of Haute-Garonne sent an immediate telegram to the new Prime Minister, the Socialist Félix Gouin, urging him to "obtain without delay a rupture of diplomatic relations with Franco, the assassin."⁹⁴ Also in Toulouse, the leadership of the Spanish UGT in exile held meetings with regional and national leaders of the CGT.⁹⁵ The execution of García was greeted with angry calls for diplomatic rupture by not only local organizations of the Communist Party, Resistance veterans, the *Union des Syndicats de la Haute-Garonne* and the local *Comité France-Espagne*, but also by a crowd of forty thousand that gathered in protest at Toulouse's *Place de la Capitole* the evening of 25 February.⁹⁶ Two days later, in Tarbes, another five thousand gathered to protest.⁹⁷ Instructions were issued to police in the Midi to take extra measures in protecting Spanish Consulates and Consuls-General.⁹⁸

The Quai d'Orsay was equally stunned by the Franco regime's sentencing of García and his compatriots. Neither was it complacent about the matter. Bernard Hardion believed that part of the Western imperative in Madrid was to foster conditions for political liberalization in Spain not only by promoting economic ties, but by trying to influence the conduct of the regime and its attitude toward its opponents. In December, the Quai d'Orsay had argued that such efforts required France to maintain a diplomatic dialogue with Spain. In the García case, Hardion presented a strong argument for the suspension of García's death sentence as a necessary step for Spain to take, emphasizing the condemned man's heroic record in the French Resistance and warning of the emotion which would be aroused in France by his execution.[99] But his efforts were futile.

The mood of the public, Resistance groups and political parties made it impossible for Communist and Socialist ministers in the Council to continue to support Bidault's cautious efforts toward Great Britain and the United States *vis-à-vis* Spain. While the García execution acted as a catalyst, both SFIO and PCF were in the midst of an important transition concerning their role in the governing coalition. Twice in late 1945, the PCF had proposed a Socialist-Communist joint effort in elections, and a large number of Socialists, led by Guy Mollet, were interested in the potential of aligning not only with the PCF, but with various Resistance movements like the MLN as well.[100] Many on the Left were frustrated with having to work alongside de Gaulle and the MRP; and, despite consistently strong results by the PCF, the MRP in particular was not losing any ground in elections such as those of October 1945. In January, 1946, the Communist party reaffirmed its desire of moving SFIO away from the MRP and in position for a potential coalition without the center-right.[101] The coincident arrival of the García case on the French political scene seemed to provide a unique opportunity.

With de Gaulle in office, neither party's ministers pressed Bidault on Spain, especially after the Quai's December note to Great Britain and the United States, which did go some way in appeasing them. After the departure of de Gaulle on 20 January, a greater opportunity to affect policy-making was found, and the debate within the Socialist party about how far left to go developed even further. In February, Mollet publicly called for SFIO to return to fundamental principles.[102] Important elements within both parties, therefore, were inclined to push the Government and its policy further to the left than had previously been done. The Spanish issue was current, and García's execution gave it a momentum that both parties were in a position to exploit. The best evidence of this was the joint rally at the *Vélodrome d'Hiver* held by the PCF and SFIO on 26 February 1946 which drew some thirty to fifty thousand people.[103] The two parties, *l'Humanité* claimed, were united by their joint desire to represent the French conscience, defend French security and defeat the right in France and Europe. All of these views meant that the Government had to move beyond the stance it had already taken toward Spain.[104] By the end of the month, divisions over Spain between SFIO and the MRP, which continued to support Bidault's position, were apparent in the Assembly and in the Council of Ministers.[105]

The new President, Félix Gouin, took a public position on the García case in the absence of any comment to the press by his foreign minister. The President made public the nature of France's diplomatic interventions in the García case, and he noted the many letters the Government had received urging intervention which indeed had prompted the Government decision to intervene. Gouin repeated the themes long cherished by the Resistance when it came to Spain, for his words gave expression of a sense of indebtedness as well as to a hope that the true democratic nature of the Spanish people would allow a better future. His decision to intervene publicly in the case, he stated, was due to "the gratitude of the French people" toward García and his colleagues, "and the promise of a fruitful understanding with the Spanish people."[106]

The Constituent National Assembly, in light of García's execution, voted on 22 February 1946 to condemn the death sentence and remind the government of the need to honor the Assembly's earlier motion (of 17 January 1946) and "prepare for" diplomatic rupture. Once the motion was brought to the floor, the speaker of the Assembly, Socialist Vincent Auriol, took the rather unusual step of speaking before the vote was taken:

> I am sure that this will be voted for unanimously, because it translates the cry, not only of the French conscience, but of the universal conscience. I can attest that all that could be done was done to save the lives of these men who defended our homeland as well as the independence of the world. Nothing more could have altered the sentence. There remains the consolation that the blood of martyrs always hastens the triumph of liberty.[107]

Auriol's comment drew great applause from the Left and Center benches of the Assembly. The motion was then voted on, and passed unanimously with the exception of abstentions from André Mutter and other members of the PRL. Their abstentions brought jeers from most of the Assembly. When Mutter requested the right to speak in order to explain his abstention, anger erupted on the benches of the Left and Auriol adjourned the session, in order to "to prevent a clash."[108]

The direction in which France could head was provided by the Communist-dominated CGT. After García's execution, the CGT and its affiliated unions announced that they would suspend all traffic and communications with Spain.[109] The Postal and Telegraphic workers (affiliated with the CGT) began a 24-hour disruption of phone service to Spain on 23 February.[110] *Franc-Tireur* claimed that "the immense majority" of the French public felt as it did, and wanted diplomatic rupture and economic sanctions.[111]

Of course, the Quai d'Orsay and its officials were absolutely against the expressed desire of the Constituent National Assembly and the governing parties to carry out a diplomatic rupture with Spain on their own, regardless of what the Anglo-Americans did. In a memorandum dated 21 February 1946, the consequences of a unilateral rupture were analyzed by the French Foreign Ministry's European section. Of significant concern were the economic impacts of a rupture. Significant short-term effects included economic and trade losses that would be "more prejudicial against France than Spain," especially as regards key products like pyrites, which France imported primarily from Spain.[112] Moreover, in the Quai's assessment, the long-term impact of a unilateral rupture was even graver. France might be permanently replaced as a supplier and trader in the Spanish market. As long as the Allies agreed on a common diplomatic policy toward Franco, there were opportunities to compete with one another economically. Indeed, in the Spanish market, France felt it had a legitimate position to defend and expand upon, for Spain was "one of the rare foreign markets where our position is still solid", due to geographic and other factors. Political and economic advisers within the Quai concluded that the Americans and British, whatever their sympathy with Quai policy-makers, were not such loyal allies as to refrain from exploiting "the advantage that our voluntary withdrawal would offer them."[113]

There were political reasons for opposing the policy desired by the Assembly as well. The Quai returned to its point of view that French sanctions alone could not topple Franco. If a policy which aimed to force the collapse of the current regime in Spain was sought, British and American sanctions were also required. A unilateral French action could only consolidate Franco's internal position and weaken France's ability to interpret the Spanish scene.[114] In what was an increasingly desperate plea for realism, the European section of the Quai d'Orsay, through its 21 February 1946 memorandum, acknowledged French weakness, but argued that only by accepting its limitations would France be in a position to influence both Spain and Allied Spanish policy. The Spanish case highlights the attitudes held by the Foreign Ministry in the early post-war era. An acceptance of France's weak international position by the Foreign Ministry required policy-makers to pursue a strategy of recovery that was apolitical, one that sought economic and other benefits in the effort to rebuild French standing.[115] Working within the Western alliance in order to influence decisions which would benefit France and its recovery was as crucial in Spain as William I. Hitchcock has argued it was in Germany. An isolated action, in a moment of passion, risked exposing France's weakness, not displaying its strength, within the Western alliance.

In response to the emotions expressed in the Assembly, Georges Bidault admitted his growing worries about the course of Spanish policy. On 25 February, he told British Ambassador Duff Cooper that the Quai's desire for a coordinated Allied policy faced the "gravest difficulties."[116] The same day, the Foreign Minister told US Ambassador Jefferson Caffrey that the continuing pressure by the French press and public opinion might very well force the Government to act alone. In a dispatch to Washington, Caffrey expressed his confusion about the turn of events within France since the December note, underlining that hitherto even the Communist ministers in Government had been quite cognizant of the need to avoid a unilateral breach with Spain.[117]

On 26 February, Bidault entered a meeting of the Council of Ministers and found his worst fears realized. Although details of Council of Ministers' meetings remain sketchy, due to the absence of official minutes, one must assume that pressure for a diplomatic break with Franco came from all Council ministers except perhaps those from the MRP. Bidault recalled that he had to argue all he could in order to prevent a vote in favor of rupture, and that pressure came from all sides of the Council table.[118] Prior to the crucial meeting, *Combat* cited a statement from Gouin's aide, Gaston Defferre, who indicated that "electoral anxiety" was increasingly the main motivation behind policy, and the decision to make French intervention in the García case public, again for internal reasons, meant that ever greater steps had to be taken in order to avoid French embarrassment.[119] Luckily for Bidault, his Secretary-General at the Quai d'Orsay had arrived at yet another compromise that could prevent a complete break with Spain. Jean Chauvel proposed that France close its border with Spain to all commercial and personal traffic and communications, in effect making official what the CGT and its members were already doing along the border.[120] The Council of Ministers adopted this proposal, and further added that France propose that the Spanish question be put on the agenda of the United Nations Security Council.

Summary

Since postal, communications and railways workers had already disrupted and limited traffic to Spain on CGT directives, the decision to close the Pyrenean border was hardly innovative. The Communist press in Toulouse claimed that the Government had acted only in response to ongoing CGT action, and thus suggested that it was the CGT and its political allies, the PCF, that forced a change in France's Spanish policy.[121] At the time, the decision was seen by American officials as exactly that, an end to Bidault's position in the face of Communist pressure.[122] However, the gesture resonated not only with Communists, but with other political parties and Resistance organizations, and it drew upon the general tone of the debate about Spain that had existed within France since the Liberation. The Spanish exile newspaper affiliated with the French MLN, *L'Espagne Républicaine*, argued that the French action, at great cost to its own economy, demonstrated "the application of the general principles of its glorious Revolution."[123] France, wrote Georges Altman in *Franc-Tireur*, was the first country to act, and it acted through a "demonstration of its own *grandeur*, for it always is the first against tyrants."[124] As earlier noted, Bidault later revealed that Council's desire to act was fairly unanimous, and it took all his efforts to avoid a diplomatic breach while at the same time gratifying the Council and the public with a gesture he called "sufficiently spectacular to satisfy their unchained passions."[125]

Since the Liberation of France in August 1944, the question of diplomatic relations with Spain had grown in importance. Foreign Minister Georges Bidault and his advisers in the Quai d'Orsay were increasingly forced to defend their own desire to continue political and economic relations with the regime of General Francisco Franco. Their critics, from the press, the political parties and broader Resistance organizations, attacked France's realism as nothing more than a betrayal of the "new politics" grounded in democracy and ideology that the Resistance experience had bequeathed to the emerging Fourth Republic. The ability of the justice argument to force the Government to act in the aftermath of Cristino García's execution revealed its legitimacy within France, as well as the failure of Government of finding balance between the arguments of justice and those of realpolitik which had been the original intent of the December Note to the United States and Great Britain.

5

France, the West and the Spanish Question, 1946

The unilateral sanctions imposed by France on Spain in the form of border closures in February 1946 suggested that the advocates of an aggressive, democratically-inspired, "just" foreign policy toward Spain had triumphed over those officials of the Foreign Ministry and Georges Bidault, the Foreign Minister, who cautiously emphasized working with France's allies before taking any action, in the tradition of realpolitik. Yet the desire of Bidault and his Ministry to find a balanced policy that satisfied both impulses remained. Technically, Bidault had preserved his position against diplomatic rupture while simultaneously answering the domestic call for action – while France did close its border to all commercial and individual traffic from Spain, its Mission in Madrid remained open. It also remained unknown whether or not France's allies might be similarly motivated to act in light of Cristino García's execution. The desire of the Foreign Ministry and Georges Bidault to position France in a place whereby both domestic opinion could be answered and Allied policy furthered was as yet unfulfilled. There was a chance that it still could be. In the aftermath of February 1946, then, France made further efforts to reconcile its anti-Franco actions with its interpretation of the importance of the western alliance in making policy on the European continent. It would do so by encouraging and cajoling its allies to join in a policy of sanction against Franco's Spain.

Yet the efforts of the French Government to respond assertively to demands for a firmer policy toward General Franco coincided with significant developments within the Alliance, particularly in the United States, that offered new reasons for arguing that the Spanish status quo should be maintained. Associated with the emergence of the Cold War, and what could best be called "proto-containment" ideas, these arguments reinforced, reasserted and made stronger the desire to pursue a policy grounded in realpolitik instead of one motivated by concepts such as that of justice. Moreover, applied within the framework of the Western Alliance, these arguments would force France into making a choice between practical international policy and principle. Over the course of 1946, the pressure to make such a choice would be starkly outlined for Georges Bidault and his colleagues. The chance of bringing into realization any policy that included France's allies in an anti-Franco position based in part upon post-war concepts of justice failed as the Spanish Question became enveloped in the geopolitics of the Cold War.

The French Proposal to take the Spanish Question to the United Nations

On 27 February 1946 France sent a note to Great Britain, the United States and the Soviet Union proposing that the Spanish Question, in light of Cristino García's execution and France's border closure, be placed on the agenda of the United Nations Security Council. The decision to make the Security Council proposal was in part forced upon Bidault by the same pressures in the Council of Ministers that led to the decision to close the border. It was seized upon by the Quai d'Orsay because it allowed the basis of French policy-making on Spain since the war, that of international co-ordination instead of unilateral action, to be salvaged. Since it could no longer coordinate western policy behind closed doors, it sought to bring Britain and the US to the French position through the forum of the United Nations. Given the inability of the French to move the western position on Spain much beyond the status quo of moral condemnation through alliance diplomacy, the decision to press on was ambitious, risky and, like Bidault's earlier initiatives, taken by the Quai d'Orsay without great enthusiasm but with the hope that something beyond unilateral sanction would result.

The first basis for the proposed discussion of Spain in the Security Council remained that of France's initial December 1945 note to the Anglo-Americans, namely that as General Franco's wartime policies became increasingly known, international public pressure for his removal grew. Moreover, France argued that since that first French initiative, the situation had worsened for three reasons: first, Franco's continued refusal to make any statement or gesture indicating that he intended to begin the process of reforming his regime; second, the presence of Francoist troops along the Pyrenean border had grown since the start of the new year; and finally, the execution of Cristino García and his associates despite French and international lobbying for a suspension of their death sentences.[1]

As a result of these actions on the part of Spain, the French Government contended that the continued presence of Franco's regime constituted "a real challenge both to the principles of international rights and democratic ideals, risks creating a situation jeopardizing peace and international security."[2] This conclusion provided the second basis for the new French initiative for it brought the United Nations into the discussion. Although not specifically mentioned, the reference to "peace and international security" was an allusion to either article 35 and/or 39 of the United Nations Charter. These articles dealt with states and their potential threat to international security, and permitted the Security Council to examine the case of a state considered to be likely to represent such a threat (article 35) or the case of a state already considered to be such a threat (article 39). The French note sought to establish UN competence to debate Spain by recalling UN resolutions concerning the Franco regime already in force most notably that of 8 February 1946 which had reaffirmed the exclusion of Spain from the international organization, a policy first articulated at the San Francisco conference.[3] In short, because the Spanish issue was already on the UN agenda, France felt it was not unreasonable to ask the Security Council to consider a debate on Spain. Furthermore, the French government argued that because of legitimate Charter reasons, the Spanish question properly belonged on the agenda of the Security Council, the UN's highest body and the only one that could consider international sanctions similar to those France had already imposed unilaterally.

On one level, the risks of the new French initiative were similar to those that had existed with previous proposals for diplomatic rupture; namely, the chance that either one or both of the other western powers would refuse to consider any action beyond the status quo of moral condemnation. Yet on another level, through their invitation to the Soviets and the appeal to the United Nations, the French risked even more. There now existed the possibility that British and American policy-makers would not only continue to prefer the status quo, but publicly separate themselves from the French for the first time. Moreover, American and British opposition to France's continued insistence on pressing the Spanish issue could now be argued on numerous grounds, extending beyond geostrategic reasoning to include arguments about the illegitimacy of international law to be applied to Spanish domestic politics. Finally, the French decision to bring the Soviet Union into the discussion threatened to propel France into an alignment with the Soviet Union and against its western allies just as rising East–West tensions began to dominate international politics. That the Soviet Union was a Permanent Member of the Security Council, and thus had considerable influence in deciding which items went onto the agenda, was reason enough for the French to suggest to Moscow that the Spanish question be placed on the Security Council agenda. In addition, through a January editorial in the Communist Party newspaper *Pravda*, the Soviet Union had made it clear that it was interested in participating in whatever discussions on Spain France, Great Britain and the United States were going to have.[4] The French note of 27 February implicitly acknowledged Soviet interest in its reference to the Yalta Declaration on Liberated Europe, a document signed by the Big Three powers, which France claimed to be honoring in raising the Spanish question at the UN. In particular, the French drew attention to the clause in the Anglo-American-Soviet agreement that stated these three powers would "aid by common accord the peoples of the former Axis satellites to solve by democratic means their pressing political and economic problems."[5] Such a specific reference, combined with the reasons for involving the Security Council, gave legitimacy to the French approach to the Soviet Union, which hitherto had not been part of France's diplomatic campaign against Franco. Nonetheless, the United Nations proposal was fraught with risk, and for France, it was "an extremely delicate political moment."[6]

For the most part, the French public welcomed the new initiative.[7] The press campaign in favor of a more aggressive French policy toward General Franco continued much as it had since Liberation. Georges Fournial, in the Communist daily *La Voix du Midi*, wrote that forcing the Allies to agree to a firmer position on Spain via the Security Council would succeed if France maintained an "energetic attitude."[8] *Franc-Tireur* reported that having led by example with its own border closure, France was in a position now to foster an international action against Spain.[9] In the Socialist party organ, *Le Populaire de Paris*, Oscar Rosenfeld wrote that France's border closure and the UN initiative provided the Allies with a logical end, and the persistence of the French Government to take on further leadership was not only admirable but necessary in the months to follow.[10] Georges Cogniot in *L'Humanité* agreed.[11]

It has been suggested that the French note of 27 February, quite different than previous French efforts due to the inclusion of the Soviet Union, suggests that either the Communist members of the government played an important role in its conception or that it was part of a larger campaign to facilitate greater French-Soviet co-operation on other matters, such as Germany, and thus contribute to the "policy of non-alignment" as the best way to restore France's international position.[12] However, there is no direct evidence to support these assumptions. In Madrid, Bernard Hardion was informed that the decision to approach the three powers with this note was made by the Council of Ministers the same day the border was closed, and as Bidault emphasized in his memoirs, pressure to act on Spain came from all sides of the Council table that day.[13] Italian historian Paola Brundu has acknowledged that the appeal to the USSR was just as likely to be motivated by the same concerns that were behind the December 1945 note to France's western allies. Bidault, caught in a difficult situation, was simply seeking another way to salvage his preferred policy of coordinated western action. Through the use of the United Nations and the appeal to the Soviets, he hoped to force the hand of the Anglo-Saxon powers in order to lessen the economic burden on France as a result of its unilateral action, and to resolve his domestic dilemma over Spain.[14]

The archival evidence supports the interpretation that the involvement of the Soviet Union was merely another tactic in pursuit of the Quai d'Orsay's original goal of a policy which reconciled domestic antagonism toward Franco with the maintenance of Allied unity on Spanish policy. If anything, Georges Bidault and his advisors were becoming more desperate in their attempt to extricate themselves from the isolation of being the only major state with economic sanctions against Franco. The quest for a policy which answered political pressure from parties and public opinion and the Quai d'Orsay's need for Allied unity continued, but at a greater risk of failure. At best, the French maintained some influence over their allies, although not decisive influence. The most hopeful expression of the reality of the situation was in *La République du Sud-Ouest* which concluded that "the destiny of Spain is in play in London and Washington, but it is not impossible that France can still influence the game."[15] Publicly, of course, both the risk of failure and the unwillingness of the Quai d'Orsay to take further action without its Allies were denied. In an appearance before the Foreign Affairs Commission of the Constituent National Assembly, Bidault stated that if the United States and Great Britain refused to support the Security Council proposal, "We alone will take the initiative."[16] Yet in an internal memo, the Quai d'Orsay's *Sécretariat des Conférences*, the body responsible for United Nations affairs, developed an argument that outlined the end sought through the Security Council proposal. The goal of the French initiative was not portrayed as anything more than salvaging France from its isolation on Spanish policy:

> What goal does our request seek to achieve? And what practical conclusion do we want really to find in the Council? It must appear that the decision that we have made to close our borders and to break economic relations was not only a unilateral act, but in some way an international sanction taken in relation to the [Yalta] Declaration of 13 February 1945, and motivated at the present by the new evidence that the Government of General Franco did act, and continues to act ... as a 'satellite of the Axis'. We must ask members of the Security Council to take equivalent economic sanctions.[17]

Increasingly there was some public expression of support for the Quai's need to find an Allied solution instead of continuing down the road of unilateral French action. As before, the official newspaper of the MRP supported to the letter the Government policy and congratulated Bidault on his tenacity, maintaining his desire to associate the United States and Great Britain with any French action.[18] In Paris, François Mauriac, writing in the conservative daily *Le Figaro*, warned that France had to abandon its "personal policy" and align with its Western Allies in a policy of realpolitik that tolerated the Franco regime not on its record, but because it represented anti-Communism in a country of strategic importance.[19] Most surprisingly, *Combat* abandoned its calls for unilateral French action just before the border closure, and came to support the policy of the Foreign Minister. "France alone is not in a position to greatly intimidate Franco," the editorialist wrote, and it was "curious foreign policy" to allow internal politics guide diplomatic tactics any longer. It concluded that many on the French Centre and Left were "naïve" if they thought otherwise.[20]

Proto-Containment and the Spanish Case: The American Debate

France was not the only country to react to the García execution. In early February, Britain's Foreign Secretary Ernest Bevin warned Sir Victor Mallet that if Franco continued to defy world public opinion and not change the nature of his regime, then Parliament, in particular the Labour Party's left-wing, would increase its pressure on him to take action beyond moral condemnation.[21] The potential for a change in British policy seemed quite high when Prime Minister Clement Attlee, at a meeting of Cabinet on 25 February, drew attention to García's execution, and the impact that it had and would have on public opinion worldwide, but especially in France. The Minister of Health, the leftist Aneurin Bevan, argued that a Labour Government had to do something to give anti-Francoists "spiritual reinforcement". The Cabinet agreed that Attlee should review Britain's Spanish policy and consider "further steps" in order to "expedite a change in the present political regime in Spain."[22] The following day, the Parliamentary Group of the Labour Party adopted a resolution which sought to break British diplomatic relations with Spain.[23] Yet unlike in France, these debates did not immediately lead to policy change. While the Attlee Cabinet debated the Spanish Question in the aftermath of García's execution, the traditional position of British non-intervention was reinforced in the days after the closure of the French–Spanish border. Treasury officials, as well as those in the Foreign Office, argued that Britain's economic relationship with Spain was a significant one that should not be tampered with.[24]

Moreover, as the García case dominated French politics in February 1946, there simultaneously appeared within the Truman Administration an argument against changing Spanish policy at all. Despite the fact that in December 1945 the State Department appeared more willing than the British Foreign Office to consider France's request for a meeting on Spain, it was in the emotional aftermath of the García execution that those who wished to abandon Franklin Roosevelt's March 1945 policy directive on Spain – and not expand upon it – emerged most forcefully. They no longer agreed with the premise that Spain must be pressured into a gradual political evolution of the regime. As the French initiatives on Spain developed in early 1946, these policy-makers in the United States began to view Spanish policy in light of the emerging conflict with the Soviet Union, and they deserted the anti-fascist perspective which had informed

Roosevelt's letter to the US Embassy in Madrid in the spring of 1945. The development of Spanish policy thus became a part of the emerging East–West conflict in that Rooseveltian assumptions were replaced by Cold War perspectives. An important aspect of the American policy change on Spain was the role played, early in 1946, by the Chargé d'Affaires in the US Embassy in Moscow, George F. Kennan. On 3 February 1946, just after the French Assembly vote on Spain and prior to the García execution, Kennan, on his own initiative, wrote to Washington on the subject of France and Spain. He wrote again on 1 March, after García's execution and the French Cabinet's decision to raise the Spanish issue in the Security Council. In between, on 22 February, he would write the so-called 'Long Telegram', which had a seminal role in defining the Cold War mentality of American policy-makers through its argument that Soviet leaders, motivated by Communist ideology and traditional Russian insecurity, were entirely expansionist in their foreign policy and could not be trusted in any negotiation.[25]

With his two interventions on Spain, Kennan would play a significant role in moving anti-Communism and "proto-containment" ideas to the forefront of American perspectives on Iberia. This, in turn, implied an abandonment of US pressure for political democratization inside Spain and an acceptance of the Franco regime more or less on its own terms. Furthermore, his interventions strengthened the positions of those in the British Foreign Office and British Embassy in Madrid who had been trying to push the US toward acceptance of the Spanish status quo. That Kennan should promote this line of thinking is not, of course, surprising. He was, after all, one of the fathers of the "Riga axioms", and his Long Telegram helped push ideas that had been circulating amongst many to the forefront of the Truman Administration's foreign policy.[26] Though not invited to participate in the formation of Spanish policy, Kennan outlined his ideas with particular reference to Spain and found considerable success.[27]

Kennan's 3 February dispatch considered Soviet attitudes toward Spain in light of "interest shown by foreign Communists in mobilizing international pressure for overthrow of Franco Govt."[28] He reviewed Soviet policy in the Spanish Civil War and the use of the Spanish Blue Division against Soviet troops in Second World War and he emphasized the strategic importance of Spain to Soviet expansion, both in Europe, especially France and Italy, and in Morocco and Latin America. At the same time he acknowledged the weakness of the Spanish Communists and contended that, in the short term, the Soviets relied not on direct intervention and the immediate establishment of a Communist regime in Spain but rather on "public opinion and gov[ernment] action in western countries to bring pressure for downfall of Franco regime." Kennan stated that the actions of Soviet diplomacy, such as pressing the US and Britain for a section on Spain in the Potsdam Declaration, were matched by Soviet efforts to manipulate trade unions, local western communists, women's groups, and others in mobilizing the west against Franco.[29] His implication was clear: he saw the activities of French Communist unions, parties and the role of public opinion in France as part of this Soviet scheme to influence the west, and his emphasis on these factors represented his effort to focus American policy on the Soviet threat in Iberia, which he perceived to have been a subject hitherto ignored in State Department policy-making.

Kennan's note significantly impacted the development of American and Allied policy toward Spain in 1946.[30] In Madrid, American Chargé d'Affaires Walton Butterworth had believed since his appointment as head of mission in December 1945 that there was little use in any sort of joint western action against Spain.[31] Upon receiving Kennan's analysis of Soviet goals in light of French initiatives, he was profoundly satisfied; he agreed with Kennan that the Spanish Communists did not pose a direct threat to Spain, but that disorder involving the Communists could threaten Spain and the West's position there. Butterworth responded with some surprise to Kennan's news that the Soviets took great interest in Spain, but he accepted it wholeheartedly – he found Kennan's analysis of the Potsdam Conference's resolution on Spain as a Soviet success "noteworthy", as he did Kennan's idea that the Soviets hoped to use Spain as a base for extending their influence in other areas. Butterworth echoed Kennan's conclusion that since Soviet interests were so contrary to American and British ones, western and Soviet approaches toward Spain had to be different. He argued that if the west desired a stable and liberal regime in Spain, achieved through a peaceful transition from Francoist rule, then it had to be understood that such a change would be slow and that democracy was a long way off. Butterworth clearly was abandoning the position of Roosevelt, one that held out the prospect of increased pressure on Franco, and he was moving toward the British position of scrupulous non-intervention. He strongly advocated that the United States make no public statement, such as Acheson had proposed, about its desired long-term outcome in Spain, but rather adopt an "ad hoc" approach in the near future.[32]

On the question of Spain, as on containment generally, Kennan was not the first to advocate that the intent of Soviet policy should be a primary concern in the development of America's international position. As early as 19 April 1945, a Joint Chiefs of Staff report stressed the geostrategic importance of Spain in any future war against "our most probable enemy", concluding that "Spanish-United States military cooperation is of significant importance to the implementation of our immediate, middle-range, and long-range war plans." By November 1945 the military had already begun considering the possibility of installing US bases on Spanish territory.[33] Nevertheless, as has been demonstrated, Roosevelt's legacy on Spain – which did not perceive Soviet Iberian policy as necessarily hostile to western aims – had been fairly well entrenched. Even as late as the beginning of 1946, leadership on the Spanish question was assumed by Dean Acheson through his proposal for a tripartite statement, which sought to strengthen earlier Allied declarations on Spain at the United Nations and Potsdam through an appeal to the Spanish people to oppose General Franco. Moreover, Acheson was not a member of the "containment" or "hard-line" school until much later.[34] Complete non-intervention, the idea that Franco and Spain should be left to their own devices, did not have as prominent an articulation until the exchange between Kennan and Butterworth.

If Kennan's dispatch had a major effect on Butterworth and the Madrid Embassy, its impact was even greater on British officials, who finally saw evidence that their preferred policy might be agreed to by Washington.[35] British diplomats in the United States had observed the strong anti-Franco feeling inside the State Department with trepidation and feared that Acheson or others might move the US towards a policy much closer to France's. They had felt frustrated in their efforts to counter such possibilities.[36] However, on 9 February officials at the American Embassy in Madrid showed Kennan's telegram to their British counterparts.[37] This was followed by a meeting between Butterworth and Mallet, at which the former emphasized his opposition to Acheson's proposed statement, primarily on the basis of Kennan's argument, a critical position which Mallet enthusiastically endorsed, exclaiming, "I wish I could memorize the Moscow telegram!"[38] Meanwhile, Frank Roberts of the British Embassy in Moscow, whose own position was similar to that of Kennan in the Long Telegram[39], also entered the debate. Writing to Frederick Hoyer-Millar of the Western Department in London, Roberts described Soviet interests in Spain as Kennan had, and specifically brought the French into the discussion by claiming that the French proposal to its Anglo-American allies which called for a discussion of Spanish policy was in fact the "spearhead" of the Soviet plan to prevent the US and the UK from fostering a gradual opening up of the Franco regime in Madrid.[40]

Kennan's involvement with the Spanish Question continued after the execution of Cristino García. On 1 March, he indicated that the Soviet Union was closely watching the American and British reaction to the French initiatives. He made a direct reference to Part Four of his Long Telegram, the section which dealt with the implementation of Soviet policy on the "unofficial or subterranean plane"[41] and argued that the western response to proposals emanating, in his opinion, from the French Communists and other Soviet-directed groups, "represents [a] test of efficiency of unofficial apparatus which they have created for influencing affairs in other countries." He concluded thus:

> It is not my intention here to suggest any course of action with respect to the Spanish problem or discourage any sort of action which our Govt may find

warranted by American interests. In view, however, of the admitted difference in aims between Russia and our country with respect to Iberian Peninsula as a whole I would be much surprised if an attitude based squarely on American interests involved were to turn out to be identical with that put forward as recommended by Soviet pressure groups everywhere beginning with the French Communists.[42]

From the British Embassy, Roberts sent a similar dispatch on 2 March underlining the Soviet use of pressure groups to change western policy. This came after a meeting he had had with Soviet foreign policy adviser Ivan Maisky on the subject of Spain.[43] He also indicated that he had consulted with Kennan on the subject and that Kennan was determined to ensure that American policy was "framed entirely in accordance with American and British interests and not in response to any ideological interests."[44] Those in the European section of the State Department who were inclined to lean towards the British position of non-intervention now had another reason to support such a position. Increasingly, an appreciation of Soviet intentions was a prominent part of American policy construction.[45]

Available archival sources suggest that there is little evidence the Soviet Union was very active in fomenting any action against Spain and the regime of General Francisco.[46] The Soviets were clearly opposed to the continuation of Franco in power, perceived the Spanish regime as a vestige of fascism, and had had no diplomatic relations with Spain since the Civil War. The use of the Spanish Blue Division troops alongside German forces in the Soviet Union during the war only reinforced existing opinion. However, Soviet policy on Spain was limited to diplomatic initiatives with its wartime allies. After the failure of the Spanish Communist invasion of the Val d'Aran, Stalin believed that the best way to proceed on Spain was to use the allied forums of the Conference of Foreign Ministers and the United Nations to make common policy. There was no intention of bringing the Communists to power in Spain as in the Civil War; rather, Stalin sought a coordinated policy of ostracism. The Spanish case was important for Stalin, for it was "a test for the validity of the notion that the Second World War has ushered in a new era in international relations when a grand alliance of democratic powers had learnt to act in concert."[47] At the Potsdam Conference, Stalin pushed for action on Spain and was able only to convince his Allies to release a statement which paralleled the United Nations resolution of April 1945. He also pushed for Soviet participation at the International Conference on Tangier, which was granted, but was unable at this conference to exclude Spain from the future international zone.[48] In short, the Soviet Union was inclined to push for action against Spain only through diplomatic channels and only when the possibility presented itself in the international arena. It is unclear what role the Soviet Union or the Cominform had in the development of the PCF position on Spain, but it is unlikely that it was of defining significance. The PCF had supported Bidault and de Gaulle on the Spanish issue well into the month of January 1946, even moderating the resolution of diplomatic rupture passed at the time, as earlier noted. The move to a more aggressive position came only as a result of Cristino García's execution, and this was a response that transcended partisan politics in France and had to do with the influence of the Resistance on French politics as much as anything else. The response of the Soviet Union during this period was simply to indicate, via an article in *Pravda*, that it was interested in participating in any sort of international discussion such as those with Great Britain and the United States proposed by France.[49]

The Soviet position on Spain was perhaps made clearer in terms of the USSR's attitude towards the Spanish Republican *guerrilleros* of the UNE like García. In conversation with the newly installed American Chargé d'Affaires Philip Bonsal, a Spanish Foreign Ministry official complained that the Soviet Military mission in Paris had not only made contact with and sent arms to Spanish Republican exiles, but did in fact control the actions of the French Communist party on the Spanish question. He went on to tell Bonsal that Soviet policy toward Spain was conducted with the intent of launching armed revolution, and all actions taken by the French Communists were done on orders from Moscow in order to facilitate the violent penetration of Spain by the Spanish Communist *guerrilleros*.[50] In fact, the Communist Party of the Soviet Union as early as 1944 had opposed any Spanish Communist plans for "reconquest". When the Val d'Aran invasion by UNE *guerrilleros* occurred in October 1944, Spanish and Soviet Communists based in Moscow had no idea of its planning, and had not authorized it. Spanish Communist leaders in Moscow, led by *la Pasionaria*, Dolores Ibarruri, were dispatched to France immediately following the failed attack in order to rein in renegade PCE leaders such as Jésus Monzón who had concocted the plan.[51] This contradicts the notion held by Spanish officials, Kennan, Bevin and others that the Soviet Union had geopolitical designs on Spain in the aftermath of the Second World War. Instead, Spanish Communists in France concentrated on being activists of the PCF alongside maintaining their own organizations.[52] The PCF, in turn, actively encouraged French diplomatic rupture with General Franco's regime amongst its activists, but only pressed this in Government after the García execution, in partnership with Socialist and other ministers.[53] Communist pressure on the French Government to isolate Franco's Spain must be properly seen as a part of the general French debate about the direction of French foreign policy, its claim to promote and respond to democracy, and thus the vision that the Resistance had for France in the new world order.

The Tripartite Statement on Spain

The ongoing debate in the United States about how far to go on Spain, the emergence of "proto-containment" and the continued resilience of the British position of non-intervention imposed real constraints upon the French. These were most evident in the Tripartite Statement on Spain, released on 4 March 1946. This document was representative of the state of official western opinion on Spain, and demonstrated the emerging barriers to new initiatives in Spanish policy. For the French, the statement did not go as far as their initiative to close the Pyrenean border and it did not commit its Allies to implement a similar type of sanction. For the Anglo-Americans, the statement was as far as they were ever going to go.

The idea of a joint statement, as noted earlier, was first proposed by Dean Acheson on 18 January 1946 in the aftermath of the French Assembly debate as a way to support the French desire, and also Acheson's, to "go beyond" the United Nations and Potsdam statements concerning Franco. The idea was placed on the diplomatic back burner until the execution of Cristino García. On 25 February, the United States approached the French Ambassador in Washington, Henri Bonnet, with the suggestion of a tripartite declaration, and with a prepared text.[54] Bidault agreed to the proposal almost immediately.[55] In one respect, the statement achieved its goal, because for the first time the powers called on Spaniards to act in support of a "peaceful departure" of Franco from power, the elimination of the *Falange* and the establishment of a provisional government. It asserted that these changes were necessary if Spain expected to conduct normal diplomatic relations with the three western states. The statement concluded by noting that the question of diplomatic rupture was still possible in light of events. The release of the statement, along with the American publication of the most extensive documentation demonstrating the extent of Franco's relations with Nazi Germany and Fascist Italy,[56] made it clear that Kennan's views were not yet universal. The idea that any type of intervention, especially that which originated to some degree in French political circles, was Soviet-inspired and for Soviet purposes, had not yet taken hold completely.

However, the most significant aspect of the Tripartite Statement was in the second paragraph, where the intent of the three Governments not to intervene in Spanish internal affairs was underlined and their condemnation of any prospective violence or civil war was expressed. Furthermore, the future of Spain was clearly made the responsibility of the Spanish people alone.[57] This was contained in the original American proposal which was agreed to by both Great Britain and the United States in advance of bringing the proposal to Bonnet.[58] Acheson, for all his expressed desire to "do more", could not come up with an exact policy prescription of how to carry that out, and the views of Kennan,

Butterworth and others within the State Department did not support such initiatives. Furthermore, as Kennan's intervention demonstrated, Acheson's line of argument was beginning to lose support. In Great Britain, despite Attlee's desire to rethink British policy on Spain, and the continued presence of domestic criticism from within and without the Labour Party, the Government as a whole was firmly opposed to doing more, a point that was underlined by Foreign Office officials in London, Washington and Madrid, and by Foreign Secretary Ernest Bevin.[59] In spite of the García execution and French proposals developed from December, the Tripartite Statement was really a reiteration of Western policy as embodied in the Potsdam Declaration and elsewhere.[60]

The weakness of the Tripartite Statement was not lost on Spanish opposition groups who had seen in the early French initiative hopes for a more aggressive western policy. The Republican Government-in-exile of José Giral thanked the French Government for its efforts on behalf of Spain, but reaffirmed its belief that the only way for a "civil, diplomatic and peaceful" solution to the Spanish problem was for the West to break relations with Franco and recognize the Giral Government as the only legitimate Spanish Government. In France, the exiled Spanish Socialist Party and UGT (both with members in the Giral Government) also acknowledged French efforts but maintained that more forceful action was required.[61] The Tripartite Statement was especially disappointing for the PSOE. They had welcomed the French note of December, had believed that the new Socialist-Communist dominated French coalition government would be more vigorous than de Gaulle's Government in addressing the Spanish question, and thus had instructed its members living in France in December 1945 to become active in contacting their French Socialist and Communist local parties and deputies in order to pressure them for action in order to ensure just such an outcome.[62]

The Government of General Franco also concluded that the Tripartite Statement represented a result far less severe than earlier initiatives had led it to believe possible. Since France's note to the United States and Great Britain in December 1945, the Spanish Government had alternatively feared and attacked French policy. On 29 December 1945, just after the French note was made public, the Spanish Council of Ministers issued a statement attacking the "new campaign of snares and slanders promoted against our Nation by extreme sectors of the foreign press, and [the Spanish Government] lamented the political sectarianism predominant in some countries that permits participation in this campaign, against the most elemental customs of international courtesy."[63] Yet in January, Foreign Minster Artajo spoke to Hardion and expressed great concern at the deterioration of Franco-Spanish relations, arguing that a healthy relationship was necessary not only for the two countries, but for Western Europe as well. He concluded that "only the Soviets will profit" from French policy aimed against Spain, and urged France to reconsider.[64] Once the Spanish

Government was convinced Great Britain and the United States would not follow France's lead, its response was firmer. Spain sealed the Spanish side of the Pyrenean frontier immediately, the night of 26 February, two days before the French planned to initiate their own border closure.[65] Hardion was told in no uncertain terms that France would suffer more than Spain, for the Iberian nation would continue to trade with Britain, the United States, Italy, Switzerland and others.[66]

In a formal note to the French Government, the Spanish Government argued that it was a victim of a French reactionary act inspired by the Soviet Union.[67] Franco was a great promoter of his regime as fervently anti-Communist since before the end of the Second World War, and he hoped to benefit from the resurgence of similar sentiments in the west.[68] In the winter of 1946, anti-communism was developed as a strategy of response designed, in part, to separate France from its Allies, and reaffirm among United States and British policy-makers fears of the instability that Communism could engineer in Spain. The weakness of the Tripartite Statement, which was symbolic of the French inability to move Anglo-American opinion substantially in the previous months, was followed immediately by Churchill's Fulton, Missouri "Iron Curtain" speech. Churchill's characterization of the threat posed by local Communist parties in the west as one against "Christian civilization" only added to an atmosphere which made a favorable hearing of Spain's argument more and more likely.[69]

Bidault, forced against his will to carry out a unilateral action against Spain, and unable to use the Tripartite Statement as an example of effective Western action to appease domestic critics, was not yet thwarted. In fact, he became more than ever committed to his original goals as defined in December 1945. Despite the evidence that both Britain and the United States were approaching their limit in terms of policy change towards Spain, he wished to continue his increasingly difficult attempt to construct a policy that both satisfied the expressed domestic desire to enforce sanctions against Spain and yet maintained a common Allied front toward the Franco regime. Even before the release of the Tripartite Statement, he understood that it was unlikely to represent a significant enough commitment on the part of the three powers to work in concert and effect real democratization in Spain. Thus the proposal to move debate to the United Nations Security Council remained a significant part of French policy concerning Spain.

Anglo-American Responses to France's UN Plans

The French Security Council proposal coincided with the British decision that the Tripartite Statement represented the full extent of intervention they were prepared to undertake. Fear of renewed civil war inside Spain, and fear of communist success and Soviet influence in any Spanish conflict, remained the primary factors behind the Foreign Office's consideration of policy options in Spain. The French Ambassador in London, René Massigli, reported that British policy toward Spain was motivated by anti-Communist and anti-Soviet motives which were increasingly dominant over other, traditional reasons for non-intervention.[70] Like George Kennan in the United States, Foreign Secretary Ernest Bevin was, in 1946, even more fearful of proceeding within the UN because of his belief that the Soviet Union was "only too anxious to make trouble over Spain" and that "by suggesting reference of the Spanish question to the Security Council the French are simply playing the Russian game."[71]

In light of this analysis, it was not surprising that economic sanctions such as proposed by France were quickly rejected. Frederick Hoyer-Millar, Head of the Foreign Office's Western Department, returned to long-standing arguments in his articulation of the British opposition to sanctions:

> we should not apply any form of economic sanctions unless and until we are virtually certain that their imposition will bring about the almost immediate collapse of Franco and his replacement by a Government at the same time acceptable to the majority of Spaniards and to ourselves; and furthermore even in that event we should not impose economic sanctions unless we are convinced that this is the only way of getting rid of Franco . . . [72]

Hoyer-Millar's opposition to sanctions was supported by the Treasury and other departments concerned with trade and economic matters. Again, traditional reasons for non-intervention in Spain complemented Bevin's anti-Soviet stance. The decision against sanctions also developed from an ongoing economic approach to Spain typified by a Board of Trade survey of October 1945 which indicated that Spain, due to its need to replace Germany as a trading partner, offered "special opportunities of trade development for United Kingdom manufactures" in competition with countries such as Switzerland.[73] Sanctions, they concluded, would harm Britain in the short-term as raw material and foodstuff deliveries would be lost, and opportunities such as the ongoing program to recover German assets in Spain would be compromised. Furthermore, sanctions on items such as oil would only be effective if a large number of countries participated, which was unlikely. In addition, there was the fear that the enforcement of sanctions would require British monitoring at Gibraltar and Portugal, which would stretch British resources and potentially harm relations with Portugal. Finally, there was a concern that sanctions applied against Spain would set a precedent and lead to calls for sanctions against Juan Péron's similarly authoritarian Catholic regime in Argentina, where Britain also had important economic interests.[74] For the British the decision was clearly against sanctions and diplomatic rupture.

The British position against any further initiative was reinforced on 15 March 1946 with a report from the Joint Intelligence Sub-Committee of the British Chiefs of Staff. Its conclusion was that foreign pressure on Spain, such as the imposition of French sanctions and the issuance of the Tripartite Declaration, had only served to reinforce the position of General Franco in power, and that Franco had been able to exploit the population's fear of renewed civil war and Communist infiltration so as to represent himself as the only leader capable of defending Spain from foreign interference. The result was that there was little chance of any popular uprising, and absolutely no indication that the monarchist generals in the army planned to overthrow Franco in the near future. The French proposal to move the debate to the Security Council would serve no purpose other than as "an easy rally cry for Spanish nationalism and xenophobia" which Franco would further exploit, and "even if considerable quantities of arms were sent into the country, economic sanctions would only make a rising likely if they were applied for a considerable time and on such a scale as to cut off wheat from all sources, including the Argentine, and to cause economic chaos and widespread hunger." Such devastation would only bring civil war, not regime transition, and foreign intervention, primarily Soviet, but potentially French as well. The Joint Intelligence Sub-Committee supported a continuation of the current Anglo-American policy, one of quiet diplomatic pressure.[75] As early as 2 March, Ernest Bevin informed British Ambassador in Paris Alfred Duff Cooper that he considered the French proposal "most ill-advised." Duff Cooper delivered Bevin's objections to the Quai d'Orsay on 4 March.[76]

Within the Truman Administration, it appeared as if the French note received a better reception than in London, although the end result, rejection, was the same. From Washington, Ambassador Georges Bonnet informed the Foreign Ministry that the State Department's Director of the Office of European Affairs, H. Freeman Matthews, had told him the United States was "sympathetic" to the French proposal, although Matthews's own minutes of that meeting do not indicate that any hint of support was given.[77] In the end, the conclusion that there was no basis for moving to the Security Council was quickly reached. The American response was particularly focused on the use of the United Nations Charter by France to achieve certain ends. To American Ambassador Jefferson Caffrey, Secretary of State James Byrnes wrote that "we do not understand how failure of Franco to give impression abroad that he was preparing evolution of internal regime brings [the] matter within [the] terms of charter." Similarly, on the subject of political executions like García's, "deplorable as these may be, we do not understand how they can be considered as being likely to endanger the maintenance of international peace and security." The troop movements of Franco's army on the Pyrenean border were also not considered a threat.[78] The American note was delivered to Bidault by Caffrey on 9 March 1946. Unlike the British note, it did not ask the French to abandon their proposal, but reaffirmed American opposition to Franco and declined association with the French initiative based on Charter issues.[79]

Despite this more gracious response to France's Security Council note, the growing role of anti-Communism was strong, and becoming stronger, within the American Administration. Bonnet reported that while there remained divisions within the State Department on the question of intervention in Spain, he could not neglect the growing belief within the United States that only the Soviets could benefit from a more interventionist policy towards Spain. He emphasized that the question of Soviet policy had played "an important role" in the final decision.[80] As noted earlier, it was George F. Kennan's 1 March 1946 comment on the Soviet Union, France and the Spanish issue that had featured prominently in both American and British discussions. Therefore, as a result of both traditional positions of non-intervention and developing viewpoints that placed the policy toward Spain in a broader international context, both the United States and Great Britain rejected Bidault's proposal to take the Spanish issue to the United Nations Security Council. The Soviet Union, however, responded favorably to Bidault's proposal.[81] The Soviets believed, like many French, that the UN might be just the instrument to use in order to achieve a unified position against Franco.[82] Yet in light of France's continued effort to maintain Allied coordination on the Spanish question and make an effort to appease domestic pressure, this was the worst case scenario. Soviet support, in light of the increased influence of anti-Communism *vis-à-vis* Spain in Britain and the United States, foreshadowed defeat.[83]

Georges Bidault was growing more and more frustrated with the course of France's Spanish policy and his inability to reconcile domestic pressure with allied unity. He openly displayed his attitude to both his American and British allies by stating that he personally did not support any further action on Spain, including the proposed move to place the issue on the Security Council agenda. He cast the policy decision almost entirely as an aspect of the French Government's domestic policy. In conversation with Duff Cooper, Bidault indicated his lack of enthusiasm for the project but concluded that Spain was not a matter on which he wished to oppose other ministers and thus threaten to break up the French Government.[84] After the positive Soviet reply, Bidault confided to Caffrey that he was "on the spot" over the way the whole thing had worked out.[85]

The purpose of such frankness was to counteract Anglo-American suspicions that French policy was increasingly directed by the Communist Party and that Bidault was a weak figure within the government. It was hoped that France's Allies might have some sympathy for the position Bidault found himself in, and thus help create a "way out" for the Quai d'Orsay. Other French officials followed Bidault's lead in attempting to portray the French government as one whose policy-making options were defined almost entirely by the passions of an entire population. In Washington, French Embassy official Armand Berard attempted with little success to convince an American newspaper reporter that the anti-Franco reaction in France was being misinterpreted in the US as Communist-inspired, when in fact it was a much broader "national reaction."[86] At the end of March, the French Parliamentary Under-Secretary for Foreign Affairs, Pierre Schneiter, a member of the MRP like Bidault, met with US Undersecretary of State Dean Acheson. He stated that while Bidault was unsatisfied with the fact that France now stood aligned with the Soviets over Spain, the Foreign Minister was under "unrelenting" pressure domestically and Schneiter hoped that "there would be a greater recognition ... of the delicacy of M. Bidault's present position in the French Government and that this recognition would take concrete form through the aligning of this government [the United States] with some of the foreign policies which M. Bidault is advocating."[87] Acheson expressed interest in this situation, but he promised nothing.

Such openness on the part of Bidault and his officials falls in line with the interpretation of historians that France could achieve more within the Western Alliance by acknowledging its weaknesses.[88] In this instance, it seemed to produce two distinct, and contradictory, responses from the Anglo-Americans. There was a real fear in London and Washington that the constraints of domestic politics the Foreign Minister complained about were real. There is evidence that this approach did elicit, at the least, some sympathy for Bidault and the Quai d'Orsay. Elements within both the Foreign Office and the State Department did acknowledge that the precariousness of post-war parliamentary politics had played a role in all of France's efforts since December 1945. In London, René Massigli gave newly-appointed Deputy Undersecretary of State Sir Oliver Harvey the distinct impression that he was also opposed to the Security Council plans, but explained at length the weak position of Bidault within the Government.[89] There was a small group in the Foreign Office that acknowledged that Bidault was "simply a victim of the unreasoning passions of powerful sections of the French public."[90] Harvey even went so far as to ask Duff Cooper to assess the possibility of Bidault's MRP being thrown out of the coalition government to be replaced by a Socialist-Communist *Front Populaire* that would begin its term by linking French policy on Spain closer to the Soviet position, and would in turn demand more action in the UN and elsewhere.[91] Certainly, then, the tried and true strategy of France to influence the western alliance from a point of weakness seemed to elicit the desired sympathy.

However, after months of dealing with the Spanish question, a very real frustration with Bidault and the Quai d'Orsay for their collective inability to "manage" foreign policy properly was also evident. French behavior, noted Peter Garran on 5 March, gave the Spanish a "very strong case" at "playing the injured innocent."[92] The next day, Frederick Hoyer-Millar went even further, chastising Bidault for being the "feeble creature that he is", unable to control his own foreign policy. Bevin's frustration with the French reflected that of his Foreign Office advisors, for he concluded, "We have impression that M. Bidault is so obsessed by his own domestic political difficulties that he is thinking merely of the day to day issues and shirking the long-term complications."[93] American Secretary of State James Byrnes was equally unsympathetic, commenting that regardless of domestic politics, all three Governments were "on the spot" due to French actions that "do not appear to have been thought through and which we regard as fundamentally contrary to the best interests of the three governments . . . and particularly the French themselves."[94] By the middle of March, the *New York Times* reported that French diplomatic exchanges increasingly represented "an embarrassed effort to justify a policy in which the [French] Foreign Office does not believe."[95]

French efforts to appeal for sympathy did not change Anglo-American policy, but rather softened the blow when the Allies finally rejected France's proposal to discuss Spain at the Security Council. When Byrnes made the decision to reject Bidault's plan, he told Caffrey that while he desired the Ambassador to give Bidault a sense of Byrnes's own personal anger with the French Government over Spain, how Caffrey chose to inform the French was left to him alone "in view of the internal political situation in France, particularly Bidault's personal position."[96]

If anything, the emphasis the French placed on domestic constraints reinforced anti-Communist motivations that State Department officials used to reject France's own proposals. The strategic role of both Spain and France in the developing Cold War became linked to France's UN proposals. There was a real fear, at this point, that the Communists could come to power in France and that the PCF was a "powerful, disciplined, totalitarian political machine slavishly obedient to Moscow."[97] On 22 March 1946, the head of the State Department's French Desk, Warner, stopped in Madrid on his way to France. He met with José Maria Doussingue, the Political Director of the Spanish Foreign Ministry. Warner told Doussingue that both Great Britain and the United States believed France's policies towards Spain were increasingly under the influence of the PCF and its trade union, the CGT, despite Bidault's personal opposition to such a scenario. Warner expressed confidence that Bidault and the civil servants of the Foreign Ministry would ultimately prevail, but he emphasized the "gravity" of current circumstances, and warned that Spain must be prepared for more public criticism of its regime. The visit was an effort to reassure the Spaniards that the West was not against them. The Spanish minutes of this meeting note with some surprise that Warner spoke of his "admiration" for Spanish reconstruction efforts and emphasized that the US official did not raise any complaints about Spanish internal politics, which was considered a first for someone from the State Department.[98] Warner also met French minister Bernard Hardion and left him with the impression that "the State Department judges the Spanish question more and more as part of the French problem." He also reported that "in order to find on our soil a pressure point necessary for Anglo-Saxon resistance against the Soviet Union, the American and British Governments are resigned to place their hostility to Franco momentarily aside."[99] Any move toward a Spanish regime that included Communists was seen as a victory for the French Communists and thus for the Soviet Union. This now became a far more important aspect of the US analysis than it had been previously.

Looking for a Way Out

While yearning to appease both Allies and internal critics did seem to drive French policy-making toward Spain in this period, there is also evidence that policy-makers understood the risks inherent in the project, and anticipated that the Security Council proposal would not result in success. Officials in the Foreign Ministry, never strong supporters of a policy of sanctions against Franco, seemed to have taken some lessons from the experience of January and February. There was an underlying acknowledgment that the potential for further developments was not great, and that the Tripartite Note most likely represented the extent that Great Britain, and increasingly the United States, were prepared to move vis-a-vis Spain.

One of the most interesting issues that demonstrates the Quai d'Orsay's preparation for retreat was that of Spanish troops on the Pyrenean border. The French note of 27 February 1946 stressed that the Spanish case should be presented to the Security Council "as a *situation*, not a *dispute*."[100] This difference was important, for if the question was a dispute, the other party, Spain, even if not a United Nations member, would be permitted to appear in front of the Security Council, an outcome none of the three western powers wanted. Moreover, such an approach allowed France to claim that the Spanish issue was not a conflict between nations which threatened French security, but rather that the existence of the Franco regime was a threat to broader international peace and security. Critics on the left were stunned by this decision. Resistance and party propaganda on the Spanish issue had consistently portrayed opposition to Franco not only as a matter of principle, but also as one of security. The linkage of Hitler, Mussolini and Franco in the French press sought not only to draw ideological parallels, but historical ones, for these were the men that had attacked the French Republic. In March 1946, as the Security Council proposal was being considered, *L'Humanité* printed detailed maps which showed extensive Spanish troop deployment along France's border, highlighting not only the numbers of armed forces, but also the existence of German Nazis within them.

The war was not really over, and the security of France was why international actions had to be taken, in the eyes of the PCF organ.[101] In the Foreign Affairs Commission of the Assembly, Edouard Herriot wondered why France had not chosen to stress the immediate crisis situation which the troops represented. Salomon Grumbach, the Chair of the Commission, concurred with Herriot's implication that the absence of any reference to the Spanish military only weakened France's argument.[102] Grumbach met privately with Bidault to stress the military threat, and the Foreign Minister refused to budge. The United States and Great Britain, he reported, did not believe that Spanish troop deployments represented a threat to international peace and France would not challenge Anglo-American judgment on that point. Bidault's conclusion, as reported by Grumbach, emphasized not only that the troop issue was moot, but that retreat from a position of principle was not that far off. "The Government has done what was asked of it," Grumbach reported Bidault as saying, "and now we will wait to see what follows."[103]

The idea that Spanish troops on the Pyrenees represented a threat to French and international security infuriated the French Minister in Madrid, Bernard Hardion. Although the French Foreign Ministry indicated to the Americans and the British that this was not, in fact, the basis for their claim on Security Council competency, the publicity given to the issue in France did not go unnoticed. To counter the effect of such reports, Hardion met with his American and British colleagues, Philip Bonsal and Sir Victor Mallet, both of whom had sent their military attaches to the border region to investigate. Their conclusions, relayed to Paris by Hardion on 17 March 1946, indicated that the total number of troops in the border area was half that at the time the war ended. Furthermore, new units arriving were there in part to stop infiltrations from France but also because the end of winter marked the normal time of troop movements in Spain. Finally, no extra reservists had been called up by the Spanish government. Taken together, these troop deployments were not unusual and were "entirely defensive."[104] Hardion told Mallet that he was completely occupied with "disabusing" Paris of the notion that there was a serious chance of Spanish aggression or threat and that he "deplored" the position that the French Government had taken with regard to Franco's Spain.[105] The frustration of officials with a policy that was deemed not to be working was becoming evident.

In the face of the Anglo-American rejection of the Security Council proposal, Bidault made further efforts to reconcile domestic and foreign policy concerns while at the same time extracting France from a public position of alignment with the Soviet Union alone on the question of Spain. On 12 March, France attempted to propose that a Security Council review of the Spanish case need not result in UN sanctions, but could in fact lead simply to a recommendation that the Four Powers (Britain, France, United States, Soviet Union) study the issue in the Council of Foreign Ministers (CFM) meetings.[106] In preparation for this second proposal, François Coulet, head of the Quai's European section, reiterated the fact that what France desired ideologically was a broad anti-Franco policy, one built on "practical and concrete" measures instead of continued rhetoric. Most importantly, however, the real motivation for France's appeal was found in Coulet's conclusion. What France sought, in the end, was a decision by the Security Council either to take measures similar to France's unilateral border closure or direct the CFM to consider a similar measure.[107] A movement to some other forum would be good enough for France. In the Foreign Ministry office responsible for UN affairs, the *Sécretariat des Conférences*, it was argued:

> We must in this case find an honorable retreat in a procedural solution that will consist of a renewed consideration of the question by the Four Powers . . . The reason for which the texts [are] invoked [i.e. the Yalta Declaration] . . . are that these texts emerged from conferences of the Great Powers. [The solution] would be to attach France's name, whose presence, in the case of Spain, would not create great difficulties, [to future statements on Spain] in concert with the Three.[108]

A decision to move consideration of the Spanish case to a forum of Great Powers, such as the Council of Foreign Ministers (CFM), would counter fears that use of the UN for such a debate could set a precedent for UN involvement in internal affairs, and would remove the issue from the public sphere of the world body, yet at the same time it would also allow France to claim to its domestic opinion that it was continuing to lead on the Spanish question. France believed that references to both the Yalta and Potsdam Declarations gave them a basis for moving the Spanish question off the UN agenda and back to a matter for the Great Powers alone to consider.[109]

Bidault's second Security Council proposal of 12 March was quickly dismissed by the two western powers.[110] From London, it was increasingly clear to the French that the Labour Government was not going to budge. Frustration at the British Foreign Office was as strong as ever. In a note to Halifax, in Washington, Bevin chastised the French "anxiety . . . in the face of pressure from their public opinion to 'do something' about Spain." He went on to conclude that French actions to date only strengthened Franco, appeared as Communist-inspired, and any further action was "unacceptable" to Great Britain. Britain was prepared to discuss the issue with France and the United States, but only in order to reaffirm that policy would proceed on the established line. An agreement to meet was Bevin's only concession. He, like the Americans, had concerns about France's growing sense of isolation from the west.[111] In April, British immobility was reiterated when Bevin strongly defended his Spanish policy at a general meeting of the Labour Party, where he stressed in particular the economic benefits Britain received from Spanish trade and his contention that all of France's actions combined had only served to strengthen Franco's position further.[112] Even amongst American policy-makers, some of whom continued to believe Franco should be removed from power, there was an unwillingness to carry on in the UN or elsewhere. Simply put, the Americans considered any number of other international problems much more urgent, and, in light of that fact and the resolution with which the British Foreign Office continued to reject all French proposals, what State Department officials desired most of all was the removal of the Spanish question from public and private discussions amongst the Allies, at least in the short term.[113]

With the rejection of France's 12 March note, Bidault decided to withdraw his recommendation that the Security Council discuss the Spanish question.[114] Grasping at his final opportunity, namely the fact that the western powers had not officially asked him to stop discussing Spain, Bidault did not yet abandon his search for a policy option which fell short of a full retreat. France embraced the Council of Foreign Ministers (CFM) as the best place to hold the discussion on Spain. This option would allow talks to be held amongst the three western allies and the Soviet Union, just as France's Security Council initiative would have. Furthermore, behind the closed doors of four-power summitry, France hoped to find an easier ways to avoid "becoming isolated with the USSR against an Anglo-Saxon coalition."[115] Foreign Ministry officials expressed the hope that within the less legal setting of the CFM, negotiations could proceed, deals could be struck, perhaps even by suggesting that the French might concede some Ruhr issues in return for joint action on Spain. Finally, discussions about the construction of an alternative Spanish regime could be addressed.[116] None of these opportunities would have been provided in a Security Council discussion. Bidault approached both Governments to propose joint talks with the Soviets on a range of subjects such as the possibility of imposing commodity-specific economic sanctions against Franco and the nature of an alternative regime in Spain.[117] The British were completely opposed to involving the Soviet Union or having discussions on a topic such as the future Spanish regime.[118] Thus the CFM format was rejected. The Anglo-Americans did agree, however, to a tripartite meeting on the subject.[119] The French were back where they had begun in December 1945. While a public acceptance of the status quo was yet to come, the writing was certainly on the wall.

Summary

Observing French policy in March 1946 reveals the complexity, and indeed confusion, of motivations and sentiments which made it difficult to decipher. This was the moment where the tide turned from the real possibility that a justice model of foreign policy-making might have some real success in France, to the growing realization that France's weakness within the Western Alliance meant a realpolitik acceptance of failure on Spain was coming. Moreover, it meant that the Government's efforts to strike a balance between the Foreign Ministry's own realist sentiments in working within the Western Alliance and the Resistance-inspired call for sanctions had also failed. The long-standing hesitation of the Quai d'Orsay to advocate a policy of sanction, the search for domestic appeasement, Bidault's desire to maintain concerted action, and the beginnings of retreat are all evident in the proposals made during March 1946. An approach toward Spain which combined practicality and principle appeared less and less possible. The argument has been made that in the aftermath of the García execution, France moved toward a "politics of intervention."[120] In actual fact, the time during which French calls for interventionist tactics dominated foreign policy planning was before the García execution, in the heady atmosphere of December 1945 to February 1946. There was a strong belief within the Quai d'Orsay that public opinion since that time had been constraining, not empowering. Difficulty with its allies and a reawakening of the Quai's own reluctance to lead world opinion on the subject of Spain meant that, increasingly from March 1946, France was willing to consider backing away from an aggressively anti-Franco policy even if that would look like a forced alignment with other states against its will.

Bidault's evident frustration and opposition to the direction of French policy has already been noted. From London, René Massigli wondered whether or not the Quai had indeed lost control of its own policy:

> Spanish policy has, in my mind, taken a bad turn. Communist action is a strong force at home; the Socialists, who only see fire, gallop ahead in order not to be passed by themselves... here [in London] they worry about the goal that all these maneuvers aim for, and they are inclined to see, more and more in this affair, the hand of Russia. I do not know what to think. But appearances do not contradict this interpretation... this Spanish matter is so moving, it is so dominated at home by considerations of internal politics... Set me straight, if you will...[121]

Massigli's plea for guidance could not be answered by Paris. The French goal from December had been to take advantage of a unique opportunity to construct a positive and united Allied policy which sought to alter Spain's regime in a manner which internal and Resistance opinion desired. In short, it was an attempt to combine rational alliance politics with domestic idealistic ideological visions. Furthermore, especially on the question of Spain, it was an opportunity particularly open to a France enlivened by the legacy of the Resistance, building its own democracy anew and wishing to see similar efforts south of the Pyrenees. Such a vision, however, was never really shared by the Quai d'Orsay, and, faced with opposition from its Anglo-American allies, French diplomatic efforts on the question of Spain came to resemble a policy based on desperation. Especially after the public mobilization around the execution of Cristino García and the closure of the French–Spanish border, where the Resistance links to Spanish democracy were closest, Georges Bidault and his advisors seemed motivated only by a desire to avoid both isolation from the Anglo-Americans and public embarrassment. The result was a policy which sought any sort of agreement on Spain to take home, instead of one constructed on rational assessments of both domestic opinion and alliance politics. In an appearance before the Foreign Affairs Commission at the end of March, Bidault expressed only a desire to leave the Spanish case alone, for he contrasted the material benefits lost by France through border closure with the moral benefits gained. "Politics," he concluded, "is justly the art of choosing between two inconveniences."[122]

The end of French efforts to lead the Allies toward a new Spanish policy was not only apparent to Bernard Hardion in Madrid, but something which he actively sought. Hardion, already on record as opposed to most of the actions the Government in Paris had taken on Spain since January, furiously worked to oppose further French initiatives. While he acknowledged that the Tripartite Note had been received with "satisfaction" by the Spanish Ministry of Foreign Affairs due to its lack of concrete measures against Spain, he believed that in and of itself the note was sufficient as an expression of policy and that nothing need follow it. Hardion underlined that while the Spanish external opposition might call for more economic sanctions, the mass of the population wanted the exit of Franco, but without the threat of civil war or a Communist regime. The Tripartite Note, Hardion argued, helped to solidify anti-Francoism without threatening intervention and chaos, and in the final analysis that was a worthy position to hold for the long-term.[123] Alignment with Britain and the United States, even if apparently forced, would be a welcome relief.

6

French Acceptance of Franco's Spain, 1946–1948

For the West, the Spanish question was effectively over by the end of 1946. The Tripartite Statement of March 1946 represented in microcosm the Western Alliance's approach toward Spain. Initiated as an American effort to respond to the importance of the Spanish question within France, it failed to do much of anything because its arrival came alongside the beginning of the imposition of the Cold War onto the Spanish question, which gradually led to the State Department's call for normalization of relations with Franco by October 1947.[1] The Tripartite Statement of France, Great Britain and the United States represented the full extent of how far London and Washington were prepared to go to encourage an alternative Spanish regime. Paris, responding to domestic pressure, may have seemed to want more as it forged ahead with its proposal to discuss Spain at the United Nations. The reality, however, was that by the middle of 1946, the French accepted the role that Franco's Spain was to play as a bulwark against Communism and realized they had no ability within the Western Alliance to alter policy toward Franco. Over the course of 1946, privately and publicly, the French Government abandoned any effort to make "justice" and the cause of Spanish Republicanism a factor in foreign policy-making. Instead, France fell in line with its Anglo-American allies and accepted the status quo of Franco's rule. This was not done without difficulty, and it required, in many places, the continuation of a public policy of anti-Francoism, the maintenance of sanctions in the form of border closure and the continuation of contacts with the anti-Franco opposition in and outside of Spain. Only by 1948 would France's position fully conform to that of its allies and represent near-normal diplomatic relations. Yet long before that the failure of the Resistance-inspired model of policy-making in the face of new assessments of national security was clear.

French Acceptance of Franco's Spain, 1946–1948

The United Nations Security Council Debate

While the realization of the need for a retreat in the forum of the United Nations was accepted in Paris over the course of March 1946, as Chapter 5 argued, the renewal of plans for a tripartite British, American and French discussion on Spain proceeded, with a date of late April likely.[2] Before this, however, French policy would again be steered off track by other events. As the French announced their decision to abandon the forum of the Security Council in pursuit of a Spanish policy, Poland decided to take up the cause within the UN's highest body. This was not completely unexpected. On 18 March, in conversation with Duff Cooper, Georges Bidault had expressed not only his fear of the "unpleasant possibility" that France and the Soviet Union would oppose the western allies on the question of Spain, but that even if France abandoned their proposal, the Soviets could induce the Ukraine or Poland to raise the issue.[3] When news came of the Polish initiative, Bidault was exasperated:

> Just at the moment where we received the note of Mr. Caffrey that informed us of our first positive result of our efforts in Washington and London, the Polish request to put the subject of Spain before the Security Council risks the emergence of an element of confusion likely to slow down the development of negotiations.[4]

In the initial days after the Polish motion to the Security Council became public, Great Britain and the United States continued to renew their promise to France that discussions on Spain should be held amongst the three allies, and talks were scheduled for London near the end of April.[5] As the issue developed in the Security Council, however, talks were postponed, and there is no record of them ever taking place. Bidault's exasperation, therefore, was well founded.

The Polish decision to carry on where France had failed put the French in an extraordinarily delicate position. France's policy, from December 1945 through to its own Security Council initiatives, had been based on promoting a more aggressive policy toward Spain *only* with the support and joint leadership of its two western allies, Great Britain and the United States. The UN debate that began in April 1946 was significant because France emerged, on the surface, as "the European power the most hostile to the Franco regime" within the United Nations.[6] The reality, however, was that the public position France was forced to adopt did not reflect the underlying combination of complication and confusion behind French policy toward Franco's Spain. The leadership of the Quai d'Orsay, from Bidault through to Hardion in Madrid, was extremely reluctant to have had France play the role of international moral crusader on its own. When they finally seemed to be moving closer to abandoning policies which placed France in an increasingly risky position within the western alliance, the Polish proposal forced them publicly to return to earlier ideological stances which Great Britain and the United States could not support.

By March, the Foreign Ministry sought room to prepare for a retreat from the burdens of ideological leadership. Domestic politics, however, imposed real and imagined constraints on French diplomats that meant even such a retreat had to conform to very specific conditions. By the end of March, the Foreign Ministry seemed willing to accept that, for a time, France's unilateral sanction against Spain would stand, that domestic opinion and allied policy could not work in unison on Spain, and that the matter should only be discussed with the Anglo-Americans behind closed doors. The Polish initiative destroyed what little satisfaction Bidault had left, for in making policy toward Spain over the previous months not only a matter of allied exchange, but also of public record, Bidault would be unable to instruct the French delegation at the United Nations to do anything but support Poland. Henri Bonnet, temporary head of the French UN delegation, understood that France had no other option but to support Poland. If France opposed the Polish initiative, domestic criticism would be intense. Even though France had agreed to hold off on any Spanish initiatives until a meeting with the Americans and British took place, criticism of France over opposition to Poland would create a situation far worse, even "an impression prejudicial to our interests."[7]

Bidault's instructions to the French delegation emphasized the above points. If the issue of competence was raised, that is, the issue of whether or not the Security Council even had the right to examine the Spanish case, then France had to support the Polish motion in light of its own earlier initiatives, and similarly France had to argue that UN sanctions could be applied against Spain in the same manner that France had applied its own sanctions in closing the Pyrenean border. The Foreign Minister was not willing, however, to go much beyond this. He reminded the French delegates that throughout the entire affair, France's policy had been solely in pursuit of a "tangible policy" and therefore any action by the Security Council had to have the unanimous support of the five permanent members. Bidault wrote that, "under grave risk to the policy we ourselves defend, we cannot go further along the path that we have opened without the policy alignment of the other Great Powers."[8] France had abandoned its leadership role, yet Bidault could not completely walk away.

The response of Great Britain and the United States to news of the Polish initiative did not bode well for France. Britain's representative to the UN, Sir Alexander Cadogan, characterized the Security Council "solely as a sounding board for mischievous propaganda" and the debate on the Spanish case, like the debates regarding Greece and Iran, was to him "unreal."[9] The United States took a strictly legal interpretation of the UN Charter that led to two positions, both of which meant opposition to the Polish motion. First, the United States did not believe that the Charter gave the Security Council rights to intervene in internal affairs, and that therefore actions like the Tripartite Statement represented the limits of non-intervention. Furthermore, as to Poland's other claim, that the Franco regime constituted a threat to international security, the Director of the State Department's Office of European Affairs, H. Freeman Matthews, maintained that the United States must argue that there was "no information indicating that Spain has threatened or is threatening the security of France or any other state." He concluded, "If the Spanish question is raised in the Security Council we feel that the US Representative should not hesitate to state that in the view of the United States Government, based on our present evidence, the Council does not have jurisdiction."[10]

On 17 April 1946, the Polish delegate, Oskar Lange, introduced the issue of Spain onto the Security Council agenda and stated that the Franco regime was "the lone survivor of the Axis in a world of international peace and justice to which the United Nations is committed, a dangerous remnant of the enemies which they defeated at such tremendous cost of blood and wealth."[11] Lange's charges against Spain were based on four factors. The first two were historical, including Franco's involvement with the Axis powers during the Spanish Civil War and the Second World War. In addition, Lange argued that two post-war situations made Spain a threat that should concern the Security Council. The first was represented by recent troop movements along the Pyrenean border which, Lange argued, were part of "the constant intrigues of the Franco regime against the French Republic."[12] Second, the harboring of German agents and assets in Spain, including the hiding of German atomic scientists, made Spain a threat to international peace and security. Lange proposed that the Security Council declare Spain a threat to international peace and security under articles 34 and 39 of the Charter, and thus request all UN members maintaining diplomatic relations with Spain to break them, as per article 41.[13]

Immediately following Lange's opening comments, Henri Bonnet spoke on behalf of France. Bonnet reviewed the international and inter-allied approach France had taken toward the question of Spain since December, and asserted that what France sought was not only another statement on Spain, but practical action by the international community similar to France's unilateral border closure. In comments aimed particularly at the United States and Great Britain, Bonnet supported Lange's proposed resolution by arguing that it was legitimate for the Security Council to consider the issue of Spain as one that was not about internal politics, but rather about "international peace and security" as stated in Article 2, paragraph 6 of the Charter.[14] In short, moving to the forum of the UN via the Polish motion, despite France's previous failures, forced France to stick to its established policy. In this spirit, Bonnet concluded with a statement that was at once both an appeal to the ideologically dominated domestic opinion and a plea to the Security Council to end France's isolation:

Moral condemnations, however valuable, are no longer sufficient . . . [France] has given tangible proof of this attitude in the problem now before us: first, it welcomed the Spanish Republican Government to French territory; secondly, anticipating the measures which might be adopted by the Council, it severed economic and frontier relations with Spain in spite of the losses and damages involved.[15]

Just as the French argument had not convinced the United States or Great Britain in inter-allied notes and talks, it was unable to do so within the forum of the Security Council. Sir Alexander Cadogan, speaking for Great Britain, not only rejected claims of competency for the Security Council to deal with the matter, but he also attacked the nature of the Polish charges. Cadogan claimed that Polish accusations against Spain were based primarily on Franco's early wartime policy, between 1940–3, and that between 1943–5, Franco had in fact aided the Allies in important ways. He further argued that Polish estimates of Spanish troop deployment along the Pyrenees were grossly exaggerated.[16] Edward Stettinius concurred, and stated that the United States Government could not agree with the Polish charges as presented.[17]

United States policy, however, differed from the British in one important aspect which suggested to the French that there was a still path open toward honorable retreat. The policy advocated by the United States allowed that while the United States stood against the Polish motion, there was no need, at this point, to dismiss the Spanish case from the Security Council agenda altogether. In reality, US delegates did not want to vote at all on the Polish motion, for the US was fearful of the propaganda value Spain and Franco could derive from a motion that would clearly be defeated by the United States and Great Britain. With Spain on the continuing agenda, the Security Council could appoint a sub-committee or refer matters to the General Assembly, which had already censured Spain, and thus send the message that "the situation in Spain still continues to be of concern to the international community."[18] Officials at the State Department were not the only ones thinking along these lines, and on the second day of debate in New York, the Australian delegate, Colonel William Hodgson, presented a resolution to create such a sub-committee in order to establish facts for the Security Council members before they considered possible resolutions or action.[19] Bonnet welcomed the Australian proposal, seeing in it a "compromise" that was ideal for France, for it clearly placed Spain on the Security Council agenda. Moreover, Bonnet observed, it seemed to be sufficient for the United States to accept the proposal in order to appease its own liberal opinion. An American move, Bonnet observed, might force Cadogan to abandon his "completely negative attitude."[20] The Ambassador pledged to work on promoting the Australian resolution in order to ensure that France's fear of another "divergence between the Great Powers on the Spanish situation" would not come to pass.[21]

Once again, subtle differences amongst the Anglo-Saxon powers regarding Spain gave the French a glimmer of hope that their goal might be able to be realized. And once again, the differences between the United States and Great Britain were not as wide as France suspected. To the British, who strongly opposed the Australian motion, the United States argued that its aims were the same as Cadogan's, namely to discourage any Security Council action on Spain. However, the US argued, public and international tension over the Spanish question would not dissipate, and thus had to be addressed in a manner that the Sub-Committee could offer. Furthermore, the Americans argued that, if anything, the Committee could reveal information about the activity of French and Spanish Communists in France on the subject of Spain, which would be an advantage to the west.[22] The British abstained from voting, and in London Sir Oliver Harvey wrote that any effort to remove Franco had been "completely wrecked by this policy of intervention" on the part of France and other countries.[23] On 29 April, after some re-writing of Hodgson's initial resolution, the Security Council referred the Spanish question to a Sub-Committee that consisted of the Australian, Brazilian, Chinese, French and Polish delegates.[24]

The Security Council Sub-Committee on Spain

The Sub-Committee, under the Chair of the Australian Herbert Evatt, set about its task by soliciting Security Council and other United Nations members to provide it with any information regarding the activities of the Spanish Government. Not surprisingly, the primary documentation was provided by the American, British and French governments. In addition, a presentation from José Giral, head of the Spanish Republican Government-in-exile, was heard. Nine questions posed by the Sub-Committee constituted the range of the enquiry. These were the nature of the Franco regime; the attitude of the regime towards the Axis during the Second World War; the extent of German involvement in Spain; the current military situation in Spain; the extent of military and war goods production ongoing in Spain; the persecution of Republicans and others for political reasons; the detention by Franco of non-Spanish nationals; pro-fascist and pro-Falangist activities outside Spain; and the international repercussions of the existence of the Franco regime.[25]

The Sub-Committee process left the French hopeful but not convinced that a solution to their dilemma existed. Exactly how to reach France's desired conclusion, some kind of UN sanction that went beyond the Tripartite Declaration and ended France's isolation on the question of sanctions, was unclear to the French themselves. Forced into the Security Council action after a reluctant acceptance of defeat, unable to speak freely for fear of alienating public opinion, unable to pursue a sanctions option aggressively for fear of further eroding its alliance with Great Britain and the United States, French officials confined themselves to watching, listening and speculating as to how the Sub-Committee situation could give them the way out they had been seeking for so long. Initially the French delegation was hesitant about making its own submission to the Sub-Committee.[26]

The French Foreign Ministry eventually decided that a contribution to the Sub-Committee based on the nine areas of concern had to be made, although the final French submission reflected the wait-and-see attitude adopted by Bonnet and his delegation in New York. No strong desire for a particular result in the Security Council was overtly visible. The French submission was prepared in large part by Bernard Hardion, French Minister in Madrid, who, as has been demonstrated, had long been reluctant to engage in the public anti-Franco stance taken by the Quai d'Orsay. In his report, Hardion was forceful enough in outlining his criticisms of the regime, while at the same time he drew attention to areas in which he believed France had benefited from relations with Spain. For instance, in response to the question about Franco's attitude during the war, Hardion clearly demonstrated that for much of the war Spain had favored the Axis, yet also underlined the beginnings of Spanish relations with Algiers and the Free French in early 1943. On the military question, Hardion refuted Poland's assertion that Spain had aided Nazi Germany in atomic research and while he admitted that Spanish troops and fortifications had increased along the Pyrenees since the *guerrillero* attacks of 1944–1945, he emphasized that the "one cannot speak of serious fortifications" and that although one hundred and seventy thousand troops were in the Pyrenean region, their orders and disposition were "entirely defensive." Even on the subject of political internees and executions, Hardion noted that while the situation was serious, it was in decline compared to the period immediately following the civil war in 1939.[27] As a result, Hardion's answer on the subject of repression was augmented by a report from the Ministry of Foreign Affairs in Paris that detailed those cases of political prisoners which France had intervened in. These included those with ties to the French Resistance, such as Cristino García, as well as those who did not, such as thirty seven Spanish Socialists condemned in Alcala de Henares in early 1946. As of May 1946, France had intervened in one hundred and eighty seven cases.[28]

On the question of the wartime role of Franco's Government, the United States provided information from its collection of captured German and Italian documents that had previously been released in March alongside the Tripartite Statement.[29] Henri Bonnet observed that the opinion of the American delegate, Edward Stettinius, was at times closer to the French position than it was to British delegate Cadogan's. If the US delegate's attitude was symbolic of a possible change in the American position, then Bonnet believed that there was a possibility that would "permit the Sub-Committee to move much more quickly toward satisfactory conclusions," such as the consideration of collective action on the part of the Security Council.[30] Based on the British submission to the Sub-Committee, however, this scenario seemed unlikely. The British delegation focused its efforts on refuting the Polish allegation that Spanish troops along the Pyrenees represented a threat to France and international peace. Within Spain, British Military Attaché Brigadier William Torr had spent much of April assessing the frontier situation, as he had consistently since the end of the war. In an interview with the Spanish Army's Chief of Staff, General García-Valiño, on 3 April 1946, Torr, "in strictest confidence," was provided with exact figures on the Spanish Army's frontier strength.[31] In short, as Peter Garran noted in a Foreign Office minute, Cadogan had enough to "show that the Spanish army dispositions are purely defensive and to counter the exaggerated allegations" made in New York.[32] This was done, and Bonnet complained to Paris that the British delegate's response to the Sub-Committee, the first received, was "completely founded on the opinions of the British Ambassador in Madrid."[33]

While the Sub-Committee itself did not include any of the Permanent Members except France, it certainly had to be aware of their positions, as it wished to avoid seeing some of the first vetoes used when presenting its report. The Quai d'Orsay, through Hardion's submission, had not provided the new French representative to the United Nations, Alexandre Parodi, with a very strong mandate to act aggressively. By this stage the Quai d'Orsay probably preferred Parodi to be in such a position. While publicly France still appeared as a leader amongst nations concerned with the Spanish question, the opportunity for real French stewardship had ended in March when Bidault abandoned his own Security Council proposal. France's support of Poland's motion was, with few exceptions, not undertaken with enthusiasm. Within the Sub-Committee, France only hoped to avoid a situation that it appeared the British desired, namely the announcement of another statement of moral condemnation along the lines of the Tripartite Statement. The Quai d'Orsay hoped, at best, that the Sub-Committee might call for sanctions that paralleled the Pyrenean border closure. At the very least, they sought a motion that allowed France to retreat honorably from the Security Council by keeping the issue on the United Nations agenda and avoiding a conclusion of UN non-competence. Within the Sub-Committee, then, Parodi argued only for a recommendation in favor of some United Nations action, a position supported by the Polish representative Lange, while the Brazilian representative preferred a policy that corresponded more directly with the Tripartite Statement.[34]

The final report ended up being a compromise fostered by the Australian chair, Evatt. It rejected the Polish assertion that Spain posed an immediate threat to peace under article 39 of the Charter. It did agree, however, that the activities of the Franco regime could, in the future, present a threat to peace as defined under article 34. Thus it proposed that the Security Council endorse the Tripartite Statement and encourage the General Assembly to pass a motion recommending that all member states end diplomatic relations with Franco.[35] Representing the two extreme points of view within the Committee, Poland reserved decision on the question of immediate threat and Brazil reserved decision on the idea of recommending action to the General Assembly. Sir Alexander Cadogan was angry, for he deemed the Sub-Committee report "a put-up job by the Soviet Government" and he believed that the recommendations made "were doing violence to the Charter."[36] Alexandre Parodi, however, was very satisfied with the result of this process. He wrote to Bidault that the Sub-Committee's condemnation of the Franco regime, combined with the recommendation that the General Assembly act in calling for member states to end relations with Franco, constituted a "happy result and the promise that such a result should pass the Security Council without great difficulty."[37] Cadogan's comment gave René Massigli in London some trepidation, and he emphasized to Paris that the British attitude toward Franco had not changed at all, and in fact was further solidified by the return of Peter Garran from Madrid and his news that Franco was growing stronger domestically in light of the international pressure.[38] The Americans wished to avoid any direct action on the part of the UN, but they also hoped that they would not have to use their Security Council veto to stop this. The Sub-Committee proposal seemed to allow them such an outcome.[39] British officials, meanwhile, still detested the fact that the issue had appeared at the Security Council in the first place, but they conceded that the Sub-Committee's report "might have been worse."[40] Both powers wished to get the issue off the Security Council agenda and pass it onto the General Assembly.

In New York, Parodi was willing to live with the limitations sought by the United States and Great Britain. As long as the Security Council did not explicitly instruct the General Assembly to abandon the option of calling for diplomatic rupture, or cut out the Sub-Committee's recommendations from the text of the resolution, Parodi would be satisfied.[41] France, finally, appeared to have the international solution it had been seeking, one that could be held up at home as an initiative that responded to domestic concerns as well as one that ended France's isolated position of sanction enforcer *vis-à-vis* the Franco regime. Most significantly for the Foreign Ministry, it appeared to hold out the promise that France would no longer be divided from its western allies over the question of Spain. In an act that was both a demonstration of the relief felt by French officials and a reflection of their recent desperation over Spain, Parodi advised Jean Chauvel, Secretary-General of the Foreign Ministry, to extend a French apology to British and American officials he dealt with. Now that the end seemed near, he no doubt echoed the sentiments of many within the Quai d'Orsay, in admitting that a fear of domestic backlash had blinded France to some very basic international realities. He wrote to Chauvel that the apology should be, in effect, a French admission that the UN route was not well chosen, combined with a final plea for support now that the Spanish problem finally seemed resolvable via adoption of the Sub-Committee report.[42]

Carrying on a Public Policy of Anti-Francoism

Despite this apparent end to the debate, France's dilemma reappeared and would remain a concern for the rest of 1946. A United States motion which called for the Spanish question to be passed on to the General Assembly with the Sub-Committee conclusions and the phrase "or alternatively such other action" attached to the recommendation for diplomatic rupture, was adopted as friendly by the Sub-Committee members but vetoed by the Soviet Union in a full Security Council vote.[43] The Soviet representative, Andrei Gromyko, concluded that while the Sub-Committee drew the Council's attention to numerous documents which demonstrated the threat posed by Franco, it "has not dared to draw the right conclusion from all the material it used." Gromyko stated that Spain represented a threat under Article 39 and that the Security Council, under Article 41, had the right to call on member-states to end diplomatic relations with Franco without consulting the General Assembly.[44] By this point in time, Soviet leaders had abandoned any hope of finding unity with the US and Britain on Spain and were simply hoping to further discredit the West.[45] The Soviet veto did so by ensuring that the Spanish Question stayed on the Security Council agenda.

For the remainder of June, the Security Council scrambled in an effort to come up with a resolution to the dilemma created by the Soviet veto. In Paris, Georges Bidault had had great confidence in the aftermath of the Sub-Committee report that France's delicate conditions had been met. At one point, he even assured the Spanish delegation in Paris that Parodi would advocate a more moderate position in the Security Council than Bonnet had at the start of the Sub-Committee process.[46] Yet the Soviet veto had only strengthened American and British desires to be finished with Spain, while France was again hamstrung due to its public position which advocated some form of UN action.[47] In the aftermath of the Soviet veto, French policy in the Security Council seemed, finally, to unravel in the face of all its competing pressures. During the month of June, Parodi's voting was inconsistent, at best, although he did not offer up any comment. He voted alongside Poland, Mexico and the Soviet Union, and against Britain and the United States, to break relations with Spain. Two days later, he voted alongside the US and Britain, and against a Soviet veto, for an Australian proposal that would simply keep the Spanish question on the Security Council agenda. Later, he abstained on a Soviet resolution that would mandate that such reconsideration be undertaken by 1

September 1946.⁴⁸ Eventually the main points of the Australian resolution were passed, after numerous Soviet vetoes, and the Spanish question was referred to the General Assembly while remaining on the Security Council agenda.

Domestic opinion would not accept a full retreat during 1946. While the extent of coverage in the French political press of the United Nations debate on Spain was nothing like the situation from December 1945 through March 1946, the issue of Spain still produced passionate responses on the part of French politicians. The Prefect in Pau, a member of the MRP and a Resistance veteran, defended the border closure in a meeting with the Spanish Consul there, offering only to augment the personal security of the Consul if that was deemed necessary.⁴⁹ At a meeting of the Foreign Affairs Commission of the National Assembly in August, Gilbert de Chambrun argued that France's position on Spain, while admirable, still had to be augmented through a formal end of diplomatic relations with the Franco regime. Moreover, Commission members were so taken with a debate on how to proceed that they telephoned José Giral, leader of the Spanish Republican Government-in-exile, who lived in Paris at the time, and arranged for him to join the meeting that same day. Giral expressed his gratitude to France for its position on Spain and its economic sanctions, but reiterated that "there will not be a stable peace in the world as long as fascism remains in Spain."⁵⁰ In September 1946, the Deputy from Biarritz, Guy Petit, proposed a resolution in the National Assembly calling for a re-opening of the border due to the commercial damage it had caused France without any effect on Spain. This motion was harshly dealt with by the Commission and its *rapporteur*, Socialist Paul Rivet, who wrote that the policy, however unsuccessful to date, would ultimately prevail and that the "honor of France" was at stake.⁵¹ In an appearance before the Commission the same month, Bidault assured the members of the Assembly that France continued its policy of isolation toward Franco and continued the attempt to win over Great Britain and the United States to the French position.⁵² In actual fact no new efforts were undertaken by the Quai d'Orsay. The Quai's position was not to initiate, but rather to fall back on the status quo until there was evidence of public and party opinion softening on Spain. Rather than seeking to shape Western policy to suit French goals, as they had set out to do, the French, at least when it came to Spain, had to admit that the constraints of their own polity had deprived them of any policy-making power. Jean Chauvel, Secretary-General of the Quai d'Orsay informed British officials that France did not wish to have talks of any kind on Spain, but that if a resolution condemning Franco came up on the floor of the General Assembly, France would be obliged to reaffirm its "known doctrinal position."⁵³ In Madrid, Bernard Hardion indicated to Spanish Foreign Ministry Political Director de Erice that domestic pressures, combined with international pressures such as the continued American refusal to upgrade their diplomatic representative in Madrid to

Ambassadorial status, meant that France would not adopt a position contradictory to general world opinion.[54]

In December, the Spanish issue returned to the agenda of the United Nations, this time in the General Assembly.[55] When the Spanish issue arose in the First Committee (Political and Security Questions) of the General Assembly, labor leader Léon Jouhaux of the CGT spoke on behalf of France, suggesting sanctions against the import of foodstuffs from Spain, which was quickly rejected.[56] Jouhaux's position mirrored that of Parodi's in the Security Council Sub-Committee. France desired UN action above all, but was prepared to go with any action short of a moral condemnation, whether that was the ideal goal of UN sanctions which would end France's isolation on that question or something less severe. Beyond Jouhaux's one initiative, however, France played an almost non-existent role in the General Assembly debate. Along with its western allies and the Soviet Union, France on 12 December 1946 voted for a successful resolution which called for a continuation of the UN ban on Spanish membership and urged all member states to withdraw their Ambassadorial-level representatives from Madrid.[57]

Ending French Sanctions against Spain: 1946–1948

The French Mission in Madrid had opposed the border closure of February 1946 before it occurred and did not let up in its opposition when the measure was implemented. By the summer of 1946, its dissent was articulated in a paper submitted to Paris. The document emphasized that French suppliers and manufacturers who had markets in Spain would be replaced by British and American firms and advocated an immediate resumption of individual traffic across the border and a gradual resumption of commercial traffic by autumn, 1946.[58] In July 1946 French Minister Bernard Hardion traveled to Paris to reaffirm his belief that the time to preserve and develop France's economic interests in Spain was short.[59] By August, Hardion was permitted to open negotiations with the Spanish Foreign Minister, Martín Artajo, in order to lessen controls on the movement of individuals and families crossing the border. In return, France was allowed to participate in the Allied Trusteeship Council which was charged with the dispersal of German assets in Spain.[60]

As France's economic sanction remained unilateral, and the failure to bring the various elements of the Spanish opposition together sunk in, Hardion and his colleagues in the European Section of the Foreign Ministry argued that maintaining France's policy of sanctions against General Franco served little purpose. Indeed, as the European section emphasized in a note to Bidault, the United States and Great Britain, by remaining active in Spain economically and otherwise, and by limiting their criticism of the regime to the rhetoric of the

Tripartite Statement, had done more to encourage change inside Spain than had French policy.[61] These arguments had been made before, in 1946, to no avail. By 1947, however, they were quietly embraced as the basis for French policy toward Spain.

The most significant reason for this change was due to changes in the domestic context of French foreign policy-making. By 1947, the Spanish issue was no longer the focus of national attention that it had been. As with other debates about renewal and justice in the reconstruction of France, a pessimism about the potential for change set in. Spain was no longer the touchstone for French democrats that it had been in 1936 and early 1946. In his memoirs, Georges Bidault argued that he was nothing if not an antifascist, but he had bitter memories of the passions that were stirred up in the aftermath of Liberation over the question of Spain. In his mind, Franco was in Madrid to stay, and discussion of any harsh policy toward him could only be "abundantly, eloquently, passionately and uselessly discussed."[62] Thus French policy after 1946 gradually moved to match that developed by the United States and Great Britain. This meant that the western powers not only recognized Franco as the legitimate ruler of Spain, but also sought effective partnership with Spain economically and otherwise. The impact of the Cold War, and France's inability to influence its Allies on a peripheral issue like Spain, played a significant role here. A general pessimism about the inability of the Fourth Republic to be innovative in its foreign policy came to dominate the thinking of many who had been active with regard to the Spanish Question, as it did on other matters of foreign and international policy.[63]

Pessimism about the potential for change was accompanied by a strong dose of realism. In the southwest, where anti-Franco sentiment had been most lively, Chambers of Commerce began to press the government to reopen the border to trade in response to economic losses suffered by the various businesses in the region.[64] Even left-wing opinion in the region began to make the argument that the cost to the French economy outweighed the gain for democratic policy-making. The local head of the CGT in the Basses-Pyrénées publicly criticized the policy of closure and the Prefect reported to Paris that with the exception of Communists and some Socialists, the union leader spoke for most of the left in the area.[65] By the summer, coverage of French involvement in the Spanish question in the Socialist organ *Le Populaire de Paris* was reduced to a report covering a press conference of the Paris branch of the *Association France-Espagne*.[66] Only the most committed activists and the Communist Party maintained their established positions on the Spanish question.[67]

On 5 May 1947, Georges Bidault forwarded a series of letters on Spain to the Premier, Paul Ramadier. This batch of correspondence primarily came from local Chambers of Commerce, parliamentarians and other protesting the French policy of border closure with Spain. This was not an insignificant date, for it was the same day that the French Communist Party left the government.[68] By the summer, the Foreign Minister was willing, for the first time, to speak openly in the National Assembly about the possibility of opening the border to commercial traffic.[69] In September, French officials in Paris and Washington held talks with American officials prior to the UN General Assembly meeting, which once again considered the Spanish case.[70] The Quai's instructions to the French delegation were clear: the French delegation would abstain from voting on any anti-Franco measure, as Hardion, the US and Great Britain had all requested.[71] Negotiations with the Spanish government, directed by Jean Chauvel and Bernard Hardion, resulted in a reopening of the Pyrenean frontier in February 1948 and by May, the September 1945 trade agreement between the two states was restored.[72] At the same time, the Ministry of the Interior officially adopted a policy, shared with the Spanish Government, to "encourage the movement of certain Spanish exiles" from the southwest to the interior of France as they represented a "threat to public order."[73]

The trends in international and European politics which had made acceptance of General Franco and his regime viable continued to develop. Certainly Spain remained an exception in Europe, and the United States did not seriously consider making Franco's regime eligible for Marshall Plan economic aid.[74] Yet the process of increasing openness toward the Spanish regime began. In the United States, Ambassador José Lequerica orchestrated a Spanish Lobby in Congress which drew upon Catholics, Republicans and committed anti-communists.[75] The more the Cold War developed, the more important Spain became as a necessary strategic point in American strategic planning, a point underlined by George Kennan's Policy Planning Staff October 1947 document which called for a "normalization" of US-Spanish relations and thus laid the groundwork for what was to come.[76] The American rationale increasingly changed from a focus on economic and democratic reconstruction issues which had defined the Marshall Plan program to a more overtly military definition of security (although the two were not mutually exclusive).[77] By 1950, with the Korean War raging, the United Nations rescinded its December 1946 resolution which had called upon all member states not to appoint Ambassadorial-level representatives to Madrid, and Great Britain and the United States immediately appointed fully-fledged diplomats to Madrid. US Department of Defense officials initiated discussions with the State Department concerning Spain's military role in a potential war with the Soviet Union, which would primarily be to provide installations for US forces. In 1951, President Truman authorized military talks with the Spaniards and by September 1953, agreements which allowed US access to Spanish military bases, military aid for the Spanish army, and economic assistance for Spain were signed.[78]

Naturally there were still some limits on what the French government could do, and they could not join their allies in completely parallel policies. Public opinion may have been willing to accept a renewal of trade, but overt military cooperation remained out of the question. This was true not only in France, but in a number of European states, and it led, in 1948, to French and European insistence that Spain not even be considered for admission to the military alliance known as the Western European Union (WEU).[79] Ultimately, however, the importance of Spain could not be denied. Quietly, where security issues of mutual interest existed, as in North Africa, French military officials pursued contacts and arrangements with the Spaniards.[80] The strategic value of Spain was not overlooked, and due to North African colonial defense, it has been rightly argued that France's strategic interests in Spain were greater than those of the United States.[81] Indeed, colonial issues came to dominate French–Spanish relations in the 1950s, and created a number of rough spots as Morocco headed toward independence in 1956.[82]

In general, the primary goal of French policy after 1947 was to move toward accepting Spain and avoiding any repeat of the intense debate of 1946.[83] Economic exchanges grew tremendously, and the May 1948 commercial accord was renewed and expanded upon in June 1949. Traditional cultural exchanges between the two states also were reinvigorated.[84] Thus, just as the Americans were doing, the French slowly opened the door to Spain internationally, opposing Spanish exclusion from the Organization for European Economic Cooperation (OEEC) in 1948 and allowing Spain to participate in the technical organizations of the United Nations.[85] The development of improved relations with General Franco's regime did not come without consequences, and required France to grant Spain the occasional political favor. An end to privileges and protections for Spanish exiles culminated on 7 September 1950 when the Spanish Communist Party in exile (PCE) and its sister party, the Catalan Unified Socialists (PSUC), were banned in France, and two hundred and eighty-eight Spanish communists were arrested and either deported or assigned designated residences by the French Government. Operation Boléro-Paprika, as it was called, was inspired not only by growing anti-communism in the French Government and the Ministry of the Interior, but also by repeated Spanish complaints about the many activities of Spanish political refugees which were tolerated within France.[86] By the end of the year, Bernard Hardion was named a full ambassador in Madrid, ending the final French sanction against the regime of General Francisco Franco.

Summary

In a December 1946 note to Bidault summarizing Franco-Spanish relations, the Quai's European section made an attempt to account for the year's dilemmas on the Spanish question, and began with the acknowledgment that French action had failed and the policy that had been attempted was now "inoperable." The blame for the direction taken, however, was not the Quai's, but rather the "near unanimity of French opinion that demanded the departure of Franco and the closure of our Spanish border and the interruption of all commercial relations with the Madrid government in order to achieve this goal." The value of the French attempt to coordinate policy with the Anglo-Americans was defended, and the Quai argued that if the US and Britain had joined France, tripartite action would have had "a considerable effect, potentially engendering agitation and contributing to the eventual departure of Franco." Without such joint initiative, however, the Quai accepted the fact that an isolated French effort had been used by Franco to rally support behind him, and had thus contributed to the strengthening of his position, and weakened the already divided Spanish opposition.[87] From this point on, there was no real option open to the French other than to wait for domestic opinion to change and then align France's policy toward Spain with that of its western allies. As has been shown, this became possible over the course of 1947 and 1948.

The Quai's year-end assessment concluded with an acknowledgment of 1946's key lesson: the United States and Great Britain had growing interests in Spain, economic and otherwise, and these permanent interests would not be risked, even if the Americans and British detested Franco.[88] Fear of conflict, civil war, and the potential for Soviet-influenced Communist success in Spain, as well as growing economic benefits derived from trade, limited the Anglo-Americans to a policy of moral condemnation alone. The consequences of the Cold War not only impacted Anglo-American policy in Spain, but also led France's Allies to be increasingly wary when it came to considering policy initiatives that came from a French Government dominated by leftists. As Keith Hamilton has written, the British throughout 1946 were determined that "neither an ungodly France nor an unholy Russia would have their way in Spain."[89] On the subject of Spain, France was forced to remain an ally without real say or sway in inter-allied councils until coming to conclusions that resulted in the same policy toward Franco pursued by its Allies.

The policy-makers from the Quai d'Orsay, on the one hand, may have seemed to have beaten back the arguments of the Resistance-affiliated movement in favor of Spanish Republicanism. They themselves, and particularly those who served in Madrid like Bernard Hardion, believed that France could accomplish much as a western power and as an economic force by remaining in Madrid. Yet as the tone of the document from late 1946 suggests, they also took some pride in the effort made to reconcile this realpolitik assessment of the situation with the domestic calls for a more assertive, pro-democratic, pro-Republican policy in Spain. The role of France in the Spanish Question was not only one of retreat back to the position of the Great Britain and the United States, but also one of attempting to forge ahead and shape western European reconstruction in a particularly French and a particularly Republican manner. That this failed when it came to Spain was evident, and it was accepted. But it was done so with only some regret.

CONCLUSION

France, Spain and Post-War Foreign Policy in Europe

The intensity of the domestic debate over Spain that occurred in France between 1944 and 1946 led the government down a number of roads that were unanticipated, such as refugee protection and intervention for Spanish Republicans facing deaths sentences in Spain. Ultimately such actions did not represent the policies that emerged from France's Allies in Britain and the United States as the Cold War developed. Nor, ultimately, did they represent the inclinations of French officials in Madrid and the Quai d'Orsay. By focusing on the debate that occurred in France, however, and not simply on a narrative description of French–Spanish relations, one can appreciate some truths about the "lingering" impact of the Second World War and its ideological discourses, and the direct connection between those and the reconstruction of France and Europe.

When in early 1946 the French Government imposed sanctions on the Franco regime through the closure of their common Pyrenean border to all individual and commercial traffic, it became the only western state to take action against Spain that moved beyond a policy of rhetorical condemnation. This action was preceded and followed by intense efforts to convince the United States and Great Britain to join in the sanctioning of Franco's Spain. Indeed, France sought Allied support for their policy both in private, within the alliance, and publicly, in the forum of the United Nations. All these efforts failed. What was behind the French effort to adopt a policy of sanction and what motivated the effort to broaden it? Did the Spanish case demonstrate a real division between the leftist, Resistance-inspired French and the emerging Cold War realpolitik of the United States? The purpose of this work has been to examine that question and extrapolate what significance the Spanish case had for our understanding of the post-war era and the foreign policy aspects of European reconstruction and the onset of the Cold War.

Recent historiography concerning France's foreign policy has emphasized that it was the French who were as much the realists as anyone. Georges-Henri Soutou has written that France was 'deeply committed' to the Cold War conflict and the emerging western alliance.[1] William I. Hitchcock has asserted that France successfully influenced alliance policies in the remaking of Western Europe, economically, militarily and politically as it pursued a 'national strategy' to reclaim a leadership role in the world.[2] Many have argued that the groundwork for this successful period of influence was laid early on in the post-war, amidst many other pressing concerns including the political and social tensions that arose from the Resistance experience and reorganization of the constitution.[3] Where differences between the realpolitik inclinations of French leaders and their Allied counterparts have been found, it is now argued that domestic politics, and especially the strength of the French Communist Party, accounted for this, rather than a fundamental difference in worldview; the practical impact of this was simply to curtail France's public display of pro-alliance sentiment, at least until the Communist Party left government in May 1947.[4] In private, however, French foreign policy-makers, alongside their American and British colleagues, shared a common view of the need to rebuild Europe in the face of potential Soviet aggression. This created the likelihood that a question on the periphery of European politics, like that of Spain, would be seen through the lens of the emerging Cold War rather than from the perspective of the Resistance-inspired ideas of 'justice' and 'renovation'. As this work has shown, that motivation and its corresponding pro-Western Alliance sentiment was very much present in French policy-making toward Spain. In addition, it was complemented by the analysis that Franco could not be removed from power without difficulty, and the economic assessment of Spain's value for France's reconstruction efforts was considerable. The result of these impulses was to create a realist-inspired policy that saw a desire to build upon and expand wartime relations between non-Vichy France and Spain. In this sense, the argument developed by William I. Hitchcock, Michael Creswell and others with reference to French foreign policy in post-war Germany holds in other cases like that of Spain.

Yet government bureaucrats, politicians and journalists were also products of the wartime experience and the Resistance, in one way or another. In French relations toward Franco's Spain, there was a policy grounded in conceptions of democracy and morality that the ideals of the Resistance experience spoke to. The basis of that influence was the ability of the Resistance, in all its manifestations (including within the Quai d'Orsay), to cast the Spanish question in light of issues that drew upon the power of France's own Resistance myth. The rhetoric of the period after fascism enabled many to cast the Spanish nation as one of Republicans who had contributed so much to France's own liberation. Thus France had an obligation to apply its influence to their cause using the lessons of justice and dignity, not power politics, as inspiration. All of these themes repeated in the French press, helped influence the direction of the French Government's policy toward General Francisco Franco's Spanish regime. Recognition of this type of Resistance influence over conceptions of French foreign policy in the immediate aftermath of liberation is an important one.

As Tony Judt has argued, the scale of the Second World War and the devastation it created, politically and otherwise, led to a period where reconstruction and renewal was grounded in a dismissal not only of the wartime leadership and political system, but also a replacement of the pre-war conception of politics as usual.[5] While many historians, including Judt, question the longevity of this impulse, it did lead to significant policy change in areas like social welfare and economic planning.[6] Others have gone further, casting the period from the middle of the war through 1947 as a period of unprecedented "anti-fascist unity."[7] More was at work here than simply the triumph of Communism as a political force in Western Europe. As the Spanish case demonstrates, the moment was unique for the many ways in which traditional political leaders, the veterans of Resistance, and public opinion could be united by the concepts of renewal and justice. Moreover, these sentiments were powerful in the realm of international policy just as they were strong in terms of domestic reconstruction. The policies that emerged from the debate over Spain that occurred inside France confirmed the fact that many across France and in the government shared a sense of sympathy with the arguments of the Resistance to "remake" France in the aftermath of war, occupation and collaboration. The cause of Spanish Republicanism came to represent a sense of the "new politics" desired by many, both in terms of its goal, the defeat of Franco, and in its natural champion, Liberated France.

If we are to truly understand the post-war reconstruction of Europe, it is essential to see both the impulses for realistic assessments of national security and those for justice and renewal as equally legitimate. On the debate over Spain, the French Resistance, in its broadest form, succeeded in transforming French politics and policy and infusing it with a sense of justice. While in hindsight it is right to acknowledge this as a "moment" rather than a transformation, it is also correct to assert, as Geoff Eley does, that to read "Cold War divisions back into this time distorts its dynamics."[8] Yet those ideas associated with the Cold War were there, and emerging, during this same period. As the case of Spain demonstrates, as France moved toward its role within the western alliance, it did so awkwardly, with both the significance of Resistance rhetoric and imagery about an idealized new world competing with a realistic assessment of France's role as a member of the Alliance and European leader.

The inability of the French Government to balance both impulses and create a policy that combined aspects of change desired by the Resistance and the French public with a practical policy that could be adopted by France's allies in

Great Britain and the United States led to frustration, pessimism over France's role in Europe, and significant criticism of the Government. Such feelings were not just limited to political partisans of the left, but were shared by many in the Government itself. That fact alone suggests the importance of both realpolitik and justice as real factors in policy-making in Liberated France. The reality of the Cold War was accepted, even embraced by some, but for many it was also harsh. The European department of the Quai d'Orsay took the opportunity in a memorandum to underline this as early as February 1945:

> The Franco regime might last much longer than we generally think. It is necessary to take account of the example of the American government and the British government, in our relations with Spain, if we wish not to risk not only an economic rupture which will have grave repercussions on the reconstruction of our country but equally the loss of [economic] positions that will be taken up by others and will be difficult to recover later on, even if under a republican government disposed in our favor.[9]

NOTES

Introduction: **France and Spain in the aftermath of the Second World War**

1. Tony Judt, *Postwar: A History of Europe since 1945* (New York, 2005), 10.
2. Lynn Davis, The *Cold War Begins: Soviet–American Conflict over Eastern Europe* (Princeton, 1974).
3. Geoff Eley, *Forging Democracy: The History of the Left in Europe, 1850–2000* (Oxford, 2002), 287.
4. Eley, *Forging Democracy*, 288.
5. Eley, *Forging Democracy*, 288.
6. Mark Mazower, 'The Strange Triumph of Human Rights, 1933–1950', *The Historical Journal* 47:2 (2004), 386–7.
7. Jean-Pierre Rioux, *The Fourth Republic, 1944–1958*. trans. G. Rodgers (Cambridge, 1987), 48.
8. Megan Koreman, *The Expectation of Justice: France, 1944–1946* (Durham, NC, 1999), 4.
9. Koreman, *Expectation*, 4.
10. Koreman, *Expectation*, 4.
11. Paul Preston, *A Concise History of the Spanish Civil War* (London, 1996), 6.
12. Michael Richards, *A Time of Silence: Civil War and the Culture of Repression in Franco's Spain* (Cambridge, 1998), 30–1.
13. Gerhard L. Weinberg, *A World at Arms: A Global History of World War II* (Cambridge, 1994), 2.
14. Alan S. Milward, 'Bad Memories', *Times Literary Supplement*, 14 April 2000.
15. Judt, *Postwar*, 27.
16. Melvyn Leffler, *A Preponderance of Power: National Security, the Truman Administration and the Cold War* (Stanford, 1992), 10–15.
17. William I. Hitchcock, *France Restored: Cold War Diplomacy and the Quest for Leadership in Europe, 1944–1954* (Chapel Hill, NC, 1998), 2–3.
18. Andrew Shennan, *Rethinking France: Plans for Renewal, 1940–1946* (Oxford, 1989), 66.
19. Koreman, *Expectation*, 2.
20. Shennan, *Rethinking France*, 37–8.
21. Shennan, *Rethinking France*, 40–1.
22. Anne Dulphy. *La politique de France à l'égard de l'Espagne de 1945 à 1955: Entre idéologie et réalisme* (Paris, 2002), 735–773.

23 Dulphy, *La politique de France à l'égard de l'Espagne*, 684–734.
24 Patricia Clavin. 'Defining Transnationalism', *Contemporary European History* 14:4 (2005), 421–39.
25 Eugen Weber, *The Hollow Years: France in the 1930s* (New York, 1996), 141.
26 Julian Jackson, *The Popular Front in France: Defending Democracy, 1934–1938* (Cambridge, 1988), 208; Robert J. Young, *In Command of France: French Foreign Policy and Military Planning, 1933–1940* (Cambridge, MA, 1978), 139–40; Geoffrey Warner, 'France and Non-Intervention in Spain, July–August 1936', *International Affairs* 38:2 (1962). See also Paul Preston and Helen Graham, 'The Popular Front and the Struggle Against Fascism' in *The Popular Front in Europe*, eds. Paul Preston and Helen Graham (London, 1987), 12.
27 David Wingeate Pike, *Les Français et la Guerre d'Espagne, 1936–1939* (Paris, 1975), 337.
28 Cited in Narciso Alba and Jacques Issorel, 'La France des libertés vue par les intellectuels espagnols avant et après la guerre civile' in *Les Français et la Guerre d'Espagne: Actes du Colloque de Perpignan* eds. Jean Sagnes and Sylvie Caucanas (Perpignan, 1990), 414.
29 Stephen Spender, *The Thirties and After: Poetry, Politics, People (1932–75)* (London, 1978), 82.
30 'Introduction to the Morningside Edition' Robert O. Paxton, *Vichy France: Old Guard and New Order, 1940–1944* (New York, 1982), xii.
31 This included the chief of state of the new French state, Marshal Philippe Pétain, for many of the generals now in power in Spain, including Franco, had been his allies in the Moroccan colonial wars of the 1920s and he was predisposed to share, in general terms, their political views about democracy. Matthieu Séguéla, *Pétain-Franco: les secrets d'une alliance* (Paris, 1992), 18–23.
32 Séguéla, *Pétain-Franco*, 62.

1 The French Refugee Crisis and Economic Warfare in Spain, 1942–1944

1 Paul Preston, *Franco* (London, 1993), 474–81; William A. Hoisington, Jr., *The Casablanca Connection: French Colonial Policy 1936–1943* (Chapel Hill, 1984), 194–223; Arthur J. Funk, *The Politics of 'TORCH': The Allied Landings and the Algiers Putsch, 1942* (Lawrence, KS, 1974), 150–261; Michel Junot, *Opération Torch* (Paris, 2001); Keith Sainsbury, *The North African Landings, 1942: A Strategic Decision* (London, 1976); Richard W. Steele, *The First Offensive, 1942: Roosevelt, Marshall and the Making of American Strategy* (Bloomington, IN, 1973); Denis Smyth, 'Screening TORCH: Allied Counter-Intelligence and the Spanish Threat to the Secrecy of the Allied Invasion of French North Africa in November, 1942', *Intelligence and National Security* 4 (1989), 335–56; David Walker, 'OSS and Operation Torch' *Journal of Contemporary History* 22 (1987), 667–79.
2 Denis Smyth, 'Franco and the Allies in the Second World War' in *Spain and the Great Powers in the Twentieth Century*, ed. S. Balfour and P. Preston (London, 1999), 204; Javier Tussell, *Franco, España y la II Guerra Mundial: Entre el Eje y la Neutralidad* (Madrid, 1995), 357–67.
3 Funk, *Politics of TORCH*, 253–5; Hoisington, *The Casablanca Connection*, 224–32;

Julian Hurstfield, *America and the French Nation, 1939–1945* (Chapel Hill, 1985), 172–3, 185.
4 Michel Catala, *Les relations franco-espagnoles pendant la Deuxième Guerre Mondiale: rapprochement nécessaire, reconciliation impossible, 1939–1944* (Paris, 1997), 235.
5 Paxton, *Vichy France*, 480.
6 For the response of the French government to Republican refugees in 1939, see Martin S. Alexander, 'France, the Collapse of Republican Spain and the Approach of General War: National Security, War Economics and the Spanish Refugees, 1938–1940' in *Spain in an International Context, 1936–1959*, ed. Christian Leitz and David J. Dunthorn (New York and Oxford, 1999), 105–28.
7 The historiography of French–Spanish relations during the war is small: Michel Catala, *Les relations franco-espagnoles* considers all three French entities in Spain while focusing primarily on Vichy; Émilienne Eychenne, *Pyrénées de la Liberté* (Toulouse, 1998) and Robert Belot, *Aux frontières de la liberté: Vichy–Madrid–Alger–Londres, s'évader de France sous l'Occupation* (Paris, 1998) emphasize the refugee crisis itself, with Belot providing extensive detail on the nature of the refugee movement as well as on the actions of French officials in Spain but not on other issues; Matthieu Séguéla, *Pétain-Franco* is concerned with Vichy and Jean-Marc Delaunay, *Des Palais en Espagne: l'Ecole des hautes etudes hispaniques et la Casa de Veláquez au coeur des relations franco-espagnoles du XXe siècle* (Madrid, 1994) with the French community in Spain.
8 Belot, *Aux frontières*, 33–42.
9 Eychenne, *Pyrénées de la Liberté*, 107–9 and Belot, *Aux frontières*, 104–10.
10 Belot, *Aux frontières*, 612.
11 NARA, RG 59 740.0011EW1939/26442, Frost (Barcelona) to Hull, 11 December 1942; See also MAE, ACG 817, Political Affairs, Foreign Affairs Commissariat to Massigli, 8 January 1944.
12 MAE, ACG 813, Consulate, Tetuán to Resident General, Rabat, 14 January 1943.
13 MAE, ACG 813, Foreign Relations Secretariat to Malaise, 22 January 1943.
14 MAE, ACG 749, Delaye to Bergerel, 18 December 1942.
15 MAE, ACG 813, Consulate, Tetuán to Nogues, (Rabat), 14 January 1943.
16 MAE, ACG 813, Note, Foreign Relations Secretariat, 15 January 1943.
17 MAE, PAAP, Piétri, 15, Piétri to Laval, 4 March 1943.
18 MAE, ACG 749, Delaye to Bergerel, 18 December 1942.
19 MAE, ACG 1067, Malaise to Algiers, 9 January 1943.
20 NARA, RG 59, 740.0011EW1939/27003, Memo. of Meeting, Giraud's Representatives with Hull, 28 December 1942.
21 NARA, RG 59, 740.0011EW1939/27838. State Dept. to Roosevelt, 11 February 1943.
22 MAE, ACG 1275, Foreign Relations Secretariat to Giraud, 'Note sur l'attitude du Gouvernement Espagnol a l'égard des autorités d'Alger', 25 May 1943.
23 Carlton J.H. Hayes. *Wartime Mission in Spain, 1942–1945* (New York, 1945), 105.
24 Hayes, *Wartime Mission*, 114.
25 MAE, ACG 1275, Hayes to Jordana, 14 January. 1943, enclosed in Hayes to de Saint-Hardouin, 15 January 1943.
26 *FRUS*, 1943 I, 255, Hayes to Hull, 24 January 1943.

27 *FRUS* 1943, I, 257–8, Hayes to Hull, 28 January 1943.
28 NARA, RG 169, UD8-Box 79-File 900, Combined Committee on North Africa to North African Economic Board, 21 June 1943.
29 Viscount Templewood. *Ambassador on Special Mission* (London, 1946), 226.
30 Hurstfield, *America and the French Nation*, 165–6.
31 TNA: PRO, FO 371/32699/15276, Foreign Office to Farquhar, 9 December 1942.
32 TNA: PRO, FO 371/32160/Z10540, Speaight to Strang, 19 December 1942.
33 TNA: PRO, FO 371/32699/W16114, Hoare to FO, 29 November 1942.
34 Templewood, *Ambassador on Special Mission*, 226.
35 MAEE, R2182/ 6–7, British Embassy to Jordana, 29 December 1942.
36 TNA: PRO, FO 371/34738/C2146/9/41, Speaight to Creswell [Madrid], 27 February 1943.
37 TNA: PRO, FO 660/ 56, Minutes of Meeting, Political and Economic Council, 30 January 1943.
38 TNA: PRO, FO 371/34737/C11568, Hoare to FO, 31 January 1943.
39 TNA: PRO, FO 371/34738/C2231/9/41, Foreign Office to British Embassy Washington, 5 March 1943.
40 TNA: PRO, FO 371/34738/C1855/9/41,de Gaulle to Eden, 12 February 1943.
41 Catala, *Relations franco-espagnols*, 238.
42 MAE, ACG 813, Foreign Relations Secretariat to Malaise, 22 January 1943.
43 NARA, RG 169 Entry UD8-Box 68, Minutes of Iberian Peninsula Cross-Trade Committee, Washington, 11 August. 1943; Wiley (Algiers) to Hull, 28 June 1943; NARA, RG 169, Entry UD8-Box 70, Minutes of Iberian Peninsula Cross-Trade Committee, Washington, 3 November 1943.
44 NARA, RG 169, Entry UD 8 Box 68, US Embassy Madrid to Hull, 16 July 1943.
45 *FRUS* 1943, I, 260–1, Hayes to Hull, 15 February 1943.
46 MAEE, R1372/22, Notes of meeting, Franco with Moltke, 3 December 1943.
47 MAE, ACG, 1275, Malaise to Ronin, 13 December 1942.
48 Catala, *Relations franco-espagnols*, 240–1.
49 Catala, *Relations franco-espagnols*, 243.
50 MAEE, R2167/140, Piétri to Spanish Foreign Ministry, 5 January 1943.
51 MAE, PAAP, Piétri, 15, Piétri to Vichy, 5 and 19 December 1942.
52 François Piétri. *Mes années d'Espagne: 1940–1948* (Paris, 1954), 199–202; MAE, ACG 813, Malaise to Algiers, 15 February 1943.
53 Piétri, *Mes années,* 195.
54 MAE, ACG 813, Malaise to Algiers, 15 February 1943.
55 Piétri, *Mes années,* 202.
56 Belot, *Aux frontières,*196.
57 Belot, *Aux frontières,* 196–7.
58 Piétri, *Mes années,* 182.
59 This quote, which Belot thinks is from Admiral Delaye, is cited in Belot, *Aux frontières,* 201.
60 Belot, *Aux frontières,* 235–9.
61 MAE, ACG 815, 'Note sur l'attitude du Gouvernement Espagnol a l'égard des réfugiés français', 12 July 1943; MAE, ACG 813, Malaise to Foreign Relations Secretariat, 15 February 1943.

62 MAE, ACG 813, Malaise to Giraud, 7 March 1943.
63 *FRUS* 1943, I, 262–3, Hayes to Hull, 6 March 1943.
64 MAE, ACG 1275, Clarac to Saint-Hardouin, 22 March 1943.
65 MAE, ACG 813, Note, Foreign Relations Secretariat, 25 March 1943.
66 *FRUS* 1943 I, 263–5, Hayes to Hull, 8 March 1943.
67 MAE, ACG 1275, Clarac to Saint-Hardouin, 22 March 1943.
68 MAE, ACG 1275, Clarac to Saint-Hardouin, 22 March 1943.
69 MAE, ACG 813, Note, Foreign Relations Secretariat, 25 March 1943.
70 MAE, ACG 814, Note, Foreign Relations Secretariat, 19 June 1943.
71 MAE, ACG 814, De Marcel to Saint-Hardouin, 22 May 1943.
72 SHAT, 5 P 20, Bernard to Devinck, 30 June; 29 August; 25 September 1943.
73 MAE, ACG 1275, Saint-Hardouin to Giraud, 30 December 1942.
74 MAE, ACG 1275, Hayes to Jordana, 14 January 1943, enclosed in Hayes to Saint-Hardouin, 15 January 1943.
75 MAE, ACG 1275, Enclosed in Clarac to Saint-Hardouin, 28 February 1943, and Clarac, report, 22 March 1943.
76 Norman J.W. Goda, *Tomorrow the World: Hitler, Northwest Africa, and the Path Toward America* (College Station, TX, 1998), 197; Preston, *Franco*, 482.
77 MAE, ACG 1275, Note, 13 January 1943.
78 *FRUS* 1943 I, 261–2, Hayes to Hull, 28 February 1943.
79 MAE, ACG 1067, External Commerce Secretariat to Pettit, 18 January 1943.
80 MAE, ACG 1275, Foreign Relations Secretariat to Clarac, 4 February 1943.
81 MAE, ACG 1275, Report, Clarac, 22 March 1943.
82 MAE, ACG 1275, Clarac to Saint-Hardouin, 12 March 1943.
83 Smyth, 'Franco and the Allies', 191, 204; Preston, *Franco*, 482–505.
84 MAE, ACG 1275, Report, Clarac, 22 March 1943.
85 MAE, PAAP, Piétri, 15, Piétri to Laval, 17 April 1943.
86 MAE, ACG 1275, Malaise to Saint-Hardouin, 15 April 1943.
87 Smyth, 'Franco and the Allies', 204.
88 NARA, RG 59, 740.0011EW1939/29304, Beaulac to Hull, 17 April 1943.
89 MAE, ACG 1275, Malaise to Saint-Hardouin, 22 May 1943
90 MAE, ACG 1275, Giraud to Franco, 16 May 1943.
91 MAEE, R2071/10, Directorate of Foreign Economic Affairs to Sangróniz, 31 October1944.
92 MAE, ACG 1067, Saint-Hardouin to External Commerce Secretariat, 9 January 1943; MAE, ACG 813, Note, Foreign Relations Secretariat, 15 January 1943.
93 MAE, ACG 1067, Nogues to Haussaire, 12 and 22 December 1942.
94 MAEE, R2071/10 Directorate of Foreign Economic Affairs to Sangróniz, 31 October 1944; MAE, ACG 1067, External Affairs Commissariat to Resident-General, Rabat, 7 and 27 May 1943; MAE, ACG 1067, Nogues to Giraud, 5 June 1943.
95 Smyth, 'Franco and the Allies', 188.
96 Christian Leitz, 'Nazi Germany and Francoist Spain, 1936–1945' in *Spain and the Great Powers*, ed. Balfour and Preston, 137–8.
97 MacGregor Knox, *Mussolini Unleashed, 1939–1941: Politics and Strategy in Fascist Italy's Last War* (Cambridge, 1982), 240.

98 Norman J.W. Goda, 'Germany's Conception of Spain's Strategic Importance, 1940–1941' in *Spain in an International Context,* ed. Leitz and Dunthorn, 129–47. See also Goda, *Tomorrow the World.*
99 Stanley G. Payne, *The Franco Regime 1936–1975* (London, 2000), 268.
100 Goda, 'Germany's Conception', 132–8.
101 Payne, *The Franco Regime,* 271–8.
102 Gerald Kleinfeld and Lewis A. Tombs, *Hitler's Spanish Legion: The Blue Division in Russia* (Carbondale, IL, 1979).
103 Denis Smyth. *Diplomacy and Strategy of Survival: British Policy and Franco's Spain, 1940–1941* (Cambridge, 1986), 4–5.
104 W.N. Medlicott, *The Economic Blockade, vol. II* (London, 1959), 547.
105 Leitz, 'Programm BÄR: The Supply of German War Material to Spain, 1943–1944' in *Spain in an International Context,* ed. Leitz and Dunthorn, 172–3.
106 TNA:PRO, FO 837/794/Z2174, Thomson, 'Report on Allied Economic Policy in Spain', 29 February 1944.
107 Sir Llewellyn Woodward, *British Foreign Policy in the Second World War, Volume IV* (London, 1975), 14.
108 James W. Cortada, *United States-Spanish Relations, Wolfram and World War II* (Barcelona, 1971), 16–17.
109 Smyth, 'Franco and the Allies', 186–7; For Anglo-American division over wolfram and oil policy in Spain, see Christian Leitz, *Economic Relations between Nazi Germany and Franco's Spain, 1936–1945* (Oxford, 1996), 186–91.
110 TNA: PRO, FO 371/36253/Z2022, Hoare to Foreign Office, 11 February 1943.
111 TNA: PRO, FO 371/36253/Z2022, Minute, Rumbold, 13 February 1943.
112 Woodward, *British Foreign Policy, IV,* 11–12.
113 TNA: PRO, FO 837/794/ Z2174, Thomson, 'Report on Allied Economic Policy in Spain', 29 February 1944.
114 NARA, RG 169, Entry UD 8 Box 69, Georgianna Pouzzner to H. K. Fleming, 15 January 1943.
115 TNA: PRO, FO 371/36253/Z3609, Macmillan to FO, 14 March 1943.
116 TNA: PRO, FO 371/36254/Z4238, Hoare to Foreign Office, 3 April 1943.
117 TNA: PRO, FO 371/36254/Z4111, Matthews to Mack, 29 March 1943.
118 TNA: PRO, FO 371/36254/Z4327, Minute, Speaight, 13 April 1943.
119 TNA: PRO, FO 371/36255/Z4890,Yencken to Strang, 12 April 1943; TNA: PRO, FO 371/36255/Z4915, Minute, Rumbold, 23 April 1943; See also MAE, ACG 1067, Undersecretary of External Commerce to French Missions, Madrid and Lisbon, 8 April 1943.
120 Medlicott, *Economic Blockade, vol. II,* 548; MAE, ACG 1067, Clarac to Algiers, 27 April 1943.
121 TNA: PRO, FO 837/794/Z2174, Thomson, 'Report on Allied Economic Policy in Spain', 29 February 1944.
122 NARA, RG 169, Entry 157-Box 1- File BL-59, Memo., Bureau of Economic Warfare-Blockade and Supply Division, 2 December 1942; Report on Trade Program for French Africa, Bureau of Economic Warfare-Blockade and Supply Division, April 1943.

Notes to pp. 24–7

123 NARA, RG 169, Entry 157-Box 1- File BL-59, Report on Trade Program for French Africa, Bureau of Economic Warfare-Blockade and Supply Division, April 1943.
124 NARA, RG 169, Entry 161- Box 976, Murphy to Hull, 21 April 1943.
125 NARA, RG 169, Entry UD 8- Box 70, Hayes to Hull, 2 January 1943.
126 MAE, ACG 1067, Clarac to Algiers, 27 April 1943.
127 NARA, RG 169, Entry UD 8- Box 79- File 900, Culbertson to Hull, 19 April 1943.
128 NARA, RG 169 Entry UD 8- Box 70, Murphy to Hull, 17 April 1943.
129 SHAT, 5 P 20, Delaye to Giraud, 17 April 1943; various reports, Allais, 'Mission Navale de Gibraltar'.
130 Jean Lacouture, *De Gaulle: The Rebel, 1890–1944* trans. Patrick O'Brian (New York, 1990), 434–52. See also Jean-Baptiste Duroselle, *L'Abîme 1939–1945* (Paris, 1982), 413–42.
131 MAE, ACG 1275, Note, Massigli, 11 September 1943.
132 For the SR-BCRA intelligence conflict, see Belot, *Aux frontières*, 573–8.
133 MAE, ACG 815, Boyer-Mas to Massigli, 7 July 1943.
134 MAE, ACG 1067, Minutes, first meeting, 1 June 1943, and subsequent meetings; for minutes for 1944, see TNA: PRO, FO 371/42199.
135 MAE, ACG 1067, Decree, Diethelm, 21 August 1943.
136 MAE, ACG 1067, Massigli to Puaux, 2 September 1943, MAE, ACG 1067; MAEE, R2071, Directorate of Foreign Economic Affairs, Memo., 'Imports of Moroccan Phosphates, 1943–4', 15 September 1944.
137 MAE, ACG 1067, Massigli to CFLN, 13 November 1943.
138 MAE, ACG 1068, Truelle to Massigli, 18 January 1944.
139 Leitz, *Economic Relations*, 191.
140 MAE, ACG 1068, Truelle to Algiers, 3 April 1944; Diethelm to Drouin, 18 April 1944.
141 Leitz, *Economic Relations*, 191.
142 See MAE ACG 1274, Vienot to Massigli, 19 March 1944; for one example of French protest, this one involved in the recovery of German property and assets abroad, part of the Allied SAFEHAVEN program, see MAEE, R2193/18, Truelle to Lequerica, 7 May 1945. The best account of SAFEHAVEN, including its implementation in Spain, is the State Department Historian's official report, William Z. Slany, *US and Allied Efforts to Recover and Restore Gold and Other Assets Stolen or Hidden by Germany during World War II* (Washington, 1997).
143 MAE, ACG 1274, Massigli to Truelle, Vienot, 25 March 1944.
144 MAE, Z/Espagne, 82, Memo. by Foques-Duparc, 11 October 1944; in addition, Foques-Duparc also highlighted the divisions amongst Spanish opposition groups as a reason for France taking on such a policy.
145 MAE, ACG 1069, Hugues to Diethelm, 18 August 1944.
146 MAE, Z/Espagne, 2, Truelle to Chauvel, 28 September 1944.
147 MAE, Z/Espagne, 82, Foreign Affairs Commissariat, Europe to Chauvel, 25 August 1944.
148 MAE, Z/Espagne, 82, MAE Europe to Cabinet du Ministre, 17 March 1945.
149 Fernando Guirao, *Spain and the Reconstruction of Western Europe, 1945–57: Challenge and Response* (New York: St. Martin's Press, 1998), 16.

150 MAE, PAAP-Maurice Dejean , 62, 'Procès-verbaux de la Commission Mixte, Saint-Sebastian', 15 September 1945; see also AN, 457 AP 101, Memo. on the Commercial Treaty, MAE Economic Affairs to Bidault, 10 January 1946.
151 MAE, Z/Espagne, 82, Dejean to Bidault, 23 November 1945.
152 Guirao, *Spain and the Reconstruction of Western Europe*, 33.
153 Denis Smyth, 'Franco and the Allies', 185–8.
154 MAE, ACG 1276, Truelle to Massigli, 8 March 1944; Sangróniz repeated this statement to the French Consul in Tangier Lavastre. Lavastre to Massigli, 11 March 1944.
155 MAE, Z/Espagne, 82, Memo. by Foques-Duparc, 1 October 1944.

2 The Resistance and Spanish Republicanism in Liberated France, 1944–1945

1 Henry Rousso, *The Vichy Syndrome: History and Memory in France since 1944* trans. A. Goldhammer (Cambridge, MA, 1991), 18.
2 Georgette Elgey, *La République des Illusions, 1945–1951* (Paris, 1966), 106.
3 Rousso, *Vichy Syndrome*,19; Rioux, *Fourth Republic*, 50–4.
4 Rousso, *Vichy Syndrome*, 19.
5 Shennan, *Rethinking France*, 69.
6 Aline Angoustures, 'L'Opinion publique française et l'Espagne, 1945–1975' *revue d'histoire moderne et contemporaine* 37 (1990), 672–86; Antoine Bechelloni, 'Italiens et Espagnols dans la presse française de septembre 1944 à decembre 1946' in *Exils et Migration: Italiens et Espagnols en France, 1938–1946*, eds. Pierre Milza and Denis Peschanski (Paris, 1994), 287–97.
7 Jill Edwards, *Anglo-American Relations and the Franco Question, 1945–1955* (Oxford, 1999), xvii.
8 John W. Young, *France, the Cold War and the Western Alliance, 1944–1949* (Leicester, 1990), 78.
9 Tussell, *Franco, Espana y la II Guerra Mundial*, 13.
10 MAE, ACG 1277, Truelle to Algiers, 24 August 1944.
11 Shennan, *Rethinking France*, 68.
12 Peter Novick, *L'Epurtation française*, 2nd ed., trans. Helene Ternois (Paris, 1983), 196.
13 Novick, *L'Epurtation française*, 203.
14 *Le Populaire de Paris*, 8 January 1946.
15 *Le Populaire de Paris*, 27 August 1944.
16 AGA Seccion Exteriores (10)009.001 54/9539, Spanish Consulate General, Algiers to Commissariat des Affaires Exterieures, Algiers, 3 November 1943.
17 *Combat*, 7 September 1944.
18 *Le Populaire de Paris*, 24 October 1944.
19 *Combat*, 28 May 1945.
20 *La République du Sud Ouest*, 1 January 1946.
21 AN C/15274, Procès-verbaux, Commission des Affaires Etrangères, Assemblée Consultative Provisoire, 25 May 1945.
22 *Le Populaire de Paris*, 4 August 1945.
23 *New York Times*, 3 January 1945.
24 Cited in Alan Bullock, *Ernest Bevin: Foreign Secretary, 1945–1951* (London, 1983), 163.

25 On the United States, see Boris N. Liedtke, *Embracing a Dictatorship: US Relations with Spain, 1945–53* (London, 1998), 8–9; for Great Britain, see Edwards, *Anglo-American Relations*, 47–53.
26 MAE, Z/Espagne, 1, Truelle to Chauvel, 9 August 1944.
27 MAE PA-AP Maurice Dejean, 62, 'Procès-verbal de la Commission Mixte signé a Saint-Sebastien', 15 September 1945.
28 NARA, RG 59, 751.52/8-445, Caffrey to Secretary of State, 4 August 1945.
29 MAE, Z/Espagne, 82, 'Note General, Relations Franco-Espagnols', 1 December 1945.
30 *Franc-Tireur*, 12 January 1945.
31 *Franc-Tireur*, 12 January 1945.
32 *L'Espagne Républicaine*, 30 June 1945.
33 *L'Espagne Républicaine*, 30 June 1945.
34 *L'Espagne Républicaine*, 18 August 1945, 8 December 1945.
35 *Le Populaire de Paris*, 10 May 1945.
36 *Le Populaire de Paris*, 18 August 1945.
37 *La République du Sud Ouest*, 26 December 1944.
38 *Combat*, 7–8 January 1945.
39 *La République du Sud Ouest*, 26 December 1944.
40 *Combat*, 7 September 1944.
41 *L'Espagne Républicaine*, 29 December 1945.
42 Genevieve Dreyfus-Armand, *L'Exil des Républicains Espagnols en France: De la Guerre Civile á la Mort de Franco* (Paris, 1999), 34–41.
43 Louis Stein, *Beyond Death and Exile: The Spanish Republicans in France, 1939–1955* (Cambridge, MA, 1979), 8.
44 Dreyfus-Armand, *L'Exil*, 53.
45 Stein, *Beyond Death and Exile*, 125.
46 Dreyfus-Armand, *L'Exil*, 131.
47 Dreyfus-Armand, *L'Exil*, 163.
48 Marie-Claude Rafaneau-Boj, *Odyssée pour la Libération: Les Camps de Prisonniers Espagnols, 1939–1945* (Paris, 1993), 270.
49 Dreyfus-Armand, *L'Exil*, 167.
50 Pierre Bertaux, *La Libération de Toulouse et sa Région* (Paris, 1973), 99.
51 MAE, Z/Espagne, 34, Memo. Of Meeting with Consul-General of Spain, 8 September 1944.
52 *Combat*, 7 September 1944.
53 Bechelloni, 'Italiens et Espagnols', 287–97.
54 *La République du Sud Ouest*, 15 September 1944.
55 *La Voix du Midi*, 6 September 1944.
56 *L'Espagne Républicaine*, 18 August 1945.
57 *La Voix du Midi*, 15 September 1944.
58 *Combat*, 21 November 1944.
59 *La Quatrième République* (Pau), 17 July 1945. Copy in MAEE, R2223/ 6.
60 Rafaneau-Boj, *Odyssée*, 271.
61 Cited in NARA, RG 59, 740.0011EW1939/9-144, Hayes to Hull, 1 September 1944.

62 MAE Z/Espagne, 34, Embassy at London to Ministry of Foreign Affairs, Paris, 2 September 1944. Pierre Bertaux disputed the claim that the Consul in Toulouse had been assassinated and later stated that in fact he had left for the Spanish border with a French escort. Bertaux, *La Libération de Toulouse*, 104.
63 MAE, Z/Espagne, 5, Note General, MAE Direction d'Europe, 28 December 1944.
64 MAE, Z/Espagne, 34, Coiffard (Barcelona) to Truelle, 27 September 1944.
65 MAE, Z/Espagne, 34, October and November, 1944 reports.
66 MAE, Z/Espagne, 34, Lt Col Richard to MAE Europe, 1 October 1944.
67 MAE, Z/Espagne, 34, Lt Col Richard to MAE Europe, 1 October 1944.
68 NARA, RG 59, 740.0011EW1939/8-3144, Hayes to Hull, 31 August 1944, Report of US Consul-General in Barcelona, Key, on his visit to Perpignan.
69 AN, F1A/ 3346, Serreulles, Republican Commissioner Bayonne to Tixier, Minister of Interior, 20 November 1944. Collet believed that demobilization of Spanish FFI forces would be easier in the future, and too difficult, at the time, given the large number of tasks which the FFI was expected to accomplish in the southwest over the autumn of 1944.
70 MAE, Z/Espagne, 34, Lt. Col. Richard to MAE Europe, 1 October 1944.
71 Sixto Agudo, 'Participation des Espagnols à la Résistance dans le 4e région', 15 April 1976. Reproduced in Daniel Latapie, *L'Affaire du Val d'Aran: Témoignages et Documents* (Toulouse, 1984), no page.
72 NARA, RG 59, 740.0011EW1939/10-1644, Coordinated Military Intelligence Report on Iberia, 13 October 1944, copied in Hayes to Hull, 16 October 1944. The American Military Attaché, Colonel Frederick Sharp, received these figures directly from the Assistant Chief of the Spanish General Staff.
73 NARA, RG 59, 740.0011EW1939/10-1644,Coordinated Military Intelligence Report on Iberia, 13 October 1944, copied in Hayes to Hull, 16 October 1944.
74 NARA, RG 226, M1642/ Roll 20/ Frames 154–5, Donovan to Dunn, 6 October 1944.
75 Agudo, 'Participation des Espagnols'.
76 Agudo, 'Participation des Espagnols'; Agudo claims it was a Central Committee decision against the wishes of UNE military commanders; David Wingeate Pike, *Jours de Gloire, Jours de Honte: Le parti communiste d'Espagne en France depuis son arrivée en 1939 jusqu'à son départ en 1950* (Paris, 1984), 119–20 agrees. It is quite clear that the decision to invade was made without Moscow's approval and against the express wishes of French Communists involved with the Spanish guerrilleros, most notably André Marty. See Geoffrey Swain. 'Stalin and Spain, 1944–1948' in *Spain in an International Context*, eds. Leitz and Dunthorn, 246–7.
77 For a detailed account of the Val d'Aran invasion and its political motivations, see Jean-Louis Dufour and Rolande Trempe, 'La France, Base Arrière d'une Reconquete Républicaine de l'Espagne: L'Affaire du Val d'Aran' in *Les Français et la Guerre d'Espagne*, eds. Sagnes and Caucanas, 261–84; see also Pike, *Jours de Gloire, Jours de Honte*, 119–32 and Daniel Arasa, *Años 40: Los maquis y el PCE* (Barcelona, 1984), 121–241; for an account by one of the best friends of the Spanish guerrilleros, FFI commander and *Commandement Militaire de la Frontière* agent Daniel Latapie, see his self-published account, including a description of his own efforts to dissuade the UNE from action the night before the invasion. Latapie, *L'Affaire du Val d'Aran*.

78 Stein, *Beyond Death and Exile*, 59.
79 Cited in Stein, *Beyond Death and Exile*, 185.
80 MAE, Z/Espagne, 35, Auriol to Bidault, 19 May and 26 May 1945.
81 MAE, Z/Espagne, 34, Coiffard to Truelle, 18 October 1944; De Gaulle's intelligence organization, the BCRA, had learned of this agreement in July, 1944: AN, 3 AG 2/371, Note, 24 July 1944.
82 MAE, Z/Espagne, 34, Coiffard to Truelle, 1 October 1944; Truelle to Bidault, 20 Octobere 1944.
83 Jean Estebe, *Toulouse, 1940–1944* (Paris, 1996), 298.
84 MAE, Z/Espagne, 34, Massigli to MAE Europe, 24 October 1944.
85 NARA, RG 59, 740.0011EW1939/9-2644, Hayes to Hull, 26 September 1944.
86 MAEE, R 2154/8, 'Note', no date, but sometime after 19 February 1946.
87 Bertaux, *La Libération de Toulouse*, 103.
88 Bertaux, *La Libération de Toulouse*, 102.
89 Swain, 'Stalin and Spain', 246.
90 Agundo, 'Participation des Espagnols'.
91 MAE, Z/Espagne, 35, Truelle to Bidault, 27 March 1945.
92 NARA, RG 226, M1642, Roll 58/ Frame 1186, Hayes to OSS Washington, 4 September 1944.
93 MAE, Z/Espagne, 34, French Embassy, London to MAE Europe, 2 September 1944.
94 MAEE, R 2154/ 8, 'Note', no date but sometime after 19 February 1946.
95 MAE, Z/Espagne, 34, Truelle to MAE Europe, 25 October 1944.
96 MAE, Z/Espagne, 34, Lt. Col. Richard to MAE Europe, 1 October 1944.
97 MAE, Z/Espagne, 34, Coiffard to Truelle, 1 October 1944; Truelle to Bidault, 20 October 1944.
98 NARA, RG 59, 740.0011EW1939/10-2444, Hayes to Hull, 24 October 1944, following Hayes' meeting with Truelle.
99 Bertaux, *La Libération de Toulouse*, 104.
100 MAE, Z/Espagne, 34, Dejean to French Embassy, Washington, 29 October 1944.
101 NARA, RG 226, M1642/Roll 58/ Frames 1213–16, Elton to Washington, 27 September 1944.
102 MAE, Z/Espagne, 34, Lt Col Richard to MAE Europe, 1 October 1944. This action led to a complaint from the *Ligue Française pour la défénse de l'homme et du citoyen*. Dr. Sicard de Plauzoles to Bidault, 6 November 1944, found in the same file.
103 AN, F1A/ 3346, Tixier to Republican Commissioners in Toulouse, Montpellier, Bordeaux, 8 October 1944.
104 AN, F1A/ 3346, Decree of 14 October 1944; AN, F1A/ 3346, Diethelm to Tixier, 28 January 1945 indicated that border control was returned to the Army by decrees of 8 and 9 January 1945.
105 NARA, RG 59, 740.0011EW1939/10-1344, Hayes to Hull, 13 October 1944.
106 AN, F1A/ 3346, Serreulles to Tixier, 20 November 1944.
107 MAE, Z/Espagne, 34, Ministry of War, 2e Bureau to Bidault, 14 October 1944.
108 MAE, Z/Espagne, 34, Truelle to MAE Europe, 22 February 1945.
109 NARA, RG 59, 740.0011EW1939/11-2144, Coordinated Military Intelligence Report on Iberia, 20 November 1944, copied in Hayes to Hull, 21 November 1944;

Colonel Ortega of the Spanish Army provided this report to Colonel Frederick Sharp, US Military Attaché in Madrid, in November.
110 AGA Seccion Exteriores, (10)097.001 54/11288 leg 3399, Ministry of Foreign Affairs, Madrid to Hardion, 2 October 1946.
111 AN, F1A/ 3346, Serreulles to Tixier, 20 November 1944.
112 MAE, Z/Espagne, 5, Spanish Consulate-General (Paris) to MAE, 11 December 1944.
113 MAE, Z/Espagne, 5, Truelle to MAE, 28 December 1944.
114 MAE, Z/Espagne, 5, Bidault to Tixier, 6 January 1945.
115 AGA Seccion Exteriores (10)097.001 54/11290, Mateu to Lequerica, 19 January 1945.
116 MAE, Z/Espagne, 5, Spanish Consulate-General (Paris) to MAE, 1 February 1945.
117 AE, Z/Espagne, 5, Truelle to MAE Europe and MAE Economic Affairs, 3 February 1945.
118 AGA, Seccion Exteriores (10)097.001 54/11290 leg. 3292, Lequerica to Mateu, 14 February 1945.
119 AN, C/ 15274, Procès-verbaux of the Foreign Affairs Commission, 20 November 1944.
120 AN, C/ 15274, Procès-verbaux of the Foreign Affairs Commission, 2 February 1945.
121 AN, C/ 15274, Procès-verbaux of the Foreign Affairs Commission, 2 February 1945.
122 MAEE, R 2223/1, Spanish Consulate, Bayonne to Madrid, 4 January 1945; MAEE R 2223/ 2 includes reports from a number of Spanish Consulates concerning French anti-Franco activism including newspaper clippings from *Combat*, *L'Etincelle* (PCF, Pau) as well as news about the attendance of French representatives at Spanish Republican exile events, for example the anti-Franco speech of M. Albon, President of the Comité Departmental de Liberation-Rhone-Alpes at a meeting of Spanish trade unions in exile (UGT–CNT) in Lyon in December 1944; another was the participation of Prefecture officials in the Nice *Comité France-Espagne* in February, 1945.
123 *La Voix du Midi*, 24, 30, 31 March 1945, 6 April 1945; the anti-Consul campaign was also supported by the MRP organ in Toulouse, *La Victoire*, which reported the crowd as 'large' but did not give any numbers. *La Victoire* 26, 30 March 1945, 2 April 1945.
124 MAEE, R 2223/ 2, various reports from Perpignan where 10,000 rallied outside the Spanish Consulate in late March.
125 Perry Biddiscombe has argued that the Chambéry incident was one example of the Resistance's need for summary justice and violence, albeit with more complications since this attack, unlike others in post-Liberation France, directly involved a foreign state. Perry Biddiscombe, 'The French Resistance and the Chambéry Incident of June 1945', *French History* 11:4 (1997), 438–60.
126 AGA Seccion Exteriores, (10)097.001 54/11358 leg 3224A, Suñer to Lequerica, 15 May 1945.
127 AGA Seccion Exteriores (10)097.01 54/11364 leg 2271, MAEE Dirrecion Europa to Mateu, Paris, 16 July 1945.
128 *Franc-Tireur*, 23 June 1945.
129 *Franc-Tireur*, 30 June 1945.

130 *La Voix du Midi*, 18 June 1945.
131 *L'Aube*, 11 December 1945.
132 France. *JO*, 17 January 1946, 22 February 1946.
133 TNA: PRO, FO 371/60421, Minute, R. Sloan, 6 March 1946.

3 French Politics and the Cause of Spanish Republicanism, 1944–1947

1 AN, C/ 15274, Procès-Verbaux of the Foreign Affairs Commission, 20 November 1944.
2 AN, C/ 15274, Procès-Verbaux of the Foreign Affairs Commission, 20 November 1944.
3 See Chapter 2 fn 27.
4 David Wingeate Pike, *In the Service of Stalin: The Spanish Communists in Exile, 1939–1945* (Oxford, 1993), 282.
5 MAE, Z/Espagne, 34, Interior Ministry to MAE Europe, 23 October 1944. The JEL was linked to a similar organization in Mexico which ultimately helped form a Republican Government-in-exile.
6 MAE, Z/Espagne, 34, Prefect of l'Aude to Bidault, 1 December 1944.
7 Dreyfus Armand, *L'Exil*, 184–91.
8 Cited in Dreyfus-Armand, *L'Exil*, 188.
9 MAE, Z/Espagne, 34, Bidault to Tixier, 16 October 1944.
10 Claudena Skran, *Refugees in Inter-War Europe: The Emergence of a Regime* (Oxford, 1995), 102–30.
11 Vicki Caron, *Uneasy Asylum: France and the Jewish Refugee Crisis, 1933–1942* (Stanford, 1999), 52.
12 AN, 457 AP (Bidault) 100, Ministry of Foreign Affairs to League of Nations High Commission for Refugees-Representative in France, 31 October 1944.
13 Lester was informed 6 October 1944. AN, 457 AP 100, Direction des Etrangers et Conventions Administratives, MAE to Massigli, 22 February 1945.
14 MAE, Z/Espagne, 34, Massigli to Bidault, 12 December 1944.
15 AN, AJ(43), 584-136-1 no. 3, Patrick Murphy-Malllon, Inter-Governmental Committee for Refugees (IGC) to Martha Biele, US Representative to IGC, 5 January 1945.
16 AN, 457 AP 100, Direction des Etrangers et Conventions Administratives, MAE to Massigli, 22 February 1945.
17 MAE, Z/Espagne, 34, MAE to Massigli, 22 February 1945.
18 AGA Seccion Exteriores, (10)097.001 54/11358 leg 3224A, Lojendio (Paris) Memo, 6 February 1945.
19 AN, AJ(43) 584-136-1 no. 14, Paul Mason to Herbert Emerson, 18 April 1945.
20 Michael Marrus, *The Unwanted: European Refugees in the Twentieth Century* (Oxford, 1985), 171, 216–18, 285–6.
21 MAE, Z/Espagne, 34, Massigli to MAE, 7 February 1945.
22 AN, AJ(43) 584-136-1 no. 4, Valentin-Smith to IGC HQ, 10 January 1945.
23 MAE, Z/Espagne, 34, Bidault to Tixier, 16 October 1944.
24 FPI, AE-103-4, Assembly of UGT Departmental Groups in France, 26–27 August 1945.

25 AN AJ(43) 584-136-2 no. 27, Valentin-Smith to Kuhlman, 25 February 1947.
26 Dreyfus-Armand, *L'Exil*, 204.
27 MAE, Z/Espagne, 35, Mateu, to Bidault, 25 April 1945.
28 AGA Seccion Exteriores, (10)097.001 54/11358 leg 3224A, Mateu to Spanish Consulates-General in France, 2 March 1945.
29 AGA Seccion Exteriores, (10)097.001 54/ 11358 leg 3224A, Responses from the Consuls-General in Pau, Lyon, Strasbourg, Sète, Bayonne, Paris, Marseilles and Nice, all March or April 1945.
30 MAE, Z/Espagne, 37, National Police to MAE, 28 February 1946.
31 MAE, Z/Espagne, 35, Andre Mattei to Truelle, 18 April 1945.
32 Richards, *A Time of Silence*, 1.
33 Richards, *A Time of Silence*, 30–1.
34 Cited in MAE, Z/Espagne, 34, French Embassy Madrid to Bidault, October 14, 1944.
35 MAE, Z/Espagne, 34, Commissioner of the Republic, Bordeaux, to Ministries of Interior, Foreign Affairs, War, January 18, 1945.
36 *La République du Sud Ouest*, 8 December 1944.
37 IFHS, Fonds Lamberet 14 AS 599 (38). 'Terreur Sur L'Espagne: Rapport du Congrès National de l'Assocation France-Espagne', 8 June 1947.
38 For the text of the resolution, see *La Victoire* 10 April 1945 and *Le Voix du Midi* 6 April 1945.
39 *Le Voix du Midi*, 27 April 1945.
40 MAE, Z/Espagne, 35, MAE to Truelle, 29 April 1945.
41 *Le Populaire de Paris*, 15 September 1945.
42 MAE, Z/Espagne, 36, Spanish Embassy, Paris to MAE, 12 October 1945.
43 MAE, Z/Espagne, 36, Cabinet du Ministre to MAE Europe, 28 November 1945.
44 MAE, Z/Espagne, 36, Cabinet du Ministre to MAE Europe, 28 November 1945.
45 AGA Seccion Exteriores, (10)097.001 54/11304 leg 3313, Mateu to Artajo, 7 November 1946, 27 November 1946.
46 MAE, Cabinet du Ministre/Bidault (1944–48), 18, Letter to Ministry of Foreign Affairs, December 1946; Raoul Calad, Deputy for Herault, to Bidault, 10 February 1947; Madelain Braun, Gilbert de Chambrun, Maurice Schumann, et al to Bidault, 5 February 1947.
47 MAE, Z/Espagne, 36, Hardion to Coiffard, 5 November 1945.
48 MAE, Z/Espagne, 35, Coiffard to Hardion, 29 June 1945.
49 MAE, Z/Espagne, 36, Hardion to Paris, 9 January 1946.
50 MAE, Z/Espagne, 37, Hardion to Paris, 4 January 1946.
51 MAE, Z/Espagne, 37, 38, Hardion to Paris, 28 February 1946 and 18 March 1946.
52 MAE, Z/Espagne, 36, Hardion to Paris, 9 January 1946.
53 MAE, Z/Espagne, 38, Coiffard to Paris, 17 April 1946 and 29 April 1946.
54 See, for example, MAE, Z/Espagne, 38, Coulet to Hardion concerning methodology of Francoist trials, 21 March 1946.
55 MAE, Z/Espagne, 40, Hardion to Paris, 8 October 1946.
56 See, for example, MAE, Z/Espagne, 38, Frederico Minana, Left Republican Party, and Jean Montala, Socialist Unified Party of Catalonia, to Georges Bidault, 15 May and 19 May 1946 respectively.

57 Copied in MAE Cabinet du ministre/Bidault (1944–48), 18, Carmen de Pedro Zoroa to Maitre de Moro Giafferri, 28 November 1946.
58 MAE, Z/Espagne, 37, Hardion to Paris, 4 January 1946.
59 MAE, Z/Espagne, 36, Hardion to Paris, 9 January 1946.
60 AN, C/ 15286, Bidault testimony to Constituant Assembly's Foreign Affairs Commission, Procès-Verbaux of the Foreign Affairs Commission, 12 December 1945.
61 MAE, Z/Espagne, 35, 'La Junta Española de Liberación ante la Conferencia de San Francisco de California', April 1945.
62 AN, 457 AP 99, Memo. for Bidault, 24 June 1945.
63 David J. Dunthorn, *Britain and the Spanish Anti-Franco Opposition, 1940–1950* (London, 2000), 3.
64 Dunthorn, *Britain and the Spanish*, 62.
65 Edwards, *Anglo-American Relations*, 76–7.
66 Stone, 'The Degree of British Commitment to the Restoration of Democracy in Spain, 1930–1946' in *Spain in an International Context*, eds. Christian Leitz and David J. Dunthorn, 209.
67 AN, 457 AP 99, Memorandum for Bidault, 13 July 1945.
68 Dunthorn, *Britain and the Spanish*, 62–3.
69 Dunthorn, *Britain and the Spanish*, 63.
70 MAE, Z/Espagne, 35, De los Ríos to Bidault, 31 August 1945.
71 TNA: PRO, FO 371/ 49557/ Z13136, Duff Cooper to FO, 29 November 1945.
72 MAE, Z/Espagne, 36, Bonnet to MAE Europe, 21 September 1945; TNA:PRO FO 371/ 49556/ Z10497 Hoyer-Miller Minute, 7 September 1945 for the British view; see also Dunthorn, *Britain and the Spanish*, 55.
73 MAE, Z/Espagne, 36, Bonnet to MAE Europe, 21 September 1945.
74 TNA: PRO FO 371/ 49557/ Z13136, Minute by Peter Garran, 1 December 1945.
75 MAE, Z/Espagne, 36, Memo., 31 October 1945.
76 Dunthorn, *Britain and the Spanish*, 82.
77 MAE, Z/Espagne, 38, Hardion to MAE, 1 March 1946.
78 MAE, Z/Espagne, 38, De los Ríos to Bidault, 9 March 1946.
79 MAE, Z/Espagne, 38, Henry to Torres, 18 March 1946.
80 TNA: PRO, FO 371/60333/Z290, Duff Cooper to Foreign Office, 8 January 1946.
81 Hartmut Heine, *La Oposición Política al Franquismo* (Barcelona, 1983), 328.
82 TNA: PRO, FO 371/ 60333/ Z290, Foreign Office to Duff Cooper, 13 January 1946.
83 *DBPO* Series I, vol. VII , no. 18ii, Bevin to Duff Cooper, 22 February 1946.
84 Chapter Four and David A. Messenger, 'The Spirit of Sacrifice: The French Left, Franco's Spain and the Case of Cristino García' in *Proceedings of the Western Society of French History Volume 28: Selected Papers of the 2000 Annual Meeting*, ed. Barry Rothaus (Greeley, CO, 2002).
85 MAE, Z/Espagne, 67, MAE Information and Press Service to French Embassy, Madrid, 4 March 1946.
86 FPI, AE-103-6, Joint PSOE/UGT Circular No. 28, 19 March 1946 gives the Giral Government response; for the response amongst Republicans in Madrid, MAE, Z/Espagne, 38, Hardion to Paris, 22 March 1946.

87 Heine, *La Oposicíon*, 185.
88 Jose Borras, *Polítícas de los Exilados Españoles, 1944–1950* (Paris, 1976), 109; FPI, AE-103-6, PSOE-UGT Joint Circular No. 28, 19 March 1946 for the official PSOE-UGT statement on the potential of talks with Don Juan.
89 AN, 457 AP 99, Note to Bidault, 14 February 1946.
90 MAE, Z/Espagne, 38, Direction des Renseignements Généraux, 6e Section, 1 April 1946.
91 MAE, Z/Espagne, 39, Roger de Bercegol to MAE, 17 July 1946.
92 Dunthorn, *Britain and the Spanish*, 75.
93 MAE, Z/Espagne, 39, Legenissel to MAE, 14 June 1946; MAE Europe to Falaize, 13 August 1946; TNA:PRO, FO 371/ 60336/ Z7207, Minute by Peter Garran Minute, 15 July 1946 and *DBPO*, Series I, vol. VII, no. 55 Minute by Derrick Hoyer-Millar Minute, 22 July 1946 for British dismissal of Giral.
94 AN, 457 AP 99, Memo., 26 and 30 April 1946.
95 AN, 457 AP 99, Madrid Embassy to MAE, 17 May 1946.
96 This official is referred to as 'Monsieur X' in documents contained in the papers of Georges Bidault that relate to Spain, AN, 457 AP. There is a good chance that Roger de Bercegol, a member of Hardion's' staff at the Madrid Mission, was 'X', but there is no definitive evidence for this informed guess.
97 AN, 457 AP 99, X to Bidault, 'summer 1947'.
98 MAE, Z/Espagne, 39, 40 contain these reports, Hardion to MAE, from spring, 1946 through to the end of the year.
99 AN, 457 AP 99, Madrid Embassy to MAE, 17 May 1946.
100 AN, 457 AP 99, Documentation Exterieure et Contre-Espionage to Bidault, 19 September 1946.
101 AN, 457 AP 99, X to Bidault, 'summer 1947'. See also MAE, Z/Espagne, 39, Roger de Bercegol to MAE, 16 August 1946.
102 Heine, *La Oposicíon*, 363–4.
103 AN, 457 AP 99, X to Bidault, 'summer 1947'.
104 TNA: PRO, FO 371/60379/Z9587, Clarke to Hoyer-Millar, 7 November 1946.
105 AN, 457 AP 99, Jean Chauvel, Memo., 4 October 1946.
106 TNA: PRO, FO 371/60379/Z9587, Clarke to Hoyer-Millar, 7 November 1946.
107 AN, 457 AP 99, X to Bidault, 'summer 1947'. The original French phrase of Napoleon III's (as quoted by Bidault) was 'Faites, mais faites vite.'
108 Heine, *La Oposicíon*, 364.
109 MAE, Z/Espagne, 40, Hardion to MAE, 1 November 1946.
110 MAE, Z/Espagne, 40, Hardion to MAE, 6 November 1946.
111 Dunthorn, *Britain and the Spanish*, 79.
112 MAE, Z/Espagne, 40, Hardion to MAE, 15 November 1946.
113 MAE, Z/Espagne, 40, Hardion to MAE, 28 November 1946.
114 MAE, Z/Espagne, 40, Hardion to MAE, 6 December 1946.
115 MAE, Z/Espagne, 40, Hardion to MAE, 22 November 1946.
116 AN, 457 AP 99, X to Bidault, 'summer 1947'.
117 AN, 457 AP 99, X to Bidault, 'summer 1947'.
118 AN, 457 AP 99, X to Bidault, 'summer 1947'.

119 Dunthorn, *Britain and the Spanish*, 80.
120 MAE, Z/Espagne, 40, Foques-Duparc to Chalron, 23 December 1946; Lapie to José Giral, 13 January 1947.
121 MAE, Z/Espagne, 40, Memo., 7 February 1947.
122 TNA: PRO, FO 371/67872/Z1950, Duff Cooper to Foreign Office, 20 February 1947; MAE, Z/Espagne, 41, Memo. by Vasse, 6 March 1947.
123 MAE, Z/Espagne, 41, Memo. by Vasse, 6 March 1947; TNA: PRO, FO 371/ 67872/ Z1950/ Z3208, Duff Cooper to Foreign Office, 20 February 1947 and 28 March 1947, Foreign Office to British Embassy Madrid, 31 March 1947 gives details of the British relationship with Llopis, which was more extensive than their contacts with Giral as Llopis met with Duff Cooper in Paris and traveled to London to meet Minister of State H. McNeil, although not Bevin; MAE, Z/Espagne, 41, Massigli to MAE Europe, 27 March 1947 for French reports of the British gesture.
124 TNA: PRO, FO 371/ 67876/ Z4980, Minute by Hogg, 20 May 1947.
125 Dunthorn, *Britain and the Spanish*, 103.
126 MAE, Z/Espagne, 41, Memo., 16 June 1947.
127 MAE, Z/Espagne, 41, Memo., 'Le Problème Espagnol', 20 June 1947.
128 *FRUS* 1947, III, 1067, Acheson to Douglas, 7 April 1947.
129 *FRUS* 1947, III, 1069, Douglas to Marshall, 19 April 1947.
130 *FRUS* 1947, III, 1075, Douglas to Marshall, 1 May 1947.
131 MAE, Z/Espagne, 42, Hardion to MAE Europe, 3 September 1947.
132 Dunthorn, *Britain and the Spanish*, 108.
133 TNA: PRO, FO 371/ 67877A/ Z10788, Howard to Crosthwaite, 10 December 1947; TNA: PRO, FO 371/ 67908A for British analysis of these talks; see also David J. Dunthorn, 'The Prieto-Gil Robles Meeting of October 1947: Britain and the Failure of the Spanish Anti-Franco Coalition, 1945–50', *European History Quarterly* 30:1 (2000), 49–75.
134 AN, 457 AP 99, X to Bidault, 'summer 1947'.

4 French Initiative on Spain, 1945–1946

1 MAE, Z/Espagne, 66, Ministère des Affaires Etrangères to United States Embassy, Paris and British Embassy, Paris, 12 December 1945; the State Department translation can be found in *FRUS*, 1945, V, 698–9.
2 AN, C/ 15286, Procès-verbaux of the Foreign Affairs Commission, 12 December 1945.
3 MAE, Z/Espagne, 66, Note for Bidault, 3 December 1945.
4 Hitchcock, *France Restored*, 6–7.
5 William I. Hitchcock, 'Response to 'France and the German Questions 1945–1955' by Michael Creswell and Marc Trachtenberg' *Journal of Cold War Studies* 5:3 (2003), 36.
6 Georges-Henri Soutou, 'France and the Cold War 1944–63' *Diplomacy and Statecraft* 12:4 (2001), 35–6; see also Michael Creswell and Marc Trachtenberg, 'France and the German Question, 1945–1955', *Journal of Cold War Studies* 5:3 (2003), 9 and their 'Rejoinder: New Light on an Old Issue' in the same issue, 48.
7 Creswell and Trachtenberg, 'France and the German Question', 9.

8   Charles Cogan, 'Response to Michael Creswell and Marc Trachtenberg' *Journal of Cold War Studies* 5:3 (2003), 29.
9   Guirao, *Spain and the Reconstruction of Western Europe*, 24.
10 Jean Peyrade, *Situation de la presse dans la région de Toulouse (20 aout 1944–1er octobre 1947)* (Paris, 1976), 25; In June, 1945, the new French Minister in Madrid Bernard Hardion (he replaced Jacques Truelle upon the latter's death) spoke to Bidault in Paris about the need to keep the exiled Spanish press shut down; he later met with Spanish Embassy chargé Tomás Suñer and reported that 50 tonnes of newsprint destined for Spanish clandestine publications had been seized by the French Government, MAEE, R 2223/ 5. Suñer to Madrid, 11 July 1945.
11 MAE, Z/Espagne, 5, Memo., 9 February 1945.
12 *Franc-Tireur*, 7 September 1945.
13 TNA: PRO, FO 371/ 49634/ Z11156, Holman to London, 25 September 1945.
14 MAE, Z/Espagne, 82, Hardion to Paris, 7 November 1945.
15 Dreyfus-Armand, *L'Exil*, 180.
16 Jean Chauvel, *Commentaire: D'Alger à Berne (1944–1952)* (Paris, 1972), 172.
17 Pierre Gerbet, *Le Rélevement, 1944–1949* (Paris, 1991), 117.
18 Paola Brundu, 'L'Espagne franquiste et la politique etrangère de la France au lendemain de la Deuxième Guerre Mondiale', *Rélations Internationales* 50 (1987), 170; *JO*, 16 January 1946 has reference to d'Astier de la Vigérie's initiative by Gilbert de Chambrun (who had supported it) in France.
19 AN, C/ 15286, Bidault testimony to the Assembly's Foreign Affairs Commission. Procès-verbaux of the Foreign Affairs Commission, 12 December 1945.
20 MAE, Z/Espagne, 65, MAE Europe to Bidault, 3 December 1945.
21 MAE, Z/Espagne, 82, Memo., 'Rélations France-Espagne', 1 December 1945.
22 MAE, Z/Espagne, 82, MAE Europe to Bidault, 3 December 1945; NARA, RG 59, 751.52/9-1345 Armour to Secretary of State, 13 September 1945, indicates that the US Embassy in Madrid received a report in September, 1945 from a 'dependable' source inside the Spanish Government that certain French officials had suggested that France's entire Spanish policy could be 'reoriented' toward greater cooperation if Spain turned to France instead of the United States for economic, industrial and technical assistance.
23 MAE, Z/Espagne, 82, Memo., 1 December 1945.
24 NARA, RG 59, 751.52/12-1545, Caffrey to Byrnes, 15 December 1945.
25 Florentino Portero, *Franco aislado: la cúestion española, 1945–1950* (Madrid, 1989), 128–32.
26 Portero, *Franco aislado*, 128.
27 Bullock, *Ernest Bevin*, 163.
28 *DBPO*, Series I, V, 13ii(c), Mallet to Foreign Office, 6 October 1945; MAE, Z/Espagne, 80, MAE to Madrid Embassy, 17 October 1945; Cited in *DBPO*, Series I, V, 104 fn 3, Washington Embassy to Foreign Office, 7 December 1945.
29 *FRUS* 1945, V, 695–7, Armour to State Department, 1 December 1945.
30 MAE, Z/Espagne, 66, Hardion to MAE, 14 December 1945.
31 MAE, Z/Espagne, 66, Bonnet to MAE, 19 December 1945 for Dunn's response; Hardion to MAE, 15 December 1945 for Howard's response.

32 Brundu, 'L'Espagne franquiste', 171.
33 AN, C/ 15286, Procès-Verbaux of the Foreign Affairs Commission, 19 December 1945.
34 *L'Espagne Républicaine*, 29 December 1945.
35 Mark S. Sheetz 'France and the German Question: Avant-garde or Rearguard? Comment on Creswell and Trachtenberg', *Journal of Cold War Studies* 5:3 (2003), 37.
36 Chauvel's fear of domestic opinion is cited in Anne Dulphy, 'La politique de la France à l'égard de l'Espagne franquiste, 1945–1949', *Revue d'histoire moderne et contemporaine* (1988), 125.
37 *Franc-Tireur*, 5 January 1946. See also *Le Populaire de Paris*, 4 January 1946 for criticism of economic relations, in particular the shipment of French potatoes to Spain.
38 For example, *L'Aube*, 18 December 1945. For the 'realist' attitude of *Le Figaro* and *Le Monde*, see Bechelloni, 'Italiens et Espagnols', 290.
39 *Franc-Tireur*, 18 December 1945.
40 FPI, AE-102-1, *PSOE* Circular no. 32, 22 December 1945.
41 Great Britain. House of Commons. *Parliamentary Debates* 20 August 1945.
42 For Attlee's views, see Portero, 'Spain, Britain and the Cold War' in *Spain and the Great Powers*, eds., Balfour and Preston, 211–18.
43 CAB 128/ 45(45), 23 October 1945 in *Cabinet Papers: Series Three, CAB 128/129 Part I and II*, Great Britain, Cabinet Office (London, 1996).
44 MAE, Z/Espagne, 66, Hardion to MAE, Direction d'Europe, 15 December 1945.
45 TNA: PRO, FO 425/423 34176, Mallet to Bevin, 3 December 1945.
46 Bullock, *Ernest Bevin*,164.
47 *DBPO*, Series I, V, 104, Attlee to Duff Cooper, 21 December 1945.
48 Portero, 'Spain, Britain and the Cold War', 218.
49 *FRUS* 1945, V, 699–704, Memo. by James Dunn, 19 December 1945.
50 *FRUS* 1945, V, 704–6, Memo. by James Dunn, 20 December 1945.
51 *FRUS* 1945, V, 706–7, Acheson to Caffrey, 22 December 1945.
52 Cited in *DBPO*, Series I, V, 104 fn 10, Halifax to Foreign Office, 23 December 1945.
53 *DBPO*, Series I, VII, 18i, Halifax to Foreign Office, 19 January 1946; Halifax reported that Acheson's position was in contrast to his subordinates in the Office of European Affairs, John Hickerson and Paul Culbertson, who agreed with the British viewpoint.
54 *DBPO*, Series I, VII, 18i, Halifax to Foreign Office, 19 January 1946.
55 *FRUS*, 1946, V, 1030–1, Acheson to Byrnes, 18 January 1946.
56 *DBPO*, Series I, VII, 18i, Halifax to Foreign Office, 19 January 1946.
57 Portero argues that only British pressure held back the United States from agreeing to France's proposal to discuss diplomatic rupture, Portero, 'Spain, Britain and the Cold War', 218; Edwards agrees that the British felt the need to restrain both the French and the Americans, Edwards, *Anglo-American Relations*, 65; indeed, as the December, 1945 Conference of Foreign Ministers approached, even the Soviet Union believed that the United States 'was increasingly hostile' toward Franco and was considering possible policy changes, Swain, 'Stalin and Spain', 252.
58 IFHS, Fonds Lamberet, 14 AS 599 (38), 'Terreur Sur l'Espagne: Congès de

l'Association France-Espagne', 8 June 1947, identified both Chambrun and d'Aragon as leading members of the *Association France-Espagne*'s parliamentary caucus.
59 *JO*, 15 January 1946.
60 *JO*, 16 January 1946.
61 The original quote was: "*C'est la pire des choses dans votre métier*", *JO*, 17 January 1946.
62 *JO*, 17 January 1946 quoted Mutter as expressing his position by simply stating, 'We are not in Spain'; in the 1930s, Mutter had been a member of Colonel de la Roque's *Parti Social Français* but had been a major figure amongst right-wingers in the Resistance. For more on Mutter and the *PRL*, see Joseph Algazy, *La tentation néofasciste en France, 1944–1965* (Paris, 1984), 67 and especially Richard Vinen, *Bourgeois Politics in France, 1945–1951* (Cambridge, 1995), 116–21.
63 *JO*, 16 January 1946.
64 *JO*, 16 January 1946.
65 NARA, RG 59, 751.52/1-1846, Caffrey to Byrnes, 18 January 1946.
66 *JO*, 17 January 1946.
67 *JO*, 17 January 1946.
68 *JO*, 17 January 1946.
69 NARA, RG 59, 751.52/2-546, Caffrey to Washington, 5 February 1946.
70 United Nations. General Assembly. *Official Records*, Session 1(1), vol. I. (London, 1946), Minutes of the Plenary Meeting, 9 February 1946.
71 *Le Populaire de Paris*, 17 January 1946.
72 *L'Humanité*, 6/7, 16 January 1946.
73 *L'Aube*, 18 January 1946.
74 *JO*, 17 January 1946.
75 MAE, Z/Espagne, 66, Hardion to MAE, 20 January 1946.
76 TNA: PRO FO 371/ 60349/ Z666, Mallet to Foreign Office, 21 January 1946.
77 NARA, RG 59, 751.00/1-1946, Wright to Office of European Affairs, 19 January 1946.
78 TNA: PRO, FO 371/ 60421/ z698, Minuted by Sloan, 24 January 1946.
79 This aspect of the accord was given great publicity in the Communist press, especially in Toulouse and the southwest, where it was reported that the agreement called for the implementation of all measures already passed by the Constituent National Assembly and not yet enforced, 'notably those relative to relations with the Government of Franco.' *Le Voix du Midi*, 25 January 1946; see also Jacques Dalloz, *Georges Bidault: Biographie Politique* (Paris, 1992), 129; the new government saw an increase in Communist ministers from 5 to 6, almost saw the exit of the *MRP* from the tripartite coalition, and coincided with a deeply divisive debate within *SFIO* about whether or not the party should move away from the *MRP* and become closer to the Communist Party, see B.D. Graham, *Choice and Democratic Order: The French Socialist Party, 1937–1950* (Cambridge, 1994), 287–314.
80 Elgey, *La République*, 106; it is interesting to note that at the time, the lack of French action on previous motions seemed to give assurance to many outside France that this agreement would not alter French policy; commenting on the three-party state-

81 *Le Voix du Midi*, 26 January 1946.
82 MAE, Z/Espagne, 67, Memo., 1 February 1946; see also *DBPO*, Series I, VII, 18ii Bevin to Madrid, 3 February 1946 and Minute by Hoyer-Millar, 12 February 1946; for similar expression of concern by Bidault to the Americans, see NARA, RG 59, 751.00/1-2846 Caffrey to Byrnes, 28 January 1946.
83 NARA, RG 59, 751.52/1-3046, Butterworth to Washington, 30 January 1946.
84 Dreyfus-Armand, *L'Exil*, 166, 200.
85 MAE, Z/Espagne, 36, 37, Cabinet du Ministre to MAE Europe, 26 November 1945 and Hardion to MAE, 9 January 1946, respectively.
86 *L'Humanité*, 2 February 1946.
87 See, for example, *L'Humanité*, 3/4, 7, 8, 10/11, 16 February 1946.
88 IFHS, Fonds Lamberet 14 AS 599 (38), 'Terreur sur l'Espagne: Congrès de l'Association France-Espagne', 8 June 1947.
89 *Le Populaire de Paris*, 23 February 1946.
90 *Franc-Tireur*, 26 February 1946.
91 *La Voix du Midi*, 23 February 1946.
92 *Le Voix du Midi*, 12 February 1946.
93 MAE, Z/ Espagne, 84, Service des Renseignements Generaux, Sète to Ministère de l'Interieur, Service de Renseignements Generaux, Auch to Ministère de l'Interieur, 27 & 28 February 1946.
94 *Le Voix du Midi*, 26 January 1946.
95 *Le Voix du Midi*, 30 January 1946.
96 *Le Voix du Midi*, 23, 25, 26 February 1946.
97 *Le Voix du Midi*, 28 February 1946.
98 MAE, Z/Espagne, 84, MAE Europe to Hardion, 28 February 1946.
99 MAE, Z/Espagne, 37 include Hardion's García dispatches.
100 See, for example, Graham, *Choice and Democratic Order*, 267–309.
101 Stéphane Courtois and Marc Lazar, *Histoire du Parti communiste français* (Paris, 1995), 224.
102 Graham, *Choice and Democratic Order*, 297.
103 *L'Humanité* and *Le Populaire de Paris*, 27 February 1946 cite crowds of 50,000. *The Times*, 27 February 1946 claimed 30,000.
104 *L'Humanité*, 27 February 1946.
105 Vinen, *Bourgeois Politics*, 153.
106 *Le Populaire de Paris* and *L'Humanité*, 17 February 1946.
107 *JO*, 22 February 1946.
108 *New York Times*, 23 February 1946.
109 *New York Times*, 24, 26 February 1946.
110 *New York Times*, 24 February 1946. For more on the Communist takeover of the CGT leadership over the course of 1944–1946 and in particular within the postal and communications section, see Michel Dreyfus, *Histoire de la C.G.T.* (Paris, 1995), 213–27; also Courtois and Lazar, *Histoire du parti communiste*, 226–7.
111 *Franc-Tireur*, 26 February 1946.

112 MAE, Z/Espagne, 67, Memo.,'Consequences d'une rupture unilaterale de nos relations diplomatiques avec le Gouvernement Franco', 21 February 1946.
113 MAE, Z/Espagne, 67, Memo., 'Consequences d'une rupture unilaterale de nos relations diplomatiques avec le Gouvernement Franco', 21 February 1946.
114 MAE, Z/Espagne, 67, Memo., 'Consequences d'une rupture unilaterale de nos relations diplomatiques avec le Gouvernement Franco', 21 February 1946.
115 Hitchcock, *France Restored*, 2.
116 *DBPO*, Series I, vol. VII, 18ii, Duff Cooper to Foreign Office, 25 February 1946.
117 NARA, RG 59, 751.52/2-2646, Caffrey to Secretary of State, 26 February 1946.
118 Georges Bidault, *D'une Résistance à l'Autre* (Paris, 1965), 137.
119 *Combat*, 23 February 1946. See the harsh reply of editorialist Oscar Rosenfeld to this charge in *Le Populaire de Paris*, 24–25 February 1946.
120 Chauvel, *Commentaire, vol. II*, 172.
121 *Le Voix du Midi*, 27 February 1946.
122 NARA, RG 59, 751.52/2-2746, Butterworth to State Department, 27 February 1946; Caffrey to State Department, 1 March 1946.
123 *L'Espagne Républicaine*, 9 March 1946.
124 *Franc-Tireur*, 27 February 1946.
125 Bidault, *D'une Résistance à l'Autre*, 137.

5 France, the West and the Spanish Question, 1946

1 MAE, Z/Espagne, 67, MAE to Great Britain, Soviet Union and United States Embassies, Paris, 27 February 1946; *FRUS*, 1946, V, 1043–4, Caffrey to Washington, 27 February 1946 for English translation.
2 MAE, Z/Espagne, 67, MAE to Great Britain, Soviet Union and United States Embassies, Paris, 27 February 1946.
3 MAE, Z/Espagne, 67, MAE to Great Britain, Soviet Union and United States Embassies, Paris, 27 February 1946.
4 *New York Times*, 14 January 1946.
5 MAE, Z/Espagne, 67, MAE to Great Britain, Soviet Union and United States Embassies, 27 February 1946.
6 Brundu, 'L'Espagne franquiste', 175.
7 MAE, Z/Espagne, 68, Ligue des Droits de l'Homme et du Citoyen, section Beausoleil/Monaco to Félix Gouin, President, 17 March 1946; in Monaco, local party sections (SFIO, PCF, MRP, Radicals), trade unions and the *Ligue des Droits de l'Homme et du Citoyen* gathered in March to rally in favor of the government initiative.
8 *La Voix du Midi*, 28 February 1946.
9 *Franc-Tireur*, 6 March 1946.
10 *Le Populaire de Paris*, 5 March 1946.
11 *L'Humanité*, 5 March 1946.
12 Brundu, 'L'Espagne franquiste', 174.
13 MAE, Z/Espagne, 67, MAE to Hardion, 26 February 1946; Bidault, *D'une Résistance à l'Autre*, 137.
14 Brundu, 'L'Espagne franquiste', 174.

15 *La République du Sud-Ouest*, 7 March 1946.
16 AN, C/ 15286, Procès-verbaux of the Foreign Affairs Commission, 27 February 1946.
17 MAE, Z/Espagne, 72, Note General, Secretariat des Conférences, 4 March 1946.
18 *L'Aube*, 28 February 1946.
19 *Le Figaro*, 26 February 1946.
20 *Combat*, 23 February 1946.
21 TNA: PRO, FO 800/504, Bevin to Mallet, 3 February 1946; See also MAEE, R 1372/22, Memo., 4 February 1946, where Mallet indicated to the Head of the Spanish Foreign Ministry's Diplomatic Cabinet, the Marques de Miraflores, that public opinion in Britain required political evolution in Spain and that without such evolution, Anglo-Spanish relations would only become 'more difficult'.
22 TNA: PRO, CAB 128/ CM 18 (46), 26 February 1946.
23 MAE, Z/Espagne, 67, Massigli to Bidault, 27 February 1946.
24 Keith Hamilton. 'Non-Intervention Revisited: Great Britain, the United Nations and Franco's Spain in 1946' in *FCO Historians Occasional Papers No. 10: United Kingdom, United Nations and divided world, 1946* (London, 1995), 55.
25 Melvyn P. Leffler. *The Specter of Communism: The United States and the Origins of the Cold War, 1917–1953* (New York, 1994), 52.
26 Leffler, *Specter*, 53 and idem, *Preponderance of Pow*er, 108. The 'Riga axioms', as first defined by Daniel Yergin, were those ideas formed by the State Department's Soviet experts based in Riga, Lativa in the 1920s and later refined by the Moscow Embassy in the 1930s (which included Kennan). They were based on a belief that because of the revolutionary nature of Communism, Soviet Union foreign policy would inevitably seek to expand Communism and thus conflict with American policy. Yergin calls the Long Telegram, 'a classic restatement of the Riga axioms, indeed the most important such statement of those attitudes ever made.' See Daniel Yergin, *Shattered Peace: The Origins of the Cold War and the National Security State* (Boston, 1977), 17–41, 168.
27 The only other time Kennan had participated in a discussion of Spanish policy had been in 1944, when he opposed the idea of US intervention against Franco in a debate with other State Department officials. See Anders Stephanson, *Kennan and the Art of Foreign Policy* (Cambridge, MA, 1989), 306 fn 112.
28 *FRUS*,1946, V, 1033, Kennan to Secretary of State, 3 February 1946.
29 *FRUS*,1946, V, 1035–6, Kennan to Secretary of State, 3 February 1946.
30 Jill Edwards notes that it was circulated widely in the State Department as well as being passed on to Foreign Office officials. Edwards, *Anglo-American Relations*, 65–6.
31 MAE, Z/Espagne, 66, Hardion to MAE, 21 December 1945.
32 FRUS, 1946, V, 1038–42, Butterworth to Secretary of State, 15 February 1946.
33 Cited in Liedtke, *Embracing a Dictatorship*, 8.
34 John Lamberton Harper, *American Visions of Europe: Franklin D. Roosevelt, George F. Kennan and Dean G. Acheson* (Cambridge, 1994), 269–75; Robert L. Beisner notes that as late as August 1946 Acheson's response to the criticism of Soviet broken agreements since Yalta made in a report for President Truman by Clark Clifford and

George Elsey was 'mild'. Robert L. Beisner, 'Patterns of Peril: Dean Acheson Joins the Cold Warriors, 1945–46' *Diplomatic History* 20:3 (1996), 325. A recent Acheson biographer notes that the Undersecretary had not perceived Kennan's 'Long Telegram' favorably and, on the question of Spain in particular, he had in 1945 complained that Britain's desire for strict non-intervention prohibited a more forceful American policy. James Chace, *Acheson: The Secretary of State who Created the American World* (New York, 1998), 150–1, 94.

35 Swain, 'Stalin and Spain', 253, argues that Kennan's 3 February note 'put right' any differences the US and Great Britain had over Spain.
36 TNA: PRO, FO 371/ 60349/ Z882, Halifax to Bevin, 28 January 1946.
37 *DBPO*, Series I, vol. VII, 18iii, Madrid Embassy to Foreign Office, London, 9 February 1946.
38 *DBPO*, Series I, vol. VII, 18iii, Mallet to Harvey, 22 February 1946.
39 See John Zametica, 'Three Letters to Bevin: Frank Roberts at the Moscow Embassy, 1945–46' in *British Officials and British Foreign Policy, 1945–1950*, ed. John Zametica (Leicester, 1990), 39–97; Sean Greenwood, 'Frank Roberts and the "Other" Long Telegram: The View from the British Embassy in Moscow, March 1946' *Journal of Contemporary History* 25 (1990), 103–22.
40 *DBPO*, Series I, VII, 18iii, Roberts to Hoyer-Millar, 14 February 1946.
41 *FRUS*, 1946, VI, 703–6, Kennan to Secretary of State, 22 February 1946.
42 *FRUS*, 1946, V, 1044–5, Kennan to Secretary of State, 1 March 1946.
43 Edwards, *Anglo-American Relations*, 66.
44 *DBPO*, Series I, vol. VII, 18iii, Roberts to Hoyer-Millar, 2 March 1946.
45 See, for example, NARA, RG 59, State Department Lot Files: Office of European Affairs 1935–1947 (Matthews-Hickerson Files) 'Spain', Memo. Matthews to Cohen, 10 April 1946. Reprinted *FRUS*, 1946, V, 1065–9 as Hiss to Stettinus, 12 April 1946.
46 Swain, 'Stalin and Spain', 245–64.
47 Swain, 'Stalin and Spain', 250.
48 Luis Suárez Fernández, *Franco y la URSS* (Madrid, 1987), 22–4.
49 *New York Times*, 14 January 1946; Swain, 'Stalin and Spain', 253.
50 *FRUS*, 1946, V, 1047–8, Bonsal to Washington, 8 March 1946.
51 Pike, *Jours de Gloire*, 119–41.
52 Pike, *Jours de Gloire*, 154.
53 Swain, 'Stalin and Spain', 255–61 notes that only after the Cold War clearly was underway did Stalin return to a more aggressive policy, encouraging the guerilla activity of the Spanish Communists based in France.
54 MAE, Z/Espagne, 67, Bonnet to Bidault, 25 February 1946.
55 MAE, Z/Espagne, 67, Bidault to Bonnet, 27 February 1946.
56 United States. Department of State. *The Spanish Government and the Axis* (Washington, 1946).
57 MAE, Z/Espagne, 67, Ministère des Affaires Etrangères, Service de l'Information et de Presse to French Embassy, Madrid, 4 March 1946.
58 MAE, Z/Espagne, 67, Bonnet to Bidault, 25 February 1946.
59 TNA: PRO, FO 371/ 60421/ z1998, Minute by Sloan, 4 March 1946, Foreign Office official R. Sloan wrote: 'It has hitherto seemed to me expedient to preserve the

Anglo-US-French front and to make some concession to French feelings; hence the statement. But I think now we ought to consider again the dangers of such a policy ... If she (France) is intent on gambling with her own interests- either for the 'beaux yeux of Moscow or simply through misdirected post-war exasperation, let her do so.'; See also *DBPO*, Series I, VII, 18ii, Foreign Office to Washington, 27 February 1946 and Mallet to Foreign Office, 27 February 1946; *DBPO*, Series I, VII, 26, Bevin to Cadogan, 24 March 1946; TNA: PRO, CAB 128/ CM (20) 46, 4 March 1946 for Bevin's comments to Cabinet; all these reflect the British view that the statement represented a way to address domestic opinion in France and the United States rather than as a policy statement with new implications, and they worked hard to bring the wording of the statement in line with existing policy of strict non-intervention.

60 Preston, *Franco*, 554–5, has argued that the impact of the declaration was negligible, and in fact called it 'milder than the Potsdam Declaration' because it essentially repeated the earlier statement but this time without Soviet participation; Liedtke, *Embracing a Dictatorship*, 1, calls the statement 'a weak condemnation of Spain as a fascist regime.'
61 FPI, AE-103-6, Joint *PSOE/UGT* Circular no. 28, 19 March 1946.
62 FPI, AE-102-1, *PSOE* Circular no. 32, 22 December 1945.
63 A.J. Lleonart y Amselem, ed., *España y ONU*, I (Madrid, 1978), 49, 'Ministerial Declaration against the Foreign Campaign', issued by Sub-Secretary of Popular Education, 29 December 1945.
64 MAE, Z/Espagne, 66, Hardion to MAE, 19 January 1946.
65 MAE, Z/Espagne, 84, Coiffard to MAE, 27 February 1946.
66 MAE, Z/Espagne, 84, Hardion to MAE, 27 February 1946.
67 Fernández, *Franco y la URSS*, 37.
68 Portero, *Franco aislado*, 72–6.
69 Fernández, *Franco y la URSS*, 37–8.
70 MAE, Z/Espagne, 72, Massigli to Jean Chauvel, 5 March 1946.
71 *DBPO*, Series I, VII, 18, Bevin to Duff Cooper, 2 March 1946.
72 *DBPO*, Series I, VII, 26i (a), Minute by Hoyer-Millar, 27 February 1946.
73 Great Britain. Board of Trade. Economic Survey. *Spain: Review of Commercial Conditions, October 1945* (reprinted on microfiche, Cambridge, 1977), 48.
74 *DBPO*, Series I, VII, 26i (a), Sir Oliver Harvey to Sir Victor Mallet, 8 March 1946.
75 *DBPO*, Series I, VII, 26ii 'Possible Developments in the Situation in Spain: Report by the Joint Intelligence Sub-Committee' J.I.C. (46) 23 (0), 15 March 1946.
76 *DBPO*, Series I, VII, 18, Bevin to Duff Cooper, 2 March 1946; MAE, Z/Espagne, 72, Duff Cooper to Bidault, 4 March 1946.
77 MAE, Z/Espagne, 72, Bonnet to MAE, 6 March 1946; NARA, RG 59, State Department Lot Files, Office of European Affairs, Records of the French Desk, 1941–1951, Memo., 5 March 1946..
78 *FRUS*, 1946, V, 1048–9, Byrnes to Caffrey, 8 March 1946.
79 *FRUS*, 1946, V, 1049–51, Byrnes to Caffrey, 8 March 1946; MAE, Z/Espagne, 72 , Caffrey to Bidault, 9 March 1946.
80 MAE, Z/Espagne, 72, Bonnet to MAE, 9 March and 11 March 1946.

81 MAE, Z/Espagne, 72, USSR Embassy, Paris to Bidault, 6 March 1946.
82 Swain, 'Stalin and Spain', 253.
83 Qasim Ahmad, 'Britain and the Isolation of Franco' in *Spain in an International Context*, eds. Lietz and Dunthorn, 228, has written, 'Real or imagined, the communist bogey served to justify further the refusal of the West to take or endorse precipitate actions against the *Generalissimo*.'
84 TNA: PRO, FO 371/60421/Z2077, Duff Cooper to Foreign Office, 4 March 1946.
85 NARA, RG 59, 751.52/3-1246, Caffrey to Byrnes, 12 March 1946.
86 NARA, RG 59, 751.52/3-1446, J. Edgar Hoover, Director, Federal Bureau of Investigation to Frederick B. Lyon, Chief, Division of Foreign Activity Correlation, State Department, 14 March 1946.
87 NARA, RG 59, 751.52/3-2746, Memo., 27 March 1946.
88 Hitchcock, *France Restored*, 80–1.
89 TNA: PRO, FO 371/ 60421/Z1998, Minute by Oliver Harvey, 5 March 1946.
90 TNA: PRO, FO 371/ 60421/ z2077, Minute by R. Sloan, 6 March 1946.
91 CAC, DUFC 4/6, Sir Oliver Harvey to Alfred Duff Cooper, 13 March 1946.
92 TNA: PRO, FO 371/60421/Z2028, Minute by Peter Garran, 5 March 1946..
93 *DBPO*, Series I, VII, 18, Bevin to Duff Cooper, 2 March 1946.
94 *FRUS*, 1946, V, 1051–2, Byrnes to Caffrey, 12 March 1946.
95 *New York Times*, 14 March 1946.
96 *FRUS*, 1946, V, 1051–2, Byrnes to Caffrey, 12 March 1946.
97 Irwin Wall, *The United States and the Making of Postwar France, 1945–1954* (Cambridge, 1991), 44. See also Edward Rice-Maximin, 'The United States and the French Left, 1945–1949: The View from the State Department', *Journal of Contemporary History* 19 (1984), 730–1.
98 MAEE, R 1372/22, Minutes of Meeting, 22 March 1946.
99 MAE, Z/Espagne, 68, Hardion to MAE (Paris), 28 March 1946.
100 MAE, Z/Espagne, 72, Memo., Secretariat des Conférences, 4 March 1946. Italics are from the original.
101 *L'Humanité*, 15 March 1946,
102 AN, C/ 15286, Procès-verbaux of the Foreign Affairs Commission, 15 March 1946.
103 AN, C/ 15286, Procès-verbaux of the Foreign Affairs Commission, 20 March 1946.
104 MAE, Z/Espagne, 68, Hardion to Ministère des Affaires Etrangères, 17 March 1946; See also NARA, RG 59, 751.52/3-2246 Philip Bonsal to Secretary of State, 22 March 1946 for US Military Attaché Col. Wendell Johnson's report, and TNA: PRO, FO 371/ 60421/ Z2234, Brigadier Torr, British Military Attaché, Madrid to War Office, 4 March 1946 and FO371 60421/Z2608, Torr to Foreign Office, 16 March 1946.
105 TNA: PRO, FO 371/ 60421/ Z2601, Mallet to Foreign Office, 16 March 1946.
106 MAE, Z/Espagne, 72, Bidault to Duff Cooper, Jefferson Caffrey, 12 March 1946.
107 MAE, Z/Espagne, 72, Coulet to French Ambassadors in London, Madrid, Washington, 8 March 1946.
108 MAE, Z/Espagne, 72, Memo., Sécretariat des Conférences, 4 March 1946.
109 MAE, Z/Espagne, 72, Coulet to Ambassadors in London, Washington, Madrid, 8 March 1946.
110 MAE, Z/Espagne, 72, British Embassy, Paris to Bidault, 18 March 1946; Jefferson

Caffrey to Bidault, 20 March 1946; FRUS, 1946, V, 1056–8, Byrnes to Caffrey, 19 March 1946 for the American response.
111 *DBPO*, Series I,VII, 26iii, Bevin to Halifax, 30 March 1946; MAE, Z/Espagne, 72, Massigli to MAE, 14 March 1946, emphasized that Bevin underlined his dislike of Franco but argued the most effective way to change the Spanish regime was through non-intervention and quiet diplomacy.
112 CAC, DUFC/ 4–5, P. Dixon, Private Secretary to Bevin, to All Heads of Mission, 4 April 1946; *The Times*, 13 June 1946, demonstrates that Bevin repeated his message in public at the Labour Party Congress at Bournemouth.
113 MAE, Z/Espagne, 72, Bonnet to MAE, 16 March 1946.
114 MAE, Z/Espagne, 72, Sécretariat des Conférences to French Embassies, 24 March 1946 and Bidault to Soviet Union Embassy, Paris, 25 March 1946; MAE, Nations Unies et Organisations Internationales/ Sécretariat des Conference 1945–1959, 194, Bidault to Lie, 18 March 1946, was a formal request to UN Secretary-General Trygve Lie to place the item on the agenda under article 35-1 of the Charter, which dealt with situations that threatened international peace and security.
115 MAE, Nations Unies et Organisations Internationales/ Secretariat des Conférences, 194, Memo., 19 March 1946.
116 MAE, Nations Unies et Organisations Internationales/ Sécretariat des Conférences, 1945–1959, 194, Memo., 19 March 1946.
117 MAE, Z/Espagne, 72, Bidault to British Embassy, Paris, 21 March 1946, to United States Embassy, Paris, 25 March 1946.
118 *DBPO*, Series I, VII, 26iii, Bevin to Duff Cooper, 30 March 1946.
119 MAE, Z/Espagne, 72, Bonnet to MAE, 8 April 1946.
120 Anne Dulphy, 'La politique de la France', 129; Brundu, 'L'Espagne franquiste', 176–7, states that although France gave up the role as 'motor' against Spain in April, it was not until July 1946 that it would resume a policy of coordination with the western powers.
121 MAE, Z/Espagne, 72, Massigli to Chauvel, marked 'Personal', 7 March 1946.
122 AN, C/ 15286, Procès-verbaux of the Foreign Affairs Commission, 27 March 1946.
123 MAE, Z/Espagne, 67, Hardion to Bidault, 8 March 1946.

6 French Acceptance of Franco's Spain, 1946–1948

1 *FRUS*, 1947, III, 1092–5, Policy Planning Staff/12 'US Policy Toward Spain', 24 October 1947.
2 *DBPO*, Series I, VII, 26iii, Duff Cooper to Foreign Office, 11 & 12 March 1946; Minute by Sir Oliver Harvey, 12 April 1946.
3 *DBPO*, Series I, VII, 26 fn 2, Duff Cooper to Foreign Office, 18 March 1946; MAE, Z/Espagne, 72, Bonnet to Direction d'Europe, 13 March 1946, the Polish Ambassador in Washington approached Henri Bonnet and indicated that Poland wished to coordinate Security Council policy with France on the Spanish question.
4 MAE, Z/Espagne, 72, Bidault to the French Delegation, United Nations, 10 April 1946.
5 *DBPO*, Series I, VII, 26iii, Duff Cooper to Foreign Office, 11 April 1946, 12 April 1946; Minute by Sir Oliver Harvey, 12 April 1946.

6 David Wingeate Pike, 'Franco et l'admission aux Nations Unies' *Guerres mondiales et conflits contemporains* 162 (1991), 110.
7 MAE, Z/ Espagne, 72, Bonnet to MAE, 7 April 1946.
8 MAE, Z/ Espagne, 72, Bidault to French Delegation, United Nations, 10 April 1946.
9 *DBPO*, Series I, VII, 36, Cadogan to Bevin, 18 April 1946.
10 NARA, Matthews-Hickerson Papers, H. Freeman Matthews to Acheson, Cohen and Bohlen, 21 March 1946.
11 United Nations, Security Council, *Official Records,* First Year, First Series, no. 2 (London, 1946), Minutes of 34th Meeting, 17 April 1946.
12 United Nations, Security Council, *Official Records,* First Year, First Series, no. 2, Minutes of 34th Meeting, 17 April, 1946.
13 United Nations, Security Council, *Official Records,* First Year, First Series, no. 2, Minutes of 34th Meeting, 17 April, 1946.
14 United Nations, Security Council, *Official Records* , First Year, First Series, no. 2, Minutes of 34th Meeting, 17 April 1946.
15 United Nations, Security Council, *Official Records,* First Year, First Series, no. 2, Minutes of 34th Meeting, 17 April 1946.
16 United Nations, Security Council, *Official Records,* First Year, First Series, no. 2, Minutes of 35th Meeting, 18 April 1946.
17 United Nations, Security Council, *Official Records,* First Year, First Series, no. 2, Minutes of 37th Meeting, 25 April 1946.
18 *FRUS*, 1946, V, 1068, Byrnes to Stettinius, 12 April 1946.
19 United Nations, Security Council, *Official Records,* First Year, First Series, no. 2, Minutes of 35th Meeting, 18 April 1946.
20 MAE, Nations Unies et Organisations Internationales/ Sécretariat des Conférences, 1945–1959, 194, Bonnet (New York) to MAE, 20 April 1946.
21 MAE, Z/ Espagne, 72, Bonnet (New York) to MAE, 26 April 1946.
22 *DBPO*, Series I, VII, 42ii, Halifax (Washington) to Foreign Office, 22 April 1946.
23 *DBPO*, Series I, VII, 42ii, Minute by Sir Oliver Harvey, 24 April 1946.
24 United Nations, Security Council, *Official Records,* First Year, First Series, no. 2, Minutes of the 39th Meeting, 29 April 1946.
25 MAE, Z/Espagne, 73, Bidault (Paris) to Parodi (New York), 24 May 1946.
26 NARA, RG 59, State Department Lot Files, Office of European Affairs, Records of the French Desk, 1941–1951, Memo. by C. Noyes, 16 May 1946.
27 MAE, Z/Espagne, 73, Hardion Report; Bidault (Paris) to Parodi (New York), 24 May 1946.
28 MAE, Z/ Espagne, 73, Annex to Hardion Report; Bidault (Paris) to Parodi (New York), 24 May 1946.
29 United States, *Spain and the Axis*.
30 MAE, Z/Espagne, 73, Bonnet (New York) to Direction d'Europe, 7 May 1946.
31 TNA: PRO, FO 371/ 60422/z3439, Torr (Madrid) to Foreign Office (London), 3 April 1946 reported fourteen divisions were in the border region, with one in reserve, totaling 165,000 troops, deployed in what García-Valiño termed a position that allowed for 'active defense', prepared to counter any infiltration from across the border, which he believed would occur on a significant scale only if the

Communists won the French elections and Russia sent troops to France for such a purpose; TNA: PRO, FO 371/ 60423/ z5307, Col. Smith-Bingham (Madrid) to MI4, 21 May 1946, reported that the Spanish Army had hosted a 'goodwill tour' of the border region for the military attachés of Great Britain, the United States, Italy, Chile and Argentina between 1–18 May 1946.

32 TNA: PRO, FO 371/ 60422/ z3957, Minuted by Peter Garran, 2 May 1946..
33 MAE, Z/Espagne, 73, Bonnet (New York) to MAE, 7 May 1946.
34 *DBPO*, Series I, VII, 52i, Cadogan (New York) to Foreign Office, 1 June 1946.
35 United Nations, Security Council, *Official Records,* First Year, Second Series Special Supplement (New York, 1946), 'Report of the Sub-Committee on the Spanish Question, 1946'; See also United Nations, Security Council, *Official Records*, First Year, First Series, no. 2, Minutes of the 44th Meeting, 6 June 1946. For a full account of the UN's consideration of the Spanish question in 1946, see Portero, *Franco aislado*, 137–218; for documents and commentary, Lleonart y Anselem, *Espana y ONU*, vol. I.
36 *DBPO*, Series I, VII, 52i, Foreign Office to UK Delegation (New York), 3 June 1946; *DBPO*, Series I, VII, 52, Bevin to Cadogan (New York), 14 June 1946.
37 MAE, Nations Unies et Organisations Internationales/ Sécretariat des Conférences, 1945–1959, 194, Parodi (New York) to Bidault, 27 July 1946.
38 MAE, Z/Espagne, 74, Massigli to MAE, 7 June 1946.
39 MAE, Nations Unies et Organisations Internationales/ Sécretariat des Conférences, 1945–1959, 194, Bonnet to MAE, 4 June and 6 June 1946.
40 *DBPO*, Series I, VII, 52 and 52i, Foreign Office to UK Delegation, United Nations, 3 June 1946 and Bevin to Cadogan, 14 June 1946; for British fears that Security Council action on Spain could set precedents for foreign intervention, including in the British colonies, see Hamilton, 'Non-Intervention Revisited', 59.
41 MAE, Z/Espagne, 74, Parodi (New York) to MAE , 11 June 1946; See also MAE, Nations Unies et Organisations Internationales/Sécretariat des Conférences, 1945–1959, 194, Parodi to Bidault, 27 July 1946.
42 MAE, Z/ Espagne, 74, Parodi (New York) to Chauvel, 8 June 1946.
43 United Nations, Security Council, *Official Records*, First Year, First Series, no. 2, Minutes of the 45th Meeting, 13 June 1946; United Nations, Security Council, *Official Records*, First Year, First Series, no. 2, Minutes of the 47th Meeting, 18 June 1946 for the Soviet veto.
44 United Nations, Security Council, *Official Records*, First Year, First Series, no. 2, Minutes of the 45th Meeting, 13 June 1946.
45 Swain, 'Stalin and Spain', 255–61 asserts that once Stalin concluded the West had failed in the attempt to forge a unified policy toward Franco, a gradual process began with the Soviet Union adopting a more and more confrontational approach toward both Franco and the West, one which ultimately included the first effort since the war to supply and support the *guerrillero* movements in Spain and southern France.
46 MAE, Z/ Espagne, 74, Spanish Delegation (Paris) to Bidault, 11 July 1946.
47 MAE, Z/ Espagne, 68, Massigli to Bidault, 1 July 1946, for Massigli's enquiries at the Foreign Office about Anglo-French relations in the aftermath of the UN debate. The British response indicated the extent to which they had become fed up with the

French; officials at the Foreign Office referred Massigli to the 1820 State Papers where Castlereagh wrote that Spaniards tolerated intervention in their affairs less than any other European nation, and detested French intervention above all. Massigli rebutted that the model of 1835, where liberal allies France and Britain intervened in Spain was a better example to follow. Clearly the existence of this debate demonstrated that France had lost significant respect.

48 MAE, Nations Unies et Organisations Internationales/ Sécretariat des Conférences, 1945–1959, 194, Parodi (New York) to Bidault, 27 July 1946; see also United Nations, Security Council, *Official Records*, First Year, First Series, no. 2, Minutes of 48th Meeting, 24 June 1946, and 49th Meeting (26 June 1946).
49 AGA Seccion Exteriores, (10) 097.001 54/11288 leg 3399, Santiago Sangro (Pau) to Artajo, 7 November 1946.
50 AN, C/ 15308, Procès-verbaux of the Foreign Affairs Commission, 7 August 1946.
51 NARA, RG 59, 751.52/9-3046, Wright to Secretary of State, 30 September 1946 includes a copy of 'Rapport fait au nom de la Commission des Affaires Etrangères sur la proposition de Resolution de M. Guy Petit,' 19 September 1946.
52 NARA, RG 59, 751.52/9-1146, Caffrey to Byrnes, 11 September 1946.
53 MAE, PAAP- Rene Massigli, 94, Chauvel to Massigli, 26 October 1946.
54 MAE, Z/Espagne, 74, Hardion to Direction d'Europe, 16 October 1946.
55 *Public Papers of the Secretaries-General of the United Nations Volume I: Trygve Lie, 1946–1953* eds. Andrew W. Cordier and Wilder Foote (New York, 1969), 63–4, Secretary-General, Supplementary Oral Report to the General Assembly, 24 October 1946 shows that Secretary-General Trygve Lie encouraged the General Assembly to pick up where the Security Council had left off; United Nations, Security Council, *Official Records*, First Year, Second Series, no. 1, Minutes of the 79th Meeting, 4 November 1946 for the decision of the Security Council to remove the Spanish question from its agenda.
56 *United Nations Journal*, no. 50, Supplement No. 1- A/C.1/112, United Nations, First Committee, Minutes of 37th Meeting, 5 December 1946.
57 United Nations, General Assembly, *Official Records*, 1946 Session 1(2), I (New York, 1946), Minutes of 59th Plenary Meeting, 12 December 1946.
58 MAE, Z/ Espagne, 86, French Mission to MAE Europe, 15 June 1946.
59 AN, 457 AP 101, MAE Administrative Affairs to Bidault, 27 July 1946.
60 MAE, Z/ Espagne, 85, Hardion to MAE, 24, 27, 28 August 1946; see also Pedro Martinez Lillo, 'Una aproximación al estudio de las relaciones bilaterales hispanosfrancescas durante la posguerra. El 'affaire' fronterizo en la perspectiva del Quai d'Orsay (1946–1948)', *Revista de Estudios Internacionales* 6 (1985), 578–82.
61 MAE, Z/ Espagne, 85, Memo., 10 April 1947.
62 Bidault, *D'une Resistance a l'Autre*, 137.
63 Koreman, *Expectation of Justice*, 262.
64 See, for instance, MAE, Cabinet du Ministre/Bidault, 1944–1948, 17, 12 April 1947, for a summary of the lobbying by the Chamber of Commerce of Perpignan over the first half of 1947.
65 MAE, Z/Espagne, 85, Prefect of the Basses-Pyrénées to Bidault, 12 April 1947.
66 *Le Populaire de Paris*, 1 July 1947.

67 IHSF, Fonds Lamberet 14 AS 599 (38), Report of the Congress of the Association France-Espagne, 'Terreur sur l'Espagne: Congrès de l'Association France-Espagne, Paris.' 8 June 1947; see also *L'Humanité*, 3 September 1947, or the *Franc-Tireur* series 'Franco, c'est Hitler', *Franc-Tireur*, 9–11 September 1947.
68 Dalloz, *Bidault*, 129.
69 AN C/ 15332, Procès-verbaux of the Foreign Affairs Commission, 9 August and 13 September 1947 for Bidault's testimony; at the second of these sessions, Bidault commented on the commercial losses of France by reminding the members of the Commission that 'there are no fascist oranges, there are only oranges.'
70 MAE, Z/ Espagne, 75, Lacoste to MAE, 8 September 1947.
71 MAE, Z/ Espagne, 75, MAE Europe to French Delegation, New York, 15 October 1947; the only member of the French delegation to react against these instructions was Léon Jouhaux of the CGT, who gave interviews and circulated a proposed anti-Franco resolution amongst the UN delegates. Bidault responded by informing Jouhaux that the instructions came not only from him, but from the Premier, see MAE, Z/ Espagne, 75, Memo., 1 October 1947, Parodi to Bidault, 18 October, Bidault to French delegation, 21 October 1947.
72 MAE, Z/ Espagne, 86, MAE Service d'Information et de Presse, 7 February 1948 for the joint Franco-Spanish statement on the border re-opening; MAE, Z/ Espagne, 93, 1 May 1948 for the May, 1948 trade agreement.
73 AGA Seccion Exteriores, (10)097.001 54/11288 leg 3399, Aguirre de Carcer to Artajo, Madrid, 15 April 1948.
74 Fernando Guirao, 'The United States, Franco and the Integration of Europe' in *The United States and the Integration of Europe: Legacies of the Post-war Era* eds. F. Heiler and J. Gillingham (New York, 1996), 95.
75 Boris Liedtke, 'Spain and the United States, 1945–1975' in *Spain in an International Context*, eds. Leitz and Dunthorn, 233.
76 *FRUS*, 1947, III, 1092–5, Policy Planning Staff/12 'US Policy Toward Spain', 24 October 1947.
77 Guirao, 'The United States, Franco and Integration', 95.
78 Liedtke, 'Spain and the United States', 237–8.
79 Antonio Marquina, *España en la politica de seguridad ocidental 1939–1986* (Madrid, 1986), 154–7, 198.
80 Marquina, *España en la política*, 198.
81 Marquina, *España en la política*, 184.
82 Dulphy, *La politique de France à l'égard de l'Espagne*, 684–734; for Franco's awkward approach to Moroccan independence and relations with France, see Mike Elkins, 'Franco's Last Stand: An Analysis of Spanish Foreign Policy regarding Moroccan Independence in 1956', *International Journal of Iberian Studies* 17:2 (2004) pp. 67–86.
83 Portero, *Franco aislado*, 323.
84 Dulphy, *La politique de France à l'égard de l'Espagne*, 562–82.
85 Dulphy, 'La Politique de la France', 138.
86 Dulphy, *La politique de France à l'égard de l'Espagne*, 404–54, 633–70; Phryné Pigenet, 'La Protection des étrangers à l'épreuve de la guerre froide: l'Opération

Boléro-Paprika', *Revue d'histoire moderne et contemporaine* 46 (1999).
87   MAE, Z/ Espagne, 69, Memo., 18 December 1946.
88   MAE, Z/ Espagne, 69, Memo., 18 December 1946.
89   Hamilton, 'Non-Intervention Revisited', 63.

Conclusion: France, Spain and Post-War Foreign Policy in Europe
1   Soutou, 'France and the Cold War', 35.
2   William I. Hitchcock, *France Restored*, 6–7.
3   Soutou, 'France and the Cold War', 35–6; see also Creswell and Trachtenberg, 'France and the German Question', 9, and the expanded version of this argument in Michael Creswell, *A Question of Balance: How France and the United States Created Cold War Europe* (Cambridge, MA, 2006).
4   Creswell, *A Question of Balance*, 9.
5   Judt, *Postwar*, 63.
6   Judt, *Postwar*, 65–77.
7   Eley, *Forging Democracy*, 288.
8   Eley, *Forging Democracy*, 288.
9   MAE, Z/ Espagne, 5, Memo., 9 February 1945.

BIBLIOGRAPHY

Archival Collections

France

AN: Archives nationales, Paris.
   Série C Archives de l'Assemblée Nationale.
   Procès-verbaux de la Commission des Affaires Etrangères, 1944–1948.
   Série F(1) Ministère de l'Interieur.
   Série F(9) Affaires Militaires/ Ministère des Prisonniers, Deportes et Refugies.
   Archives des Présidents de la République/ de Gaulle.
   Archives de l'Organisation Internationale pour les Réfugies.
   Fonds Georges Bidault.
Bibliothèque de Documentation Internationale et Contemporaine, Université de Paris X, Nanterre.
Documents Collection.
Bibliothèque Municipale, Toulouse.
   Collections Réserve.
Bibliothèque Nationale de la France- Francois Mitterrand, Paris.
   Collection de presse.
IFHS: Institut Français de l'Historie Sociale, Paris.
   Fonds Lamberet.
MAE: Ministère des Affaires Etrangères, Paris.
   Série Guerre, 1939–1945.
   ACG: sous-série Alger-CFLN-GPRF.
   Vichy .
   Z: Série Z, Europe 1944–1949.
   Série Secretariat General, 1945–1960.
   Série Secretariat des Conferences, 1944–1959/Nations Unies.
   Série Cabinet du Ministre/Bidault (1944–1948).
   Série Papiers d'Agents-Archives Privées (PAAP).
   Papiers Henri Bonnet.
   Papiers Maurice Dejean.
   Papiers Rene Massigli.
   Papiers François Piétri.

Bibliography

SHAT: Service historique de l'Armée de Terre, Vincennes.
  Série P, Guerre, 1940–1945 (Vichy, Londres, Alger, Paris).

Spain

AGA: Archivo General de Administracíon, Alcala de Henares.
  Seccion Exteriores.
MAEE: Archivo General, Ministerio de Asuntos Exteriores, Madrid.
  R: Archivo Renovado.
FPI: Fundación Pablo Iglesias, Madrid.
  Archivo PSOE en exilio.
  Archivo UGT en exilio.
Biblioteca Virtual de Prensa Histórica, Ministerio de Cultura .

United Kingdom

TNA: PRO: The National Archive- Public Record Office, Kew.
  Cabinet Office: War Cabinet Minutes and Memoranda CAB 64/65.
  Cabinet Office: Secret Information Office, CAB 121.
  Cabinet Office: Cabinet Minutes and Memoranda, 1945–1950 CAB 128/129.
  Foreign Office: General Correspondance FO 371, 1943–1948.
  Foreign Office: Confidential Print FO 425, 1943–1945.
  Foreign Office: Personal Papers FO 800.
  Ernest Bevin papers.
  Foreign Office: Office of the Minister Resident in Algiers/ British Representative to the French Committee of National Liberation, FO 660, 1943–1944 .
  Foreign Office: Ministry of Economic Warfare FO 837, 1943–1945.
  Prime Minister's Office: PREM 3/4.
CAC: Churchill Archives Centre, Churchill College, Cambridge University.
  Alfred Duff Cooper Papers.
  Ernest Bevin Papers.
Cambridge University Library, Manuscripts Room, Cambridge University.
  Lord Templewood Papers.

United States

NARA: United States National Archives and Records Administration II, College Park, MD.
  Record Group 59, General Records of the Department of State.
  Decimal Files.
  Lot Files.
  Office of European Affairs.
  Records of the Policy Planning Staff .
  Record Group 84, Records of the Foreign Service Posts of the Department of State.
  Record Group 169, Records of the Foreign Economic Administration.
  Record Group 226, Records of the Office of Strategic Services .
  Washington Director's Files.

Bibliography

United Nations Archive, New York.
Records of the Security Council Sub-Committee on Spain.

Published Primary Sources

L'Année Politique Paris, 1946–1948.
France. *Journal Officiel de la République Française (JO)*. Algiers and Paris, 1943–1948
Documentary History of the Truman Presidency, vol. VII. Edited by Dennis Merrill. Washington, 1996.
Espana y ONU, vols. I–II. Edited by A. J. Lleonart y Anselm. Madrid, 1978–1991
Great Britain. *Documents on British Policy Overseas (DBPO)* Series I, vols. V, VII. London, 1990–1995.
Great Britain. Cabinet Office. *Cabinet Papers: Series Three, CAB 128/129 Part I and II*, London, 1996.
Great Britain. House of Commons. *Parliamentary Debates*. London, 1942–1948
Great Britain. Overseas Trade Department. *Spain: Economic Survey 1946*. London, 1946.
Parti Communiste Francais. *Contre l'Hitlérisme et le Fascisme, pour une France Libre, Démocratique et Independente: Rapports du Comité Central pour le Xe Congrès National, Paris, 26–30 juin 1945*. Paris, 1945.
Parti Communiste Francais. *1945–1947: Du Congrès de Paris au Congrès de Strasbourg*. Strasbourg, 1947.
Public Papers of the Secretaries General of the United Nations: Vol. I Trygve Lie, 1946–1953. Edited by Andrew Cordier & Wilder Foote. New York, 1969.
United Nations. General Assembly. *Official Records*. New York, 1945–1948.
United Nations. Security Council. *Official Records*. New York, 1945–1948.
United Nations. *United Nations Journal: Supplement I, 1946: First Committee Summary Record of Meetings*. New York, 1946.
United States. Department of State. *Foreign Relations of the United States (FRUS) 1942–1948*. Washington, 1963–75.
United States. Department of State. *The Spanish Government and the Axis*. Washington, 1946.

Newspapers

L'Aube, 1944–1948.
Combat, 1943–1948.
L'Espagne Républicaine (Toulouse), 1945–1946.
Le Figaro, 1945–1948.
Franc-Tireur, 1944–1945.
L'Humanité, 1946–1948.
Le Monde, 1944–1948.
New York Times, 1943–1948.
Le Populaire de Paris, 1944–1948.
Le République du Sud-Ouest (Toulouse), 1944–1945.

Bibliography

Solidaridad Espanola (Toulouse), 1945.
The Times, 1943–1948.
Le Voix du Midi (Toulouse), 1945–1946.
Le Victoire (Toulouse), 1944–1945.

Biographies, Diaries, Memoirs

Acheson, Dean. *Present at the Creation: My Years in the State Department*. New York, 1970.
Alvarez del Vayo, Julio. *The Last Optimist*. London, 1950.
Alphand, Herve. *L'Etonnement d'Etre: Journal, 1939–1973*. Paris, 1977.
Beaulac, Williard. *Franco: Silent Ally in World War II*. Carbondale (IL), 1986.
Bertaux, Pierre. *La Libération de Toulouse et sa region*. Paris, 1973.
Bidault, Georges. *D'une résistance à l'autre*. Paris, 1965.
Bullock, Alan. *Ernest Bevin: Foreign Secretary, 1945–1951*. London, 1983.
Byrnes, James. *Speaking Frankly*. New York, 1947.
Cava Mesa, Maria Jesus. *Los diplomaticos de Franco: J.F. de Lequerica, temple y tenacidad (1890–1963)*. Bilbao, 1989.
Chace, James. *Acheson: The Secretary of State who Created the American World*. New York, 1998.
Chauvel, Jean. *Commentaire, vol. I: De Paris à Alger 1939–1944; vol. II: D'Alger à Berne, 1944–1952*. Paris, 1972.
Churchill, Winston S. *The Second World War, Vol. IV: The Hinge of Fate*. London, 1954.
Coulet, F. *Le vertu des temps difficiles*. Paris, 1967.
Cooper, Alfred Duff. *Old Men Forget*. London, 1953.
Crozier, Brian. *Franco: A Biographical History*. London, 1967.
Dalloz, Jacques. *Georges Bidault: Biographie Politique*. Paris, 1992.
de Gaulle, Charles. *Mémoires de Guerre, vol. II: L'Unité 1942–1944; vol. III: Le Salut 1944–1946*. Paris, 1956–1959.
de Gaulle, Charles. *Lettres, Notes et Carnets, 1941–3; 1943–5; 1945–51*. Paris, 1982–4
de Gaulle, Charles. *Discours et Messages, 1940–46, 1946–48*. Paris, 1970.
Eden, Anthony. *The Memoirs of Anthony Eden, Earl of Avon*, 2 vols. Boston, 1965.
Ferro, Marc. *Pétain*. Paris, 1987.
Hayes, Carlton J.H. *Wartime Mission in Spain, 1942–1945*. New York, 1945.
Hixson, Walter L. *George F. Kennan: Cold War Iconoclast*. New York, 1989.
Hull, Cordell. *The Memoirs of Cordell Hull*, 2 vols. New York, 1948.
Kennan, George. *Memoirs, 1925–1950*. New York, 1967.
Lacouture, Jean. *De Gaulle: La Politique, 1944–1959*. Paris, 1985.
——. *De Gaulle: The Rebel, 1890–1944* trans. Patrick O'Brian. New York, 1990.
Latapie, Daniel. *L'Affaire du Val d'Aran*. Toulouse, 1984.
Loewenheim, Francis J. et al, eds. *Roosevelt and Churchill: Their Secret Wartime Correspondence*. New York, 1975.
Macmillan, Harold. *War Diaries: Politics and War in the Mediterranean*. London, 1984.
Macmillan. Harold. *The Blast of War 1939–1945*. London, 1967.
Massigli, Rene. *Une comédie des erreurs 1943–1956*. Paris, 1978.

Bibliography

McClellan, David. *Dean Acheson: The State Department Years.* New York, 1985.
Murphy, Robert. *Diplomat Among Warriors.* New York, 1964.
Navarre, Henri. *La service des renseignements, 1871–1944.* Paris, 1978.
Orwell, George. *Homage to Catalonia.* New York, 1980.
Ott, B. *Georges Bidault.* Annonay, 1978.
Paillole, Paul. *Services spéciaux (1935–1945).* Paris, 1975.
Piétri, Francois. *Mes années d'Espagne, 1940–1948.* Paris, 1954.
Preston, Paul. *Franco.* London, 1993.
Spender, Stephen. *The Thirties and After: Poetry, Politics, People (1932–75).* London, 1978.
Templewood, Viscount. *Ambassador on Special Mission.* London, 1946.
Truman, Harry S. *Memoirs,* 2 vols. Garden City (NJ), 1955–6.
Werth, Alexander. *De Gaulle.* London, 1965.

Secondary Sources

Ahmad, Qasim. *Britain, Franco Spain and the Cold War, 1945–1950.* New York, 1992.
Algazy, Joseph. *La tentation néo-fasciste en France 1944–1965.* Paris, 1984.
Alpert, Michael. *A New International History of the Spanish Civil War.* New York, 1994.
Angoustures, Aline. 'Les Réfugiés Espagnols en France de 1945 à 1981.' *Revue d'histoire moderne et contemporaine* 44:3 (1997).
——. 'L'opinion publique française et l'Espagne, 1945–1975.' PhD Thesis, Institut des Etudes Politiques, Paris, 1987.
Angel, Miguel. *Los guerilleros españoles en Francia (1940–1945).* Havana, 1971.
Arasa, Daniel. *Años 40: Los maquis y el PCE.* Barcelona, 1984.
Aviles Farre, Juan. 'L'Ambassade de Lequerica et les relations hispano-françaises, 1939–1944.' *Guerres Mondiales et Conflits Contemporains* 158 (1990).
Balfour, Sebastian and Paul Preston, eds. *Spain and the Great Powers in the Twentieth Century.* London, 1999.
Beisner, Robert L. 'Patterns of Peril: Dean Acheson Joins the Cold Warriors, 1945–46.' *Diplomatic History* 20:3 (1996).
Belot, Robert. *Aux frontières de la liberté: Vichy-Madrid-Alger-Londres, s'évader de France sous l'Occupation.* Paris, 1998.
Bernstein, Serge, ed. *Paul Ramadier: la république et le socialisme.* Paris, 1992.
Best, R.A. *'Co-operation with Like-minded Peoples': British Influences on American Security Policy, 1945–1949.* New York, 1986.
Biddiscombe, Perry. 'The French Resistance and the Chambèry Incident of June, 1945.' *French History* 11:4 (1997).
Bloch-Lainé, F. & Bouvoir, J. *La France Restaurée, 1944–1954.* Paris, 1986.
Bossuat, Gérard. *La France, l'aide américaine et la construction européenne, 1944–1954.* Paris, 1992.
Borras, José. *Políticas de los exilados españoles, 1944–1950.* Paris, 1976.
Brinkley, Douglas, ed. *Dean Acheson and the Making of U.S. Foreign Policy.* London, 1993.
Brundu, Paola. 'L'Espagne franquiste et la politique etrangère de la France au lendemain de la Deuxième Guerre Mondiale.' *Rélations Internationales* 50 (1987).

Bibliography

Buffet, Cyril. *Mourir pour Berlin: La France et l'Allemagne, 1945–1949.* Paris, 1991.
Buton, Phillipe. *Les lendemans qui déchantent: le parti communiste français à la liberation.* Paris, 1993.
Capelle, Russell. *The MRP and French Foreign Policy.* New York, 1963.
Carlton, David. 'Eden, Blum and the Origins of Non-Intervention.' *Journal of Contemporary History* 6 (1971).
Carmoy, Guy. *The Foreign Policies of France, 1944–1968.* trans. E. Halperin. Chicago, 1970.
Caron, Vicki. *Uneasy Asylum: France and the Jewish Refugee Crisis, 1933–1942.* Stanford, 1999.
Carr, Raymond & Juan Pablo Fusi. *Spain: Dictatorship to Democracy.* London, 1979.
Catala, Michel. *Les relations franco-espagnoles pendant la Deuxième Guerre Mondiale: rapprochement nécessaire, réconciliation impossible, 1939–1944.* Paris, 1997.
——. 'Vichy, Madrid et Berline face à l'enjeu nord-africain et la neutralité de la méditerranée occidentale juin 1940–juin 1941.' *Guerres mondiales et conflits contemporains* 189 (1998).
Clavin, Patricia. 'Defining Transnationalism.' *Contemporary European History* 14:4 (2005).
Cogan, Charles. 'Response to Michael Creswell and Marc Trachtenberg.' *Journal of Cold War Studies* 5:3 (2003).
Cortada, James. *United States-Spanish Relations, Wolfram and World War II.* Barcelona, 1971.
——, ed. *Spain in the 20th Century World: Essays on Spanish Diplomacy, 1898–1978.* London, 1980.
Costigliola, Frank. *France and the United States: The Cold Alliance since WWII.* New York, 1992.
Courtois, Stéphane and Marc Lazar. *Histoire du Parti communiste français.* Paris, 1995.
Courtois, Stéphane. *Le PCF dans la Guerre: De Gaulle, Résistance, Staline.* Paris, 1980.
Cowan, Andrew. 'The Guerilla War Against Franco.' *European History Quarterly* 20 (1990).
Creswell, Michael. *A Question of Balance: How France and the United States Created Cold War Europe.* Cambridge, MA, 2006.
—— and Marc Trachtenberg. 'France and the German Question, 1944–1955.' *Journal of Cold War Studies* 5:3 (2003).
——. 'New Light on an Old Issue.' *Journal of Cold War Studies* 5:3 (2003).
Davis, Lynn. *The Cold War Begins: Soviet–American Conflict over Eastern Europe.* Princeton, 1974.
Delaunay, Jean-Marc. *Des Palais en Espagne: l'Ecole des hautes études hispaniques et la Casa de Veláquez au coeur des relations franco-espagnols du XXe siècle (1898–1979).* Madrid, 1994.
——. 'L'Espagne et la France (1940–1945).' *Guerres mondiales et conflits contemporains* 162 (1991).
DePorte, Anton. *De Gaulle's Foreign Policy, 1944–1946.* Cambridge, MA, 1968.
Dinan, Desmond. *The Politics of Persuasion: British Policy and French African Neutrality, 1940–42.* Lanham, MD, 1988.

Bibliography

Divine, Robert. *Roosevelt and World War II.* Baltimore, 1969.
Dockrill, M. and John W. Young, eds. *British Foreign Policy, 1945–1956.* London, 1989.
Dougherty, J.J. *The Politics of Wartime Aid: American Economic Assistance to France and French North Africa, 1940–1946.* Westport, CN, 1978.
Dreyfus, Michel. *Histoire de la C.G.T.* Paris, 1995.
Dreyfus-Armand, Geneviève. *L'Exil des Républicains Espagnols en France.* Paris, 1999.
———. 'L'émigration politique espagnole en France après 1939: les fonds de la BDIC.' *Materiaux pour l'histoire de notre temps* 3–4 (1985).
Dulphy, Anne. *La Politique de la France à l'égard de l'Espagne franquiste, 1945–1955: Entre Idéologie et Réalisme.* Paris, 2002.
———. 'La politique de la France a l'égard de l'Espagne franquiste, 1945–1949.' *Revue d'histoitre moderne et contemporaine* (1988).
Dunthorn, David J. 'The Prieto-Gil-Robles Meeting of October 1947: Britain and the Failure of the Spanish anti-Franco Coalition, 1945–50.' *European History Quarterly* 30:1 (2000).
———. *Britain and the Spanish Anti-Franco Opposition, 1940–1950.* London, 2000.
Duroselle, J-B. *L'Abîme, 1939–1945.* Paris, 1982.
———. 'Une création ex nihilo: le ministère des affaires etrangères du Général de Gaulle, 1940–1942.' *Relations Internationales* 31 (1982).
———. 'Le général de Gaulle et l'Espagne (1940–1944)' in *Españoles y Frances en la primera mitad del siglo XX.* Madrid, 1986.
Edwards, Jill. *Anglo-American Relations and the Franco Question, 1945–1955.* Oxford, 1999.
Elegy, Georgette. *La République des Illusions, 1945–1951.* Paris, 1965.
Eley, Geoff. *Forging Democracy: The History of the Left in Europe, 1850–2000.* Oxford, 2002.
Espadas Burgos, Manuel. *Franquismo y politica exterior.* Madrid, 1988.
Estebe, Jean. *Toulouse, 1940–1944.* Paris, 1996.
Eychenne, Emilienne. *Pyrénées de la liberté: Les évasions par l'Espagne, 1939–1945.* 2nd ed. Toulouse, 1998.
Fernández, Luis Suárez. *Franco y la URSS.* Madrid, 1987.
Foot, M.R.D. *SOE in France.* London, 1966.
Frank, R. 'France-Grande Bretagne: la mesentente commerciale, 1945–1948.' *Rélations Internationales* 55 (1988).
Fraser, Ronald. 'The Popular Experience of War and Revolution' in Paul Preston, ed., *Revolution and War in Spain, 1931–1939.* London, 1984.
Funk, Arthur Layton. *Charles de Gaulle: The Crucial Years 1943–1944.* Norman, OK, 1959.
———. *The Politics of TORCH: The Allied Landings and the Algiers Putsch, 1942.* Lawrence, KS, 1974.
Gaddis, John Lewis. *The United States and the Origins of the Cold War, 1941–1947.* New York, 1972.
Gallagher, M.D. 'Leon Blum and the Spanish Civil War.' *Journal of Contemporary History* 6 (1971).
Gerbet, Pierre. *Le Rélevement, 1944–1949.* Paris, 1991.
Giles, Frank. *The Locust Years: The Story of the Fourth French Republic, 1946–1958.*

London, 1991.
Gillingham, John R. *Coal, Steel and the Rebirth of Europe, 1945–1955: The Germans and French from Ruhr Conflict to Economic Community.* Cambridge, 1991.
Goda, Norman J.W. *Tomorrow the World: Hitler, Northwest Africa and the Path toward America.* College Station, TX, 1998.
Gosser, Alfred. *Le IVe République et sa politique extèrieure.* Paris, 1972.
Goubert, M. 'Une 'République Rouge' à Toulouse à la Libération: Mythe ou realité?' *Revue d'histoire de la Deuxième Guerre Mondiale* 131 (1983).
Graham, B.D. *French Socialists and Tripartism, 1944–1947.* Toronto, 1965.
———. *Choice and Democratic Order: The French Socialist Party, 1937–1954.* Cambridge, 1994.
Greenwood, Sean. 'Ernest Bevin, France and 'Western Union': August 1945–February 1946.' *European History Quarterly* 14 (1984).
———. 'Frank Roberts and the 'Other' Long Telegram: The View from the British Embassy in Moscow, March 1946.' *Journal of Contemporary History* 25 (1990).
Guirao, Fernando. 'The United States, Franco and the Integration of Europe' in F. Heiler & J. Gillingham, eds. *The United States and the Integration of Europe: Legacies of the Postwar Era.* New York, 1996.
———. *Spain and the Reconstruction of Western Europe, 1945–57: Challenge and Response.* New York, 1998.
Halstead, Charles & Halstead, Carolyn. 'Aborted Imperialism: Spain's Occupation of Tangier, 1940–1945.' *Iberian Studies* 7 (1978).
Hamilton, Keith. 'Non-Intervention Revisited: Great Britain, the United Nations and Franco's Spain in 1946' in *FCO Historians Occasional Papers No. 10: United Kingdom, United Nations and divided world, 1946.* London, 1995.
Harbutt, Fraser J. *The Iron Curtain: Churchill, America and the Origins of the Cold War.* Oxford, 1986.
Harper, John Lamberton. *American Visions of Europe: Franklin D. Roosevelt, George F. Kennan, Dean G. Acheson.* Cambridge, 1994.
Harrison, Joseph. *The Spanish Economy in the Twentieth Century.* London, 1985.
Heine, Hartmut. *La Oposición política al franquismo.* Barcelona, 1983.
Hermet, Guy. *Les Espagnols en France.* Paris, 1967.
Hinsley, F.H. et al. *British Intelligence in the Second World War, vols. IV-V.* Cambridge, 1990.
Hitchcock, William I. *France Restored: Cold War Diplomacy and the Quest for Leadership in Europe, 1944–1954.* Chapel Hill, NC, 1998.
———. 'Response to "France and the German Question, 1944–1955" by Michael Creswell and Marc Trachtenberg.' *Journal of Cold War Studies* 5:3 (2003).
Hogan, Michael J. *A Cross of Iron: Harry S. Truman and the Origins of the National Security State, 1945–1954.* Cambridge, 1998.
———. *The Marshall Plan: America, Britain and the Reconstruction of Western Europe, 1947–1952.* Cambridge, 1987.
Hoisington, William A. *The Casablanca Connection: French Colonial Policy, 1936–1943.* Chapel Hill, NC, 1984.
Hurstfield, Julian G. *America and the French Nation, 1939–1945.* Chapel Hill, NC, 1986.
Jackson, Julian. *The Popular Front in France: Defending Democracy, 1934–1938.*

Bibliography

Cambridge, 1988.
Jones, Randolph Bernard. 'The Spanish Question and the Cold War, 1944–1953.' PhD Thesis, University of London, 1987.
Judt, Tony. *Past Imperfect: French Intellectuals 1944–1956*. Berkeley, 1992.
——. *Postwar: A History of Europe since 1945*. New York, 2005.
Junot, Michel. *Opération Torch*. Paris, 2001.
Kersaudy, François. *Churchill and de Gaulle*. New York, 1983.
Kleinfeld, Gerald and Lewis A. Tombs, *Hitler's Spanish Legion: The Blue Division in Russia*. Carbondale, IL, 1979.
Kolko, Gabriel. *The Politics of War*. London, 1968.
—— and Joyce Kolko. *The Limits of Power: The World and United States Foreign Policy 1945–1954*. New York, 1972.
Knox, MacGregor. *Mussolini Unleashed, 1939–1941: Politics and Strategy in Fascist Italy's Last War*. Cambridge, 1982.
Koreman, Megan. *The Expectation of Justice: France, 1944–1946*. Durham, NC, 1999.
Lacroix-Riz, Annie. *La CGT de la Libération à la scission, 1944–1947*. Paris, 1983.
Langer, William L. *Our Vichy Gamble*. New York, 1947 (reprint, 1965).
Larkin, Maurice. *France since the Popular Front 1936–1986*. Oxford, 1988.
Leffler, Melvyn P. *A Preponderance of Power: National Security, the Truman Administration and the Cold War* Stanford, 1992.
——. *The Specter of Communism: The United States and the Origins of the Cold War, 1917–1953*. New York, 1994.
Leitz, Christian. *Economic Relations between Nazi Germany and Franco's Spain, 1936–1945*. Oxford, 1996.
——. *Sympathy for the Devil: Neutral Europe and Nazi Germany in World War II*. New York, 2001.
——. 'Nazi Germany's Struggle for Spanish Wolfram during the Second World War.' *European History Quarterly* 25 (1995).
—— and David Dunthorn, eds. *Spain in an International Context, 1939–1959*. New York, 1999.
Liedtke, Boris. *Embracing a Dictatorship: US-Spanish Relations 1945–1953*. New York, 1998.
Lillo, Pedro Martinez. *Una introducción al estudio de las relaciones hispano-francesas (1945–1951)*. Madrid, 1985.
Little, Douglas. 'Red Scare, 1936: Anti-Bolshevism and the Origins of British Non-Intervention in the Spanish Civil War.' *Journal of Contemporary History* 23 (1988).
Lleonart, Alberto J. 'España y la ONU: la cuestión española, 1945–1950.' *Revista de Politica Internacional* 153 (1977).
Lottman, Herbert. *The People's Anger: Justice and Revenge in Post-Liberation France*. London, 1986.
Luard, Evan. *A History of the United Nations, vol. I: The Years of Western Domination 1945–1955*. London, 1982.
Maier, Charles S. 'Hegemony and Autonomy within the Western Alliance' in Melvyn P. Leffler and David S. Painter, eds. *Origins of the Cold War: An International History*. London, 1994.
Marquina, Antonio. *España en la politica de seguridad ocidental 1939–1986*. Madrid,

Bibliography

1986.
Marrus, Michael. *The Unwanted: European Refugees in the Twentieth Century*. Oxford, 1985.
Martinez Lillo, Pedro. 'Una aproximacion al estudio de las relaciones bilaterales hispanos-francescas durante la posguerra. El 'affaire' fronterizo en la perspectiva del Quai d'Orsay (1946–1948).' *Revista de Estudios Internacionales* 6 (1985).
Mastny, V. *Russia's Road to the Cold War*. New York, 1979.
Mazower, Mark. 'The Strange Triumph of Human Rights, 1933–1950.' *The Historical Journal* 47:2 (2004).
Medlicott, W.M. *The Economic Blockade*. 2 vols. London, 1952–1959.
Messenger, David A. 'Our Spanish Brothers' or 'As at Plombières': France and the Spanish Opposition to Franco, 1945–1948.' *French History* 20:1 (2006)
———. 'Rival Faces of France: Refugees, Would-be Allies and Economic Warfare in Spain, 1942–1944.' *International History Review* 27:1 (2005)
———. 'The Spirit of Sacrifice: The French Left, Franco's Spain and the Case of Cristino García' in Barry Rothaus, ed. *Proceedings of the Western Society of French History Volume 28: Selected Papers of the 2000 Annual Meeting* (Greeley, CO: University Press of Colorado, 2002).
Michel, Henri. *The Shadow War: Resistance in Europe 1939–1945.* trans. R. Barr. London, 1972.
Milward, Alan. *The Reconstruction of Western Europe, 1945–1951*. London, 1984.
———. 'Bad Memories.' *Times Literary Supplement*, 14 April 2000.
Milza, Pierre & Denis Peschanski, eds. *Exils et Migrations: Italiens et Espagnols en France, 1938–1946*. Paris, 1994.
Miscamble, Wilson. *George F. Kennan and the Making of American Foreign Policy 1947–1950*. Princeton, 1992.
Morgan, Kenneth O. *Labour in Power, 1945–1951*. Oxford, 1984.
Morris, D.S. *Britain, Spain and Gibraltar, 1945–1990: the eternal triangle*. New York, 1992.
Noguères, H. *Histoire de la Résistance en France*. 5 vols. Paris, 1967–1981.
Novick, Peter. *L'Epuration française*. 2e ed, trans. Helene Ternois. Paris, 1983.
Ovendale, Ritchie, ed. *The Foreign Policies of the Labour Government, 1945–1951*. Oxford, 1984.
Payne, Stanley. *The Franco Regime, 1936–1975*. Madison, WI, 1987.
Paxton, Robert O. *Vichy France: Old Guard and New Order 1940–1944*. 2nd ed. New York, 1981.
Pendar, Kenneth. *Adventure in Diplomacy: The Emergence of General de Gaulle in North Africa*. London, 1968.
Peyrade, Jean. *Situation de la presse dans la région de Toulouse (20 aout 1944–1er octobre 1947)*. Paris, 1976.
Pigenet, Phryné. 'La protection des étrangers à l'épreuve de la guerre froide: l'opération 'Boléro-Paprika.' *Revue d'historie moderne e contemporaine* 46:2 (1999).
Pike, David Winegate. *Vae Victis! Los Republicanos españoles refugiados en Francia 1939–1944*. Paris, 1969.
———. *Les français et la guerre d'Espagne, 1936–1939*. Paris, 1975.

Bibliography

———. *Jours de Gloire, Jours de Honte: le parti communiste d'Espagne en France.* Paris, 1984.
———. *In the Service of Stalin: The Spanish Communists in Exile, 1939–1945.* Oxford, 1993.
———. 'Franco and the Axis Stigma.' *Journal of Contemporary History* 17 (1982).
———. 'Franco et l'admission aux Nations Unies.' *Guerres Mondiales et Conflits Contemporains* 162 (1991).
———. 'L'Immigration Espagnole en France (1945–1952).' *Revue d'histoire moderne et contemporaine* 24 (1977).
Pollard, R.A. *Economic Security and the Origins of the Cold War, 1945–1950.* New York, 1985.
Pollock, Benny. *The Paradox of Spanish Foreign Policy: Spain's International Relations from Franco to Democracy.* New York, 1987.
Pondaven, Phillipe. *Le Parlement et la politique extérieure sous le IVe Republique.* Paris, 1973.
Pon Prades, Eduardo. *Guerilleros españolas, 1936–1960.* Barcelona, 1977.
Porch, Douglas. *The French Secret Services: From the Dreyfus Affair to the Gulf War.* New York, 1995.
Portero, Florentino. *Franco aislado: la cúestion española, 1945–1950.* Madrid, 1989.
Preston, Paul. *A Concise History of the Spanish Civil War.* London, 1996.
——— and Helen Graham, eds. *The Popular Front in Europe.* London, 1987.
Rafaneau-Boj, Marie-Claude. *Odyssée pour la Liberté: Les camps de prisonniers espagnols 1939–45.* Paris, 1993.
Rice-Maximin, Edward. 'The U.S. and the French Left, 1945–1949.' *Journal of Contemporary History* 19 (1984).
Richards, Michael. *A Time of Silence: Civil War and the Culture of Repression in Franco's Spain, 1936–1945.* Cambridge, 1998.
Rieber, Alfred. *Stalin and the French Communist Party, 1941–1947.* Cambridge, MA, 1962.
Rioux, Jean-Pierre. *The Fourth Republic.* trans. G. Rodgers. London, 1987.
Rothwell, Victor. *Britain and the Cold War, 1941–1947.* London, 1982.
Rousso, Henri. *The Vichy Syndrome: History and Memory in France since 1944.* trans. A. Goldhammer. Cambridge, MA, 1991.
Rubio, Javier. *La emigración española a Francia.* Barcelona, 1974.
Rubottom, R. and J.C. Murphy. *Spain and the United States since World War II.* New York, 1984.
Sagnes, Jacques and Sylvie Caucanas, eds. *Les Français et la Guerre d'Espagne: Actes du Colloque de Perpignan.* Perpignan, 1990.
Salomon, Kim. *Refugees in the Cold War: Toward a New International Refugee Regime in the Early Postwar Era.* Lund, 1991.
Sainsbury, Keith. *The North African Landings, 1942: A Strategic Decision.* London, 1976.
Sanders, Roger F. *Spain and the United Nations, 1945–1950.* New York, 1966.
Santos, Félix. *Españoles en la liberación de Francia: 1939–1945.* Madrid, 1995.
Saville, John. *The Politics of Continuity: British Foreign Policy and the Labour Government, 1945–1946.* London, 1993.
Séguéla, Matthieu. *Pétain-Franco: les secrets d'une alliance.* Paris, 1992.
Sheetz, Mark S. 'France and the German Question: Avant-garde or Rear-guard?

Bibliography

Comment on Creswell and Tractenberg.' *Journal of Cold War Studies* 5:3 (2003).

Shennan, Andrew. *Rethinking France: Plans for Renewal, 1940–1946.* Oxford, 1989.

Sjoberg, Tommie. *The Powers and the Persecuted: The Refugee Problem and the Intergovernmental Committee on Refugees (1938–1947).* Lund, 1991.

Skran, Claudena. *Refugees in Inter-War Europe: The Emergence of a Regime.* Oxford, 1995.

Slany, William Z. *US and Allied Efforts to Recover and Restore Gold and Other Assets Stolen or Hidden by Germany during World War II.* Washington, 1997.

Smith, Gaddis. *American Diplomacy during the Second World War, 1941–1945.* New York, 1965.

Smith, Richard Harris. *OSS: The Secret History of America's First Central Intelligence Agency.* Berkeley, 1972.

Smouts, Marie-Claude. *La France à l'ONU: premier role et second rang.* Paris, 1979.

Smyth, Denis. *Diplomacy and Strategy of Survival: British Policy and Franco's Spain, 1940–1941.* Cambridge, 1986.

——. 'Les chevaliers de Saint-George: la Grande-Bretagne et la corruption des généraux espagnols (1940–1942).' *Guerres mondiales et conflits contemporains* 162 (1991).

——. 'Screening 'Torch': Allied Counter-Intelligence and the Spanish Threat to the Secrecy of the Allied Invasion of North Africa in November, 1942.' *Intelligence and National Security* 4 (1989).

——. 'Spain' in Zara Steiner, ed. *The Times Survey of Foreign Ministries of the World.* London, 1982.

——. 'The Politics of Asylum: Juan Negrín and the British Government in 1940' in R. Langhorne, ed., *Diplomacy and Intelligence during the Second World War: Essays in Honour of F.H. Hinsley.* Cambridge, 1984.

Soutou, Georges-Henri. 'Georges Bidault et la construction européenne, 1944–1954.' *Revue d'histoire diplomatique* 105 (1991).

——. 'France and the Cold War, 1944–63.' *Diplomacy and Statecraft* 12:4 (2001).

Stafford, David. *Britain and European Resistance, 1940–1945.* London, 1980.

Stead, Philip. *Second Bureau.* London, 1959.

Steele, Richard W. *The First Offensive, 1942: Roosevelt, Marshall and the Making of American Strategy.* Bloomington, IN, 1973.

Stein, Louis. *Beyond Death and Exile: The Spanish Republicans in France, 1939–1955.* Cambridge, MA, 1979.

Stephanson, Anders. *Kennan and the Art of Foreign Policy.* Cambridge, MA, 1989.

Stone, Glyn. *Spain, Portugal and the Great Powers, 1931–1941.* London, 2005.

——. 'Britain, France and Franco's Spain in the Aftermath of the Spanish Civil War.' *Diplomacy and Statecraft* 6:2 (1995).

——. 'Britain, Non-Intervention and the Spanish Civil War.' *European Studies Review* 9 (1979).

Sweets, John. *The Politics of Resistance in France, 1940–1944.* Urbana, IL, 1976.

Thomas, R.T. *Britain and Vichy: The Dilemma of Anglo-French Relations 1940–42.* New York, 1979.

Thomas, Martin. *The French Empire at War, 1940–45.* Manchester, 1998.

——. *The French North African Crisis: Colonial Breakdown and Anglo-French Relations, 1945–62.* New York, 2000.

Trachtenberg, Marc. *A Constructed Peace: The Making of the European Settlement,*

Bibliography

1945–1963. Princeton, 1999.

Trempe, Rolande, ed. *La Libération dans le midi de la France.* Toulouse, 1986.

Tussell, Javier. Franco. *España y la II Guerra Mundial: Entre el eje y la neutralidad.* Madrid, 1995.

Vilanova, Antonio. *Los Olvidados: los exilados españoles en la Segunda Guerra Mundial.* Paris, 1969.

Viñas, Angel et al. *Política commercial exterior en España (1931–1975).* 2 vols. Madrid, 1979.

Viñas, Angel. *Los pactos secretos de Franco con Estados Unidos: bases, ayuda economica, recortes de sobernia.* Barcelona, 1981.

Vinen, Richard. *Bourgeois Politics in France, 1945–1951.* Cambridge, 1995.

Viorst, Milton. *Hostile Allies: FDR and Charles de Gaulle.* New York, 1965.

Walker, David. 'OSS and Operation Torch.' *Journal of Contemporary History* 22 (1987).

Wall, Irwin. *The United States and the Making of Postwar France, 1945–1954.* Cambridge, 1991.

———. *French Communism in the Era of Stalin: The Quest for Unity and Integration, 1945–62.* Westport, CN, 1983.

Warner, Geoffrey. 'France and Non-Intervention in Spain, July-August 1936.' *International Affairs* 38:2 (1962).

Weber, Eugen. *The Hollow Years: France in the 1930s.* New York, 1994.

Weinberg, Gerhard L. *A World at Arms: A Global History of World War II.* Cambridge, 1994.

Whitaker, Arthur P. *Spain and the Defence of the West: Ally and Liability.* New York, 1962.

Wigg, Richard. *Churchill and Spain: The Survival of the Franco Regime, 1940–45.* London, 2005.

Woodward, Llewellyn. *British Foreign Policy and the Second World War.* vol IV. London, 1975.

Wylie, Neville, ed. *European Neutrals and Non-Belligerents during the Second World War.* Cambridge, 2001.

Yergin, Daniel. *Shattered Peace: the Origins of the Cold War and the National Security State.* London, 1980.

Young, John W. *France, the Cold War and the Western Alliance, 1944–1949.* Leicester, 1990.

———. 'The Foreign Office and the Departure of General de Gaulle, 1945–1946.' *The Historical Journal* 25 (1982).

Young, Robert. J. *In Command of France: French Foreign Policy and Military Planning, 1933–1940.* Cambridge, MA, 1978.

Zametica, John, ed. *British Officials and British Foreign Policy, 1945–50.* Leicester, 1990.

INDEX

Acheson, Dean, 72, 83–4, 105, 108, 114
AGE *(Agrupación de Guerrillos españoles)*, 38, 39
Agrupación Democrática Española, see JEL/Agrupación
Allies
  economic war (*see* economic war)
  need for unity on Spain, 14
  rejection of France's UN proposal, 115
  response to border crisis, 45
  Spain's relationship with, 19–20
  see also Great Britain; United States
Altman, Georges, 96
Alvarez, Santiago, 60
ANFD, 68, 69, 72
Anti-Communism
  in American perspectives on Spain, 103
  arrest of Communists in France, 136
  Franco's promotion of, 110
  motivation for British policy, 111
  and non-intervention, 111
  proto-containment, 103–5
  and rejection of France's UN proposal, 115
  and US policy on Spain, 113
  see also Cold War
Anti-fascism, 141
Anti-Francoism
  and Allied contact with Spanish opposition, 65
  appeal to common history of France and Spain, 35–7
  beginning of campaign of, 33–4
  contact with French government, 69–70
  debt element in, 37–40
  and democracy, 34
  France's analyses of, 64–5
  in French press, 88, 100
  and French Resistance, 31
  French support for, 63–74
  and García case, 90–3
  Hardion's reluctance to engage in, 128

  pressure for by Republican groups, 53
  and security, 116–17
  sympathy for within France, 52
  Tripartite Statement's solidification of, 121
  Western Alliance's support for, 63–4
Apology for France's use of UN on Spanish Question, 130–1
Arms, offered to French by Spanish, 46
Association France-Espagne, 59, 60
Attlee, Clement, 102
Auriol, Vincent, 34, 42–3, 93
Australia, 126–7
  see also Sub-Committee on Spain

Balfour, John, 83, 84
Bechelloni, Antoine, 39
Bertaux, Pierre, 43
Bevin, Ernest, 111, 118
Bidault, Georges
  concern about pressure to break relations with Spain, 89
  criticized for Spanish policies, 85
  defense of Franco-Spanish trade agreement, 88
  desire to leave Spanish case alone, 121
  desire to work with Allies on Spanish Question, 97
  encouragement of transition regime, 70
  on France's policy on Spain, 113, 134
  and interventions in death sentences, 60, 63
  invitation to Soviets to address Spanish Question, 100–1
  new policies toward Spain, 78
  opposition to rupture with Spain, 94–5
  on Polish initiative, 123, 124
  proposal for refugee protection, 54
  refusal to present Spain as security threat, 117
  in response to border crisis, 51
  in Spanish Question debate, 87
  on Spanish refugees, 56–7

Index

willingness to discuss re-opening borders, 134, 135
see also Quai d'Orsay
Bidoux, Marcel, 34
Blue Division, 48
Blum, Léon, 6
Bonnet, Henri, 125–6
Borbón, Juan de, 64, 65, 68, 71–2
Border crisis, 40–6
Borders
  France's closing of, 68, 95–6, 97, 132, 134, 135 (*see also* sanctions)
  Spain's closing of, 109–10
  Spanish troop deployment on, 116–17
Boyer-Mas, André, 16–17
Brundu, Paola, 100

Cadogan, Alexander, 124, 126, 130
Camus, Albert, 37, 80
CFLN (*Comité Français de la Libération Nationale*)
  formation of, 9, 24
  relationship with Spain after liberation, 26–8
  role in economic war, 10, 25
  treated as ally, 25, 26
  see also GPRF
CFM (Council of Foreign Ministers), 117, 118, 119
CGT (*Confedération Generale de Travail*), 89, 93, 95, 115, 133, 134
Chambéry, France, 48
Chauvel, Jean, 70, 95
Christian Democrats, *see* MRP
Churchill, Winston, 110
Civil war
  fear of renewal of in Spain, 82
  Spanish, 2, 6–7, 37–40
CLN (*Comité de Libération National*), 38
CNT (*Confederación Nacional del Trabajo*), 53, 55, 68, 69, 70, 71, 72
Cogan, Charles, 76
Cold War
  commitment of France to, 140
  importance of Spain to US in, 135
  influence on European politics, 140
  and Spanish Question, 98, 122
  and US policy on Spain, 102–3
Colonial issues in Franco-Spanish relations, 136
Comité de Libération National (CLN), *see* CLN
Comité Français de la Libération Nationale (CFLN), *see* CFLN
Comité France-Espagne, 59, 60

Commercial treaty, Franco-Spanish (September 1945), 27, 34, 77, 88
Communications, disruption of, 93, 95–6
Communists/Communism
  actions during border crisis, 45
  anti-Spanish attitudes, 78
  arrest of in France, 136
  CGT, 89, 93, 95, 115, 133, 134
  in debate over Spanish Question, 85
  departure from French government, 135
  and García case, 90, 91, 92
  PCE, 38, 44
  PCF, 32, 84–5, 92–3, 106–7, 115
  pressure from to rupture relations with Spain, 89, 107
  proto-containment, 103–5
  relationship with Giral Government, 68
  role in border crisis, 43–4
  Spanish, 38, 107
  support for Spanish activists, 43
  suspected of influencing French policy, 113–14, 115–16
  UNE, 38, 42, 43, 44, 53, 57
  view of December Note, 80
  see also anti-Communism
Confedération Generale de Travail (CGT), 89, 93, 95, 115, 133, 134
Constituent National Assembly, 37, 84–7, 93
Consulates, Spanish, 40, 41, 46, 91
Containment, 103–5
Coordination
  France's desire for, 86, 113
  need for on diplomatic relations with Spain, 83–4, 94
  US's desire for with Britain, 83
Coulet, François, 118
Council of Foreign Ministers (CFM), 117, 118, 119
Creswell, Michael, 76, 140
Cross-trade system, 23

D'Aragon, Charles, 84, 85
Darlan, François, 9
  see also French High Commission in North Africa
Death sentences, French intervention in, 58–63, 90–3, 128
Debt
  in anti-Franco campaign, 37–40
  and French intervention in death sentences, 58
  and García case, 91
December Note, 79–84, 86, 87
De Chambrun, Gilbert, 84, 85–6, 132

Index

De Gaulle, Charles
  call for new politics, 31
  resignation of, 89
  treatment of Giraud, 24
  willingness to continue diplomatic relations with Spain, 4
Democracy
  and anti-Francoism, 34
  vision for in France, 5
Diplomatic relations with Spain
  Britain's, 102
  call to end in France, 37
  compromise to rupture, 95–6
  economic impact of rupturing, 94
  France's need to maintain, 53
  France's proposed rupture of, 75–6, 78
  and García case, 90–3
  motion to prepare for rupture of, 87, 93
  need for coordination on, 94
  opposition to rupturing, 94–5
  Parodi's voting on, 131
  pressure on France to rupture, 89
  Soviet Union's lack of, 106
Don Juan, 64, 65, 68, 71–2
Donnez, François, 36, 39
"Double game," 77, 78, 81, 91
Dreyfus-Armand, Geneviève, 53
Duclos, Jacques, 85
Dumas, Charles, 33
Dunn, James, 82–3

Economic war, 10, 20–6
Edwards, Jill, 31
Eley, Geoff, 1, 141
Elgey, Georgette, 89
Embassy, French, 12, 16
England, *see* Great Britain
Escape routes, 11
Estoril agreement, 71–2
Evatt, Herbert, 127
Executions, 58, 59–63, 90–3
Exiles, Spanish
  activism of, 46–7 (*see also* guerillas, Spanish)
  desires of, 53–4
  disappointment in Tripartite Statement, 109
  end to protection and privileges of, 136
  French policies regarding, 54–7
  make-up of, 53–4
  moved to interior of France, 135
  reaction to December Note, 81–2
  see also border crisis

February Note, 98–101

FFI (*Forces Françaises de l'Interieur*), 38, 45
Fourth Republic, *see* France; policy, French
France
  acceptance of failure on Spain, 119–20
  acceptance of Franco's Spain, 122
  admission of weaknesses, 113–14
  alignment forced upon, 120, 121
  alignment with Soviet Union, possible, 99, 117, 119
  alternative governments, 14 (*see also* CFLN; Free France movement; French High Commission in North Africa)
  anti-Franco sentiment in (*see* anti-Francoism)
  apology for use of UN on Spanish Question, 130–1
  attempts to parallel Allies' policy toward Spain, 34–5
  closing of Spanish border, 68, 95–6, 97, 132, 134, 135
  commercial treaty with Spain, 27, 34, 77, 88
  contribution to diplomatic settlement with Franco, 25
  contribution to Sub-Committee on Spain, 128
  German occupation of south, 9–10
  Gouin Government, 89
  influence of, 140
  international position of, 94
  isolation of, 101, 118, 139
  loss of North African territories, 9
  maintenance of relations with Franco, 74
  obligation to support Polish initiative, 124
  policies of (*see* policy, French)
  provisional government of, 26–8, 45
  pursuit of long-term agreements with Spain, 77
  reconsideration of relations with Spain, 78–9
  reconstruction of, 26, 27
  relationship with Spain (*see* diplomatic relations with Spain; Franco-Spanish relations; Spanish Question)
  response to border crisis, 44–6
  retreat from Spanish position, 129
  risks of unilateral action to, 75–6
  vision for restoration of, 50
  see also Constituent National Assembly; Free France movement; French High Commission in North Africa; GPRF; Quai d'Orsay
Franco, Francisco
  French acceptance of, 135
  lack of action against, 34–5

190

Index

Law of Succession, 73
opposition to (*see* anti-Francoism)
promotion of regime as anti-Communist, 110
reinforcement of position, 112
repression under, 58–9
Sub-Committee's condemnation of, 130
view of Tripartite Statement, 109–10
Franco-Spanish commercial treaty (September 1945), 27, 34, 77, 88
Franco-Spanish relations
after liberation, 26–8
colonial issues in, 136
France's reconsideration of, 78–9
and popular French mood, 47–8
see also diplomatic relations with Spain
Free France movement
merger with High Commission, 9, 24 (*see also* CFLN)
refugees encouraged to join, 13
work with refugees, 14–15
Freemasons, 62
French High Commission in North Africa
desire for recognition, 11, 12, 18, 22
desire to open trade talks with Spain, 22
embassy staff's allegiance switched to, 16
formation of, 9
merger with Free France movement, 9, 24 (*see also* CFLN)
negotiations about refugees, 11
role in economic war, 10, 20–4
spies in Spain, 17
trade and recognition of, 24
US's support of, 12–13, 23
French North Africa, 9, 10, 14

García, Cristino, 90–3, 102
Germany, 20–1
Giral Pereira, José, 66, 127, 132
see also Giral Government
Giral Government, 66–7, 68, 72, 109
Giraud, Henri, 9, 24
Gouin, Félix, 89, 93
Gouin Government, 89
GPRF (Provisional Government of the French Republic), 26–8, 45
Grandeur, 4
Great Britain
contact with Spanish opposition, 65, 66
defense of policy, 118–19
diplomatic relations with Spain, 102
economic warfare, 21 (*see also* economic war)
frustration with French actions, 118–19

non-intervention policy of, 106
opposition to December Note, 83, 84
opposition to French UN proposal, 112, 113, 115
opposition to protection of refugees, 55–6
opposition to sanctions, 111–12
policy on French refugees, 13–14
policy on Spain, 102–3, 110–11
reaction to December Note, 81–2
reaction to France's admission of weakness, 114–15
reaction to Long Telegram, 105
reaction to Sub-Committee report, 130
rejection of France's UN proposal, 115
response to Polish initiative, 124, 126
role in Mediterranean, 13
support for Spanish Republicanism, 79
trade with Spain, 111
Tripartite Statement, 108–10
see also Allies; Western Alliance
Gromyko, Andrei, 131
Grumbach, Saloman, 117
Guerillas, Spanish, 40, 41, 46
see also border crisis
Guerrilla warfare strategy, abandonment of, 52, 53
Guirao, Fernando, 27

Hamilton, Keith, 137
Hardion, Bernard
attempts to save Estoril agreement, 71–2
and García case, 92
intervention in death sentences, 61–2, 92
opposition to further French initiatives on Spain, 121
opposition to sanctions, 133
preparation of contribution to Sub-Committee, 128
on Spanish troops on border, 117
Haut Commissariat de France en Afrique Française, *see* French High Commission in North Africa
Hayes, Carlton J., 12–13, 18, 24
Herriot, Edouard, 117
High Commission, *see* French High Commission in North Africa
Hitchcock, William I., 3, 76, 140
Hoyer-Millar, Frederick, 105, 111
Humanitarianism, 63

Idealism *vs.* realism in policy, 64, 86, 89, 120
IGC (Intergovernmental Committee on Refugees), 56

Index

Intervention
  in cases of Spanish political prisoners, 58–63, 128
  France's in Spain, 120
"Iron Curtain" speech, 110
Isolation of France, 101, 118, 139

JEL/Agrupación, 53, 64
  see also Giral Government
Joint Committee, 23
Jordana, Francisco Gómez, 12, 15, 17
Jouhaux, Léon, 133
Judt, Tony, 1, 141
Junta Española de Liberación (JEL), see JEL/Agrupación
Justice
  balance with realpolitik, 96
  in concept of reconstruction, 1, 2
  France's inability to build policy on, 119, 122
  influence on French policy, 74, 141, 142
  influence on post-war politics, 141
  and interventions in death sentences, 63

Kennan, George F., 103–6, 108, 109, 113

Laborers, Spanish, 48–9
Lange, Oskar, 125
Lausanne Manifesto, 65
Law of Succession, 73
League of Nations, 54, 55, 56
Leffler, Melvyn, 3
Liberation, French
  chaos following, 41
  parallels to Spanish Question, 91
  relationship with Spain following, 26–8
Liberation, Spanish, see Republicanism; Republicans, Spanish
Long Telegram, 103–5
Luque, José, 71–2

Macmillan, Harold, 23
Mail, diplomatic, 62
Malaise, Pierre, 12, 14, 15–16
Mallet, Victor, 82, 88
Maquis, 41–2
  see also guerillas, Spanish
Marco Nadal, Enrique, 71–2
Marshall Plan, 135
Marty, André, 84–5, 91
Massigli, René, 55, 120
Matthews, H. Freeman, 23, 112, 125
Mayer, Daniel, 84
Mediterranean, 13
Military, French, 11, 12, 41

Military, Spanish, 116–17, 128, 129
Military cooperation with Spain, 136
Mission in Madrid, see Hardion, Bernard; Truelle, Jacques
Mitchell, Robert, 14
MLE-CNT, 68–9
MLN (Mouvement de Libération Nationale), 32, 43, 84, 85
Monarchists/monarchy, Spanish, 64, 68–9, 72, 73
"Monsieur X," 69–70, 72, 73–4
Morocco, 20
MRP (Mouvement Républicaine Populaire), 32, 84, 85, 92
MUR (Mouvement Unifié de la Résistance), 32, 78
  see also MLN
Mutter, Andre, 85, 93

Nansen Program, 54
National security, concept of, 3
Newspapers
  associated with resistance groups, 32–3
  on French debt to Spain, 39–40
  see also press, French
Non-intervention
  and anti-Communism, 111
  British position of, 106
  France's in Spanish Civil War, 6
  intentions of in Tripartite Statement, 108
North Africa, French, 4, 9, 10, 14
North African Army, 11, 18

Occupation of southern France, 9–10
Office Commercial Français en Espagne, 25
Operation Torch, 9
Opposition, Spanish, 67–9, 70, 71–2
  see also anti-Francoism
Organization for European Economic Cooperation (OEEC), 136

Pan de Soraluce, José, 18–19
Parodi, Alexandre, 129, 130
Parti Républicain de la Liberté (PRI), 85
PCE (Partido Communista Española), 38, 44
PCF (Parti Communiste Français), 32, 84–5, 92–3, 106–7, 115
Pétain, Philippe, 36
Phosphates, 15, 16, 20, 25
Piétri, François, 15–16
Pike, David Wingeate, 52–3
Poland, proposal to bring Spanish Question to UN by, 123–6
Policy, French
  acceptance of Spain, 136

Index

acknowledgment of failure of, 137–8
attempts to match Allies', 34–5
changed to match Allies', 134
Communism's influence on, suspected, 113–14, 115–16
decrease of importance of Spain in, 134
desire for Allied support, 123
failure of Resistance model, 122
idealism in, 64, 86, 89, 120
inability to build on justice, 119, 122
influence of justice on, 74, 141, 142
influence of public on, 113–14, 132
influence of realpolitik on, 4, 27, 142
influence of Resistance myth on, 4–5, 64, 140–1
Quai's loss of control of, 120
realism of, 140, 142
realism vs. idealism in, 120
reconsideration of, 78
see also Quai d'Orsay
Political prisoners, 58–63, 128
see also García, Cristino
Popular Front, 6
Portugal, 17
Pouzzner, Georgianna, 22
Press, French
anti-Franco campaign in, 88, 100
coverage of Spanish Question, 49
on French policies toward Spain, 77
and intervention in death sentences, 62
support for Allied solution to Spanish Question, 101–2
see also newspapers
PRL *(Parti Républicain de la Liberté)*, 85
Protection for Spanish exiles, 54–7, 136
Proto-containment, 103–5
Provisional Government of the French Republic (GPRF), 26, 45
PSOE (Spanish Socialist Party), 62, 68, 69, 73, 81
Pyrenees, crisis along, 40–6

Quai d'Orsay
forced to adopt Spanish policy different from Allies, 35
loss of control of policy, 120
opposition to rupturing diplomatic ties with Spain, 94
realpolitik approach of, 27
see also Bidault, Georges; France; policy, French

Ramarony, Jules, 85
Realism
of French policy, 140, 142

vs. idealism in policy, 64, 86, 89, 120
Realpolitik
in aftermath of war, 3
approach of Quai d'Orsay, 27
balance with justice, 96
within France, 4, 51
influence on French policy, 142
Reconstruction of Europe, 1
Reconstruction of France, importance of Spain to, 26, 27
Refugees, 54
Refugees, French
Boyer-Mas's work for, 16–17
Britain's policy on, 13–14
and challenge of roles in Mediterranean, 13
and contact between Franco and North Africa, 10
cost of relief of, 15
escape routes used by, 11
High Commission's assistance of, 16
High Commission's negotiations about, 11
make up of, 11, 12
military value of, 11, 18
political role of, 18, 20
sent to North Africa, 14
Spain's desire to be rid of, 15
transport of, 15, 17–18
Refugees, Spanish
appeal to IGC, 56
French treatment of, 37–8
see also exiles, Spanish
Repression under Franco, 2, 58–9, 128
see also political prisoners
Republicanism
appeal to in anti-Franco campaign, 35–7
and Resistance ideals, 31
see also Republicans, Spanish
Republicans, Spanish
appeal to French Resistance, 35–6
divisions among, 53, 65, 77
opening of Republican Chamber of Commerce, 47
power of inside France, 51
pressure for action against Franco, 53
Resistance activities as precursor to removing Franco, 40
support for in France, 43, 53
sympathy for in France, 52
see also border crisis; exiles, Spanish
Resistance, French
anti-Franco activities (see consulates, Spanish; guerillas, Spanish)
and anti-Franco sentiment, 31, 35–6
groups involved in debate about Spanish Question, 32

Index

Resistance, French *(continued)*
  importance of ties to in death sentence intervention, 62
  influence on French policy toward Spain, 4–5, 64, 140–1
  internal *vs.* external, 31
  and interventions in death sentences, 63
  as loose coalition, 32
  myth of, 3, 30, 33, 50, 140–1
  reorganization of, 38
  and republicanism, 31
  role of Spanish refugees in, 38–9
  vision for France, 50, 107
  see also García, Cristino
Resistance, Spanish, 52, 53
Resistance myth, 3, 30, 33, 50, 140–1
Restoration, possibility of, 65, 68–9
Richards, Michael, 58
Rioux, Jean-Pierre, 30
Risks in taking Spanish Question to UN, 99–100
Roberts, Frank, 105, 106
Roosevelt, Franklin, 83, 104
Rousso, Henry, 30
Rumbold, Horace, 22

Sanctions
  border closures, 68, 95–6, 97, 132–4, 135
  British opposition to, 111–12
  France's proposal of, 75–6 (*see also* December Note)
  Hardion's opposition to, 133
  and isolation of France, 139
Santamaría, Vicente, 69, 71
Second World War, 21, 128, 141
Security, national, 3
Security, Spain as threat to, 116–17, 125
Security Council, *see* United Nations
SFIO (French Socialist Party), 32, 60, 78, 81, 84, 89, 91, 92–3
Sheetz, Mark S., 80
Smyth, Denis, 21
Socialists
  and García case, 92
  SFIO, 32, 60, 78, 81, 84, 89, 91, 92–3
  Spanish Socialist Party (PSOE), 62, 68, 69, 73, 81
  Spanish Socialist trade union (UGT), 53, 57, 89, 91, 109
  view of December Note, 80
Soutou, Georges-Henri, 140
Soviet Union
  attitude toward *guerrillos,* 107
  considered expansionist, 103
  France's alignment with, possible, 99, 117, 119
  France's invitation to debate Spanish Question, 99–101
  Kennan's analysis of goals of, 103–4
  perceived interests in Spain, 104, 105–6
  position on Spain, 106–7
  relationship with Spanish Communists, 107
  support of French UN proposal, 113
  use of pressure groups to change western policy, 106
  veto of Sub-Committee report, 131
  see also Cold War
Spain
  actions during World War II, 21, 128
  alternative governments (*see* Giral Government; monarchists/monarchy)
  banned from UN, 64, 87, 133
  beginning of campaign to end Franco's reign, 33–4
  Britain's policy on, 102–3, 110–11
  closure of borders, 109–10
  commercial treaty with France, 27, 34, 77, 88
  disruption of communication with, 93
  economic ties to French North Africa, 4, 15
  French acceptance of, 135
  government in exile, 66–7, 68, 72, 109
  importance of, 137
  neutrality of, 21
  reaction to Refugee Statute, 57
  reaction to Tripartite Statement, 109–10
  recognition of High Commission, 24
  relationship with Allies, 19–20
  relationship with France (*see* diplomatic relations with Spain; Franco-Spanish relations; Spanish Question)
  relationship with French North Africa, 10, 19–20, 24–5
  strategic value of, 136
  trade with Britain, 111
  trade with Germany, 21
  see also Franco, Francisco; Spanish Question
Spanish Chamber of Commerce, occupation of, 46–7
Spanish Civil War, French experience of, 37–40
Spanish Question
  Assembly's debate over, 84–7
  Bidault's desire to leave alone, 121
  Bidault's desire to work with Allies on, 97
  and Cold War, 98, 122
  decrease of importance of, 134
  France's attempt to retreat from, 132
  and France's international role, 86

194

Index

France's proposal to bring to UN, 98–101, 110, 112, 117–19
importance of in France after liberation, 31
need to find Allied solution to, 101
Poland's proposal to bring to UN, 123–6
Soviets invited to debate, 98–101
US's motion on, 131
Spanish Red Cross, 16
Spanish Socialist Party (PSOE), 62, 68, 69, 73, 81
Speaight, Richard, 14
Spies, High Commission's, 17
Sub-Committee on Spain, 126–31

Tangier, 26, 77, 106
Telephone service, disruption of, 93
Thomson, Malcolm, 21, 23
Torr, William, 129
Toulouse, France, 43
Trachtenberg, Marc, 76
Trade
  Britain's with Spain, 111
  Franco-Spanish commercial treaty (September 1945), 27, 34, 77, 88
  Germany's with Spain, 21
  see also phosphates
Trade unions, *see* CGT; CNT; UGT
Transport
  of French refugees, 15, 17–18
  of Spanish wartime workers, 48–9
Tripartite Statement (March 1946), 68, 70, 84, 108–10, 112, 121, 130
Truelle, Jacques, 25, 26–7, 44, 46–7, 60

UGT (*Unión General de Trabajadores*), 53, 57, 89, 91, 109
UKCC (United Kingdom Commercial Corporation), 23
UNE (*Union Nacional Española*), 38, 42, 43, 44, 53, 57
Unions
  disruption of communications with Spain, 93
  French (*see* CGT)
  Spanish (*see* CNT; UGT)
United Kingdom Commercial Corporation (UKCC), 23
United Nations
  Britain's opposition to French proposal, 112, 113, 115
  France's proposal to bring Spanish Question to, 98–101, 110, 112
  France's second proposal to, 117–19
  French presentation of Spanish case, 116
  Soviet support of French proposal, 113

Spain barred from, 64, 87, 133
Spain's participation in, 136
Sub-Committee on Spain, 126–31
US motion on Spanish Question, 131
US reaction to French proposal, 112–13, 115
vote on Spanish Question, 133, 135
United Nations Charter, 99
United States
  changes in relations with Spain, 79–80
  economic warfare (*see* economic war)
  growing support for Kennan's views, 109
  position on Spain, 83, 102–3, 128
  reaction to December Note, 82–4
  reaction to France's admission of weakness, 114–15
  reaction to France's UN proposal, 112–13, 115
  reaction to García execution, 102
  reaction to Sub-Committee report, 130
  response to Polish initiative, 124–5
  role in Mediterranean, 13
  and Spanish Question, 65, 66
  support for Spanish Republicanism, 79
  support of High Commission, 12–13, 23
  Tripartite Statement, 108–10
  see also Allies; Western Alliance
USCC (United States Commercial Corporation), 23
USSR, *see* Soviet Union

Val d'Aran invasion, 42
Vichy Regime, 7, 11, 12, 38
"Vichy Syndrome," 30
Vitini, José, 60

Western Alliance
  commitment of France to, 140
  desire to maintain Spanish status quo, 97
  division over Spain, 80–1
  "double game" with Spain, 77, 78, 81, 91
  France's place in, 75–6
  opposition to Franco, 63–4
  support for Don Juan, 64
  Tripartite Statement, 68, 70, 84, 108–10, 112, 121, 130
  see also France; Great Britain; United States
Western European Union (WEU), 136
Workers, Spanish, 48–9
Work permits for Spanish refugees, 57
World War II
  influence on politics, 141
  Spain's actions during, 21, 128

Index

Yalta Declaration on Liberated Europe, 100
Young, John, 31

Zapirain, Sebastían, 60